Field Guide
to Aftermarket Parts,
1946–1948 Dodge

Field Guide
to Aftermarket Parts,
1946–1948 Dodge

Robert K. Riley

McFarland & Company, Inc., Publishers

Jefferson, North Carolina

LIBRARY OF CONGRESS CATALOGUING-IN-PUBLICATION DATA

Names: Riley, Robert K., author.
Title: Field guide to aftermarket parts, 1946–1948 Dodge / Robert K. Riley.
Description: Jefferson, North Carolina : McFarland & Company, Inc., Publishers, 2022 | Includes index.
Identifiers: LCCN 2022000948 | ISBN 9781476684468 (print) | ISBN 9781476642673 (ebook) ∞
Subjects: LCSH: Dodge automobile—Parts—Catalogs. | Dodge automobile—Parts—Identification. |
Aftermarkets. | BISAC: TRANSPORTATION / Automotive / Buyer's Guides
Classification: LCC TL215.D6 R55 2022 | DDC 629.222/2—dc23/eng/20220321
LC record available at https://lccn.loc.gov/2022000948

BRITISH LIBRARY CATALOGUING DATA ARE AVAILABLE

ISBN (print) 978-1-4766-8446-8
ISBN (ebook) 978-1-4766-4267-3

Front cover: A 1946 Dodge D24 Custom 4-door sedan owned
by Leonard "Bud" W. Smeenk, Jr., of Osteen, Florida, and registered
as a Repeat Preservation Vehicle in Class 26A (Production Vehicles—
Excluding Fords—1946–1947) at the Fall Hershey Show Car Field
in October 2019. Vehicle number, motor number and body number
indicate this was one of the first Dodge cars built in Detroit
after the war in the fall of 1945 (author's photograph).

Printed in the United States of America

*McFarland & Company, Inc., Publishers
Box 611, Jefferson, North Carolina 28640
www.mcfarlandpub.com*

In memory of my wife, Karen,
who supported this project
from beginning to end

Table of Contents

Preface

Welcome. You hold in your hands a Field Guide that gives you admission to the largest parts store(s) in the world for the 1946–1948 D24 Dodge automobile. The counter in this parts store contains over two hundred catalogs with a listing of parts that were made in the U.S.A. by American workers with American quality materials. The store is open to you all hours of the day and night. In the past you could find parts for your car at flea markets or swap meets that meet only once or twice a year. Now with the Internet you can buy parts online 24 hours a day, 7 days a week.

The origin for this Field Guide started in my senior year in high school in the fall of 1961 when the distributor rotor broke on my 1933 Dodge Brothers DP-Six four-door sedan. I went to my local gas/repair station to buy a new rotor but the owner said he only had post-war ignition catalog information and did not have one that covered a '33 Dodge. I would probably have to go to a dealership to buy one. When I showed him my broken rotor he immediately said "I have one of those—that fits a '52 Chevrolet." He checked his current Delco catalog for a part number for a '52 Chevy rotor, reached behind into an ignition cabinet on the wall, and handed me a small box. Inside was a distributor rotor for a '52 Chevy that perfectly matched the broken rotor for my DP-Six.

The information on the box only had the name Delco and the number 820445. Nowhere did it say that it fit a '33 Dodge or a '52 Chevy. I immediately realized two important concepts that have remained with me to this day: (1) In the "automobile world" numbers are important and (2) there is an interchangeability between cars and car manufacturers. If I had an older Delco ignition catalog I could use it to look up and have available to me all the Delco ignition part numbers that fit my 1933 Dodge. I also learned that I did not have to look or ask for a rotor for a 1933 Dodge—rather I had to look and ask for Delco part number 820445. Since that time I have discovered over 150 models and years of cars that use that same distributor rotor. My first trip to a large automobile flea market was in October 1974 to Hershey, Pennsylvania. I discovered not only a world of new old stock (NOS) and used parts for antique and vintage cars but a world of aftermarket counter catalogs. I found several older Delco catalogs that included all the number information I needed for my '33 Dodge. In fact, since 1974 I have found over a dozen different aftermarket catalogs that list their ignition part numbers for my Dodge. In addition to ignition information, I found dozens of aftermarket catalogs that included the numbers of the replacement parts needed to keep my car on the road. I realized that with my ever growing stack of aftermarket catalogs I could sit at home and develop a Field Guide of aftermarket company numbers for any antique car I would ever buy.

I purchased a 1946 D24 Dodge four-door Custom sedan in the summer of 2004. This car was a future "driver" that came from a barn on a homestead farm in South Dakota. This car would need several replacement parts and a lot of work to make it a roadworthy driver. With Hershey three months away, I immediately started a Field Guide for the 1946 Dodge. It worked. In the fall of 2004 I returned home with fuel pump, thermostat, carburetor, muffler, tail pipe, brakes, master cylinder, and several other NOS parts to get the car in running condition. All of the parts were found using the Field Guide numbers—none of the parts I bought at the flea market were labeled 1946 Dodge.

Again, welcome. Enjoy the Field Guide and enjoy the thrill of finding parts for your Dodge using aftermarket catalog numbers.

RKR—February 2022

Important Notice

The information data listed in the Field Guide has been compiled from reliable catalogs, brochures and published sources of information and is correct to the best of our knowledge and belief. However, the author and publisher cannot assume any responsibility for possible error in this or any printed information source.

Introduction

What Is a Field Guide?

In general, field guides are books used in biology for on-the-spot identification of plants and animals. There are field guides to identify birds, fish, insects, mushrooms and dozens of other groups down to the genus and species level of classification. This book is different. It is designed for on-the-spot identification of 1946–1948 D24 Dodge parts, and only D24 Dodge parts, from all the other thousands of automobile parts found at flea markets, swap meets and on the internet. The Field Guide is designed as a high value research and reference parts identification book for the experienced mechanic as well as the novice. It is not a repair manual to give step-by-step repairs or a list of measurements and settings.

The first time you read the Field Guide you will notice that it does not "read" or "flow" as a work of prose. In most cases you will likely read one sentence or paragraph at a time and then reflect on what you have just read. In some cases you may stop reading altogether and visit the car with pad, pencil and tape measure, before continuing on to the next sentence or paragraph.

A Trip to the Auto Parts Store

When you enter a parts store today—for example, Auto Zone, Advance Auto, Carquest etc.—and walk up to the counter to find a part—let's say a rear wheel cylinder for a PT Cruiser—you are asked a series of questions about your car by a person standing in front of a computer screen. We have all been through this if we have done any repairs on our vehicles at home. What make of car? What year? What model? What engine (in liters)? Power steering? Power brakes? Front or rear drive? And the list goes on and on. Finally, after what seems like an endless series of questions a part number WCA610130 appears on the screen with a picture. You are shown the picture and asked if that is the part. You can say yes, no or maybe. The employee goes back into the depths of the never-ending shelves behind the counter and returns with a box with the part number WCA610130, opens it for inspection and quotes a price. You pay the price and head for home. The deal is made.

As you think back on the last few minutes, you have an impression about the interaction that just took place.

1. You have to know a lot of information about your car.

2. You have to know what the part looks like as to size and shape and be able to identify it by a picture.

3. The box you just purchased has only the company name, company logo and a part number. There is no written information on the box that indicates this part fits your PT Cruiser.

Now, imagine it is 1950 and you go into a NAPA, Sears or Western Auto parts store in your home town. When you walk up to the counter to find a rear wheel cylinder for your D24 Dodge, what happens? You are asked a series of questions about your car by a person standing in front of a counter filled with "parts books" or "counter catalogs." What make of car? What year? What model? What engine (not in liters)? And the list goes on and on. Finally, after what seems like an endless series of questions the catalog identifies part number WC-10588. There might even be a drawing of the part in the parts book. The employee goes back into the depths of the never ending shelves behind the counter and returns with a box with the part number WC-10588, opens it for inspection and quotes a price. You pay the price and head for home. The deal is made.

As you think back on the last few minutes, you have an impression about the interaction that just took place.

1. You have to know a lot of information about your car.

2. You have to know what the part looks like as to size and shape and be able to identify it by a picture.

3. The box you just purchased has only the company name, company logo and a part number. There is no written information on the box that indicates this part fits your D24 Dodge.

What you knew before you entered the store—be it 1950 or 2017—is that there was a good chance you would walk out the door with a rear wheel cylinder for your car. You would not go to either parts store if you needed a driver's side door replacement. Parts stores are today and were yesterday designed to replace most of the small parts that were necessary to pass a state inspection or to get the car running today so you could get to work tomorrow.

Many of the NOS parts that were in garages, dealerships and parts stores can now be found in the original boxes at flea markets, swap meets, yard sales and on the internet.

Why Use Only a Number for Parts?

Now why is it that a rear wheel cylinder for your D24 Dodge is packaged in a box with only a number and the box does not specifically report on the side that it fits a 1946–1948 Dodge? First of all, the wheel cylinder may have been manufactured and boxed in 1947 and the information on the box would report that the cylinder fits a 1946–1947 Dodge. Nothing about fitting a 1948 Dodge. Also time marches on and cars continued to roll off the assembly line in 1949 … 1950 … 1951 and right up to the present day.

The question then becomes how long did Dodge use this wheel cylinder on Dodge models. Actually, Dodge used this rear wheel cylinder from 1946 to 1956. Wheel cylinders for Dodge changed for the first time after the war with the 1957 models. Also, Chrysler Corporation used the same wheel cylinder on the 1946–1955 Chrysler and DeSoto, and the 1946–1956 Plymouth. Therefore, a replacement wheel cylinder manufactured and boxed in the 1940s, '50s, '60s or even later with the number WC-10588 will interchange and fit a D24 Dodge.

Not all aftermarket manufacturers used the same wheel cylinder number as NAPA and NAPA is not the only aftermarket rear wheel cylinder to be found at swap meets. Therefore the Field Guide lists the numbers from several aftermarket suppliers of rear wheel cylinders that may be found.

MoPar Numbers for Parts

Every part for a D24 Dodge has a MoPar number, be it a small lockwasher located behind the dash or the sheet metal for a rear fender. Numbers may have 5, 6 or 7 digits. The correct presentation of MoPar numbers in print is to separate the last three digits with a space as shown in the following MoPar numbers: 50 652 (rear axle drive shaft nut washer), 692 791 (5 passenger front wheel brake drum assembly) and 1117 603 (fan and generator belt).

Quite often, but not always, an aftermarket catalog included the MoPar number that was replaced by their aftermarket part and both numbers will often be found on the outside of the aftermarket box (generally without the space at the last three numbers). If an aftermarket catalog included a replaced MoPar Number, then that Mopar number is included in the Field Guide.

The MoPar numbers in the **What to Look For** section of the Field Guide used as a source of numbers the December 1948 Dodge D24 Passenger Car Parts List. It is possible that the MoPar numbers reported on an aftermarket box may not match the MoPar number in the Field Guide. It may in fact be a what is called a "superseded number" that was changed for the D24 by Chrysler one or more years after 1948. There may be more than one MoPar number for the same factory part depending on the year the part was manufactured.

A Trip to the Swap Meet

Walking around a large swap meet you quickly see the difference between working on a Model A Ford, a 1955 Chevrolet and a 1946–1948 Dodge. Large tractor-trailers are loaded with parts and catalogs of parts for the Fords and Chevys. You can sit at home at the kitchen table with one or more of these catalogs and order parts by phone or computer and with a credit card have the parts arrive at your front door in a week or less from the smallest rivet to a rebuilt engine. Not so for the Dodge. There are no large tractor-trailers of parts and the limited catalogs to be found are few in pages and few in listed parts. Welcome to the world of the late 1940s Dodge in the 21st century.

Field Kit

It doesn't take very long after buying a voltage regulator, kingpin set and carburetor to realize that there must be a better way to transport these items around a swap meet other than just carrying the items around in a plastic bag from a grocery store. Also, you may be walking around for several hours before you return to your car or truck.

The field kit I use relies on a dolly or hand truck, which I like much better than a wagon. I have balanced and pushed my dolly through the miles of Hershey, Pennsylvania, the wet and muddy infield at Canfield, Ohio, and the hilly spaces at Carlisle, Pennsylvania. A golf cart of course would be best, but motorized vehicles at most shows require a special permit that must be requested in advance—even for handicapped ticketed carts.

Start by walking to the far end of the field and work back towards your parked car. As the weight in the buckets on the dolly increases, you are always closer to your car. Keep in mind that you will always find parts and equipment needed for your garage. It is better to be pushing tools, chain hoist and jack stands towards the car rather than away.

The author with his two wheeled dolly equipped with two five gallon buckets and bungee straps. There is plenty of room on the top of the buckets to strap those large pieces that will not fit inside a bucket. Note the spare tire bolted to the back of the dolly behind the top bucket.

Below is a suggested list of field kit equipment to have on hand:

Two wheeled dolly; identification; medical information; medication; small first aid kit; copy of the Field Guide; phone; watch; water; two five gallon buckets with lids; comfortable shoes; retractable small tape measure; six inch metal machinist ruler with ⅟₃₂" gradations; notebook; pens; masking tape; hat; sunscreen; spare pair of glasses; sunglasses; magnifying glass; a dozen or so mixed bungee straps (1–3 feet in length) with hooks on the ends; pliers; small crescent wrench; side cutters; mechanics wire; volt meter; slotted and Philips screwdrivers; magnet; camera; disposable rain poncho; small to medium size shipping boxes (Walmart) folded and stored behind the buckets; small LED flashlight; roll of electrical tape.

All of the above can easily fit in the bottom of a bucket and still leave plenty of room for car parts. One trip to Harbor Freight and Walmart and you are ready for a field trip to a small local show or a large one such as Hershey with its ten thousand dealer spaces. With this set-up I have carried a starter, fuel pump, coil, added on a radio and then moved on to the next space looking for more. Keep in mind it is not only the weight of the parts you have to contend with but also the volume. I am not going to explain the need for each and every item on the list, but suffice it to say that over the years I have found each and every one useful.

Figures and Illustrations

The ink-line drawings in this field guide are adapted from factory literature, brochures and advertisements to assure accuracy of important features and details. Shadowing and stippling are held to a minimum to present a level of detail that allows the user to distinguish D24 parts from parts of other manufacturers, models and years that are designed for the same work. In the ink-line drawing there is no background clutter as in a photograph and details are clearly seen. Drawings are not to scale, but measurements of some parts are included where deemed important.

In addition, the part is shown outside the car as it would be found on a table or in a box at a swap meet or flea market.

1

Identify Your 1946–1948 Dodge

The D24 Dodge

The 1946–1948 Dodge was listed in the Chrysler-Dodge shop manuals, magazine articles, parts books and aftermarket literature as D24, D 24 or D-24. I like the D24 identification and it is the most common expression used in the Field Guide. Two "Lines" of cars were produced: (1) Deluxe (S) and (2) Custom (C). Therefore an expansion of the identification of your car would be D24S, D 24S, D-24S or D24C, D 24C, D-24C.

D24 Dodges (S and C) were built from September 1945 to February 1949. The first truly different Dodges produced after the war were the D-29 Wayfarer, the D-30 Meadowbrook and the D-30 Coronet produced from December 1948 to December 1949. The overlap D24 models produced from December 1948 to February 1949, at the same time as the 1949 production models, became known as the 1949 Series 1. All Series 1 models were identical to the 1946–1948 models and are considered as D24. Many states at the time titled the car in the year they were sold so that a D24 built in 1949 may have a 1949 title. You may have been told by a former owner that you own a 1949 Dodge when in fact you have a D24.

Engine Number

The engine number is located on a "pad" on the cylinder block on the left side of the engine between the #1 and #2 cylinders just below the cylinder head. All D24 and only D24 Dodges have the number beginning with D24. The 1946–1948 Canadian Dodge at the time, which looks like a Plymouth and uses a Plymouth engine, begins with D25. Chrysler Corporation began identifying engine blocks for make and year in the 1920s and this makes it easy for the owner or restorer to identify if the engine is original to the car. Many engines from different years are interchangeable with the D24 and if it was changed, then so were the starter, generator, fuel pump, carburetor and all the other exposed and hidden parts of an engine.

Most engines were machined and assembled to "standard" tolerances at the factory before being used on the assembly line. Some engines were machined undersize before assembly and these engines were identified with a stamping on the engine pad. If the letter "A" appears immediately following the engine number, this indicates a cylinder bore .020" larger than standard. The letter "B" immediately following the engine number indicates main and connecting rod bearings .010" smaller than standard. The letters "AB" immediately following the engine number indicate a cylinder bore .020" larger than standard and main and connecting rod bearings .010" smaller than standard. The letters in the circular pads at either end of the engine number are for use by factory inspectors only and should not be connected with the engine number. Numbers without letters indicate an engine with standard cylinder bore, standard crankshaft and standard connecting rod bearings.

Record Your Engine Number _____

Serial Number Plate

The serial number indicates where and when your Dodge was built. Chrysler, like other manufacturers, would often upgrade and make changes during the mid-year of production. Where and when your car was built becomes important when buying factory original and aftermarket replacement parts for your car.

Year	Production City	Serial Number
1946 D24	Detroit	30645001 and up
1947 D24	Detroit	30799738 and up
1948 D24	Detroit	31011766 and up
1946 D24	Los Angeles	45000001 and up
1947 D24	Los Angeles	45002146 and up
1948 D24	Los Angeles	45022453 and up

Record Your Serial Number _____

Record When Your Car Was Built _____

Record Where Your Car Was Built _____

Body Number Plate

The Body Number Plate is located under the hood, on the fire wall, on the driver's side. The number should be followed either by the letter "S" (indicating a Deluxe Body Line) or "C" (indicating a Custom Body Line).

Record Your Body Number _____

Record Your Body Line _____

Deluxe and Custom Identification

There were no major outward changes to the D24 Dodge from the first models in September 1945 to February 1949 other than a more sculptured ram emblem on the hood in 1947–1948. The Custom models were the top of the line in 1946. The Deluxe models for 1946 have the same basic appearance as the Custom models and both use most of the same sheet metal, trim, bumper, grille and glass parts. Custom models were adorned with slightly more trim and equipment from the beginning of production and the Custom interior appeared more luxurious. As you look at a 1946 Dodge from a distance, close-up, or in a photograph, the Custom instantly stands out from the Deluxe with the presence of stainless trim around the side windows and a 32¼" long stainless trim strip on the back fender above the rear tire (Figure 1-4 arrows A and B). The stainless trim around the side windows and the trim strip on the back fender above the rear tire are absent on the Deluxe D24 models (Figure 1-1 arrows A and B). Use the stainless trim as a first step to distinguish if you have a Deluxe or Custom D24 Dodge.

Body Style

Eight body styles were produced in the two lines for the 1946–1948 D24 Dodge: (1) six-passenger Four-Door Sedan, (2) six-passenger Two-Door Sedan, (3) three-passenger Business Coupe, (4) six-passenger Club Coupe, (5) five-passenger Convertible Coupe, (6) six-passenger Town Sedan, (7) seven-passenger Four-Door Sedan, (8) Limousine.

Deluxe Line (S)

Figure 1-1. Deluxe Four-door Sedan—Notice: absence of stainless trim around the side windows (A) and absence of the rear fender stainless trim strip above the rear tire (B); "suicide" rear hinged rear doors; rear quarter window behind the rear door. 119½" wheelbase. 61,987 produced.

Figure 1-2. Deluxe Two-Door Sedan—Notice: absence of stainless trim around the side windows and absence of the rear fender stainless trim strip above the rear tire; no rear quarter window. 119½" wheelbase. 81,399 produced.

Figure 1-3. Deluxe Three Passenger Business Coupe—Notice: absence of stainless trim around the side windows and absence of the rear fender stainless trim strip above the rear tire; no rear quarter window. 119½" wheelbase. 27,600 produced.

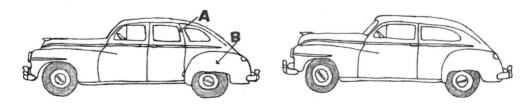

Figure 1-1. Deluxe Four-Door Sedan   **Figure 1-2. Deluxe Two-Door Sedan**

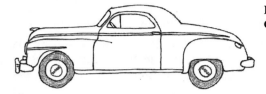

Figure 1-3. Deluxe Three-Passenger Business Coupe

Custom Line (C)

Figure 1-4. Custom Four-Door Sedan—Notice: stainless trim around the side windows (A) and a 32¼" stainless trim strip on the rear fender above the rear tire; "suicide" rear doors; rear quarter window behind the rear door. 119½" wheelbase. 333,911 produced.

Figure 1-5. Custom Six-Passenger Club Coupe—Notice: stainless trim around the side windows and a stainless trim strip on the rear fender above the rear tire; rear quarter glass behind the front door. 119½" wheelbase. 103,800 produced.

Figure 1-6. Custom Convertible Coupe (with top up)—Notice: stainless trim around the side windows and a stainless trim strip on the rear fender above the rear tire; no rear quarter window. 119½" wheelbase. 9,500 produced.

Figure 1-7. Custom Town Sedan—Notice: stainless trim around the side windows and a stainless trim strip on the rear fender above the rear tire; rear doors are front hinged; no rear quarter window; swivel vent window located within the rear door window; 119½" wheelbase. 27,800 produced.

Figure 1-8. Custom Seven-Passenger Sedan—Notice: stainless trim around the side windows and a stainless trim strip on the rear fender above the rear tire; rear doors are rear hinged; rear quarter window; jump seats for additional seating; 137½" wheelbase. 3,698 produced.

Figure 1-9. Custom Limousine (built to the same chassis specifications and looked the same as the Custom Seven Passenger Sedan from the outside)—Notice stainless trim around the side windows and a stainless trim strip on the rear fender above the rear tire; rear doors are rear hinged; rear quarter window; glass partition between driver and passengers; leather upholstery in front seat; jump seats for additional seating; additional interior lighting and additional interior leather appointments; 137½" wheelbase. Production numbers were low and it is unknown how many were actually produced.

Figure 1-4. Custom Four-Door Sedan

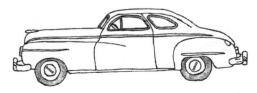

Figure 1-5. Custom Six-Passenger Club Coupe

Figure 1-6. Custom Convertible Coupe (with top up)

Figure 1-7. Custom Town Sedan

Figure 1-8. Custom Seven-Passenger Sedan

Figure 1-9. Custom Limousine

Record Your Body Style _____

Results (about the author's car)

After researching the above information, I now know the following about my car. My car is an early 1946 car that was one of the first produced after the war (there were over 700,000 D24s produced). The engine was the 28,132nd D24 engine produced and it has standard cylinder bore, standard crankshaft bearings and standard connecting rod bearings. Subtracting serial number 30645001 from my serial number identifies that my car was the 26,831st D24 built in Detroit. My body plate number identifies my car was number 8841 Custom and the body style is a four-door sedan. All of this information is important when I look for replacement parts for my car.

2

A Trip to the Dodge Showroom
and Dealership 1946–1948

Features

The 1946 D24 Dodge model was produced 32 years after the first Dodge Brothers automobile and was advertised as the "New Dodge' and the "Smoothest Car Afloat." It included a long list of new features. This New Dodge was not a hurried production of a completely new model for a car-starved civilian population, but was based on the mechanics and styling of the D22 Dodge of 1942 which in itself was advertised as the "Greatest Dodge Ever Built." Thus, the D24 was a "Fully Proven Car" even before it was built. Only a limited number of 1942 models were ever available to the buying public in late 1941 and the beginning of 1942 because production was cut short when, on February 10, 1942, the government ordered the cessation of all U.S. civilian automobile production. All Dodge assembly plants turned to the war effort and Dodge car sales ended on February 22, 1942.

The public was well aware of the economy and dependability of the D22 Dodge automobile before the war from the results of the All-American Economy Test of November 1941. Eight hundred new Dodges traveled 80,000 miles in every state of the union under all kinds of road, weather and traffic conditions with a low repair rate and a national average of 21.6 miles per gallon of gasoline.

Dodge had produced millions of cars by 1942 and many veterans had driven Dodge military vehicles during the war, so there was a huge interest in the New Dodge for 1946. Dodge answered this interest with printed information on the features of the new models in newspaper articles, magazine articles and showroom brochures starting in mid to late 1945, several months before the cars were actually available at the dealerships. The literature of the day not only reminded the public of the economy and dependability of the prewar cars, but also reported wartime performance records of Dodges on the home-front during the rationing war years. Tire mileage was high, gasoline consumption was low and repair of major mechanical items was low.

Remember that the word "Dependability" was first used by Dodge back in 1915 and it was a word well known to the automobile buying public and Dodge therefore emphasized "Dependability" in most advertisements.

The "New Dodge" of 1946 featured dozens of improvements over prewar cars. Three coordinated features were paramount in the new D24 to make it the

"Smoothest Car Afloat": (1) engineering changes added to the prewar "Floating-Power-Flow-Engine" that were developed during the war years, (2) "All-Fluid-Drive" first offered as a D24 option in 1946 was changed to standard equipment for 1947–1948 and (3) "Full-Floating-Ride" improvements to chassis, steering and suspension. Because of the importance of these three features, each is covered in a detailed outline. Dozens of comfort, style and design changes are also listed later in the Appendix, but not in as much detail.

Dealers were eager to point out the many new features of the New Dodge over any of the sixteen or so other brands that were available in showrooms across the country just after the war. Many of the D24 features were easily seen on demonstration models and could be pointed out to prospective customers by dealers in the showroom and given as reasons to buy a New Dodge.

Unseen features were well described and illustrated in showroom literature, brochures and posters and made available to prospective customers in the showroom.

Floating-Power-Flow Engine

All Deluxe and Custom D24 models were standard equipped with a six-cylinder flathead engine. This postwar engine of 1946 that was advertised in printed material as the "Floating-Power-Flow-Engine" offered many advanced and significant improvements that were developed during the war years. The two concepts of Dodge Floating-Power and Power-Flow must be discussed separately.

Floating-Power

Floating-Power is a patented method of engine suspension in the automobile that first appeared in the 1931 Chrysler automobiles, and this same method of engine suspension was refined during the war and used in the D24 postwar Dodge. The important concept here is "engine suspension." Dodge developed two important concepts in the support of an engine in the engine-bay of an automobile:

1. Most automobile manufacturers at the time bolted the engine to the frame at two, three or four points with bolts through a large rubber washer. The Dodge Floating-Power engine differs in its support of the engine at three points with motor mounts made of two metal plates separated by a center "live rubber" bushing. There is no metal-metal contact in the motor mount itself and when the engine is bolted into the engine-bay there is no metal-metal contact of the engine with the frame. Vibration from the engine to the frame and body is eliminated.

2. The weight of the engine is divided in half by an imaginary line running from the upper, front motor mount at the water pump to the two motor mounts located at the back and bottom of the bell-housing of the Fluid Drive unit (Figure 2-1). The white line with arrows in the figure illustrates where the engine is cradled in perfect balance on its natural axis to reduce rocking.

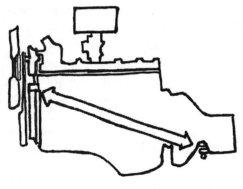

Figure 2-1. Silhouette of D24 engine driver's side with arrow showing balanced weight of engine to reduce rocking

Power-Flow Engine

The Power-Flow engine has its beginnings and development before the war with the 1941 D19 Dodge 6 cylinder engine and featured the following changes over the 1941 models: (1) piston diameter increased from 3⅛" to 3¼", (2) stroke increased from 4⅜" to 4⅝" and cubic inch displacement increased from 217.8 to 230.2. The engine became known as the "230."

Horsepower increased from 91 to 105 but the major change in the "Power" (of the Power-Flow) was the increased torque from 170 ft. lbs. to 185 ft. lbs. at the relatively low speed of 1600 rpm. It is because of this increased torque at low rpm that the 230 was used in industry as a stationary industrial engine. Many improvements and innovations were made to the 1942 Dodge 230 engine during the war years and then added to the 1946–1948 Dodge. The 230 engine of the 1942 Dodge was not the same as the improved 230 Power-Flow engine of the 1946 Dodge.

Features of the Dodge D24 Power-Flow Engine

Amola Steel: Amola steel, famous for its toughness and durability, was used for its mirror-like "super-finished" engine surfaces that virtually eliminate wear.

Water Jackets: The Dodge water jackets in the block extend the full length of the block and cylinders. Cylinders expand evenly as they are heated, maintain roundness, reduce wear and maintain compression. The oil is kept as much as 50 degrees F cooler so moving parts are lubricated better and last longer. Water jackets on many competitors' engines extend only part of the length of the cylinder and therefore cannot offer similar benefits of economy and dependability.

Water Distributing Tube: A water distributing tube, the length of the engine, is located behind the water pump to offer uniform water cooling and circulation to all cylinders, valves and valve seats. Cooler temperatures in the center of the engine give longer engine life and better performance. The water distribution tube directs water flow around the exhaust valve seats.

Crankshaft: The crankshaft is drop-forged from high-carbon steel for ruggedness and long life. Seven counterweights provide balance at rest and rotation. Four large main bearings, not three as in most competitors' engines, reduce friction for smoother operation.

Thermostat: A by-pass thermostat design offers faster engine warm-up by preventing water from circulating through the radiator until proper engine temperature is reached.

Hose: Newly developed long lasting radiator and heater hose material, developed during the war, withstands all anti-freeze solutions.

Distributor: The distributor features a fully automatic vacuum control that uses engine vacuum to advance or retard spark according to load.

Pistons: New lightweight plated aluminum "U-slot" cam ground pistons that reduce scoring and scuffing during the life of the engine and particularly during the "break-in" period. The four rings per piston are stannic coated. The piston rings are redesigned and moved down the piston to protect them from the region of highest combustion heat.

Valves: Special alloy exhaust valve seat inserts were developed to reduce valve grinding repairs and allow the valves to remain "seated" after thousands of miles.

Manifold: A new design in the exhaust manifold directs exhaust gases to travel the full length of the engine block before exiting in a 90 degree downward turn into the exhaust pipe. This design improvement allows a quicker warm-up of the intake manifold for improved fuel distribution and a more even acceleration.

Wiring: Dodge developed the "Seal-Flex" wiring harness to meet the increased distribution of electricity needs of ignition, radio, directional signals, heater, defroster, clock, wipers, etc. A flexible plastic coating is heat wrapped around the harness to protect the wiring from oil, water, battery acid and extreme temperature changes.

Oil Pump: A new high capacity "Roto-Pressure" oil pump provides increased oil pressure when idling and a more uniform distribution of increased oil pressure at all engine speeds and temperatures.

Fan: A four-blade 17" fan curved to draw air through the radiator and over and along the engine. Fan air exits the engine compartment at the curved firewall guiding the air flow down and under the car.

Additional Features of the Floating-Power-Flow Engine

See Appendix I for additional features of the Floating-Power-Flow Engine

All Fluid Drive

Fluid Drive is not a transmission, it is a "coupling unit" filled with fluid and located in place of the flywheel between the rear of the engine and the clutch of the three speed transmission. The Fluid Drive unit requires no adjusting or service except an occasional check of the fluid level and the unit is completely sealed and the oil never needs changing.

Figure 2-2A. The simple principle of how the Fluid Drive works within the D24 Dodge can best be explained by two electric fans (A and B) closely facing each other. There is no connection between fan A (on the left of the illustration)) and fan B (on the right of the illustration) other than a medium of air. If fan A is connected to an electric outlet and turned on, the moving air will turn the blades of fan B which has no electric outlet connection and is not turned on. Both fans will turn in the same direction. Chrysler Corporation engineers used the same principle to develop the Dodge Fluid Drive and replaced the flywheel at the end of the crankshaft with the fluid drive coupling.

Figure 2-2B. Illustrates an exploded view of the Fluid Drive coupling with the driving disc on the left and the driven disc on the right. The Fluid Drive unit consists of two bowl shaped 13" discs with attached fins in a fan-like arrangement in a sealed unit filled with oil.

Figure 2-2C. Illustrates the location of the Fluid Drive unit at the end of the crankshaft. The white line around the Fluid Drive in the figure illustrates the slightly larger bell-housing needed to contain the Fluid Drive coupling. There is no direct connection between the two discs other than the oil medium. Disc A (driving member disc) is connected directly to the engine and disc B (driven member disc) is directly connected to the drive train. As the engine turns, disc A drives the second disc to turn by forcing a current of oil in a spiral motion against the fins of disc B. The second disc rotates in the same direction as the driving disc. Only the oil provides the transfer of the engine power to the drive train.

Figure 2-2D. The dotted line illustrates the location of the Fluid Drive coupling in the car.

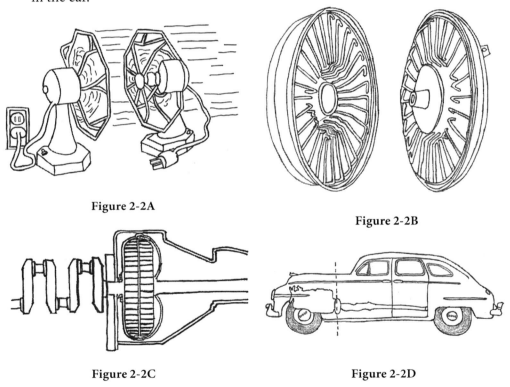

Figure 2-2A

Figure 2-2B

Figure 2-2C

Figure 2-2D

The result of Fluid Drive is a smoothness in driving as the rear wheels turn easily, smoothly and without the engine strain and jerking of a full mechanical connection from engine to rear wheel. Less strain on the engine and drive train leads to longer car life and fewer repairs.

With Fluid Drive you shift right into high gear, let out the clutch once and off you go for all-day driving in high gear without stalling. There is never a jerk or chatter as you release the clutch when you start in high gear. Start … stop … start again all day in high gear. It is unnecessary to go through the three forward gears as before and at a stop sign you brake your Dodge as usual with no need to touch the clutch. There is no need to touch the clutch in emergency stops. You can drive as slowly as one mile an hour or as fast as the top speed of the car and you can drive your Dodge in high gear up hills where before you would shift to second or first gear. From beginning of your drive to the end it is unnecessary to touch the clutch. Fluid Drive provides the driver safer and surer starts on icy and slippery roads and streets because you can start from a standstill on ice or snow without wheelspin. For maneuvering into tight spaces and parking, you still have two additional forward gears and reverse. Going down a steep hill you can remain in high gear with Fluid-Drive for it is unnecessary to shift to a lower gear. You can go as slowly as one mile per hour in high gear without danger of stalling the engine.

Full-Floating Ride

The D24 Dodge was advertised as the "Smoothest Car Afloat." The secret was in changes to the design of the frame and all the parts attached to it.

Figure 2-3A. Illustrates the frame, without axles, to show the "double kick-up" design in the front and back.

Figure 2-3B. Illustrates the buoyant "Comfort Zone" formed in the lower center of gravity between the "double kick-up" design of the frame. The Comfort-Zone cradles all passengers between the front and rear axles and free of bumps and vibrations.

Figure 2-3C. Illustrates that the rear springs were lengthened and passengers rode in front of the rear springs and not above them as in many automobiles.

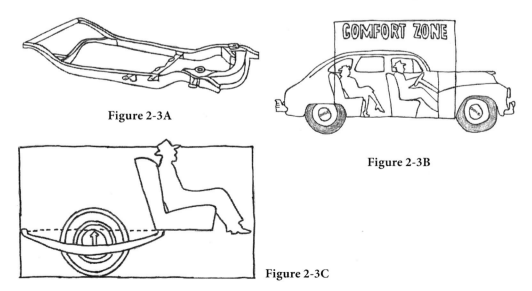

Figure 2-3A

Figure 2-3B

Figure 2-3C

3

How the Field Guide Works

Identification

Imagine you are at a large flea market or swap meet moving down the aisle from table to table. Parts are everywhere. Tables are loaded from end to end and boxes are spread over the ground. You notice a blue tarp spread out on the ground with a sign that reads "$5 tarp." On the far corner of the tarp is a cardboard banana box (what would flea market vendors do without banana boxes?) filled with new old stock (NOS) distributor caps in their original boxes. Many one, five and ten dollar blue tarps like this can be found more and more on the ground in vendors' booths with NOS boxes loaded with ignition parts, suspension parts or piston rings.

The reason for these low price tarps among so many vendors is that the parts and what they fit are unknown to the vendor. They probably acquired the box "as is" at a repair garage or dealership auction without an accompanying aftermarket catalog. They have no idea what the parts fit, the make, the year or what the value is. Do not rely on a dealer at the flea market, swap meet or internet to know if the part for sale fits your D24 Dodge. Buyer beware and all sales are final. The part is unknown to both the dealer that offers the part for sale and you as a possible client ready to purchase the part if it fits your car. It is surprising how many unmarked, mismarked and unknown parts are actually out there. Enter the Field Guide.

What to Buy

Back to the blue tarp. Six of the distributor caps in the banana box have the name Echlin and a number printed on the side of the box (Figure 3-1) . There is no information on the box as to what year or make it fits.

Above and top of following page: **Figure 3-1**

The Field Guide works in reverse to the events at the parts store at the beginning of this book. At the parts store you started with an aftermarket catalog number and ended up with a part in a box for your D24 Dodge. With the Field Guide you start with a part in a box and end up with an aftermarket catalog number for your D24 Dodge.

Step 1. Look up the Echlin page (129) in the Field Guide. Information is given about the company: **ECHLIN—IGNITION**. Echlin Manufacturing Company advertised itself as "The Largest Independent Parts Manufacturer in the World." Replacement parts for Auto-Lite, Delco-Remy, Ford and Foreign Car Systems were equal to or better than the products they replaced. Echlin was located in Branford, Connecticut, and parts were distributed through NAPA and independent jobbers.

Step 2. Look down the list of Echlin parts and locate "distributor cap."

Step 3. Identify the number to the left—**AL-63**. This is the Echlin aftermarket number for the distributor cap that fits a 1946–1948 D24 six cylinder Dodge.

Step 4. Check the six NOS boxes in the banana box for **Echlin AL-63**. Bingo. The Field Guide informs you that one of the six distributor caps does fit your D24 Dodge.

Step 5. Ask for permission from the dealer to open the box to inspect the cap. Make sure the cap actually is an NOS cap and not a used cap returned by someone in a new box. Check for chips and cracks.

Step 6. Check the **What to Look For** section to match the distributor cap with the illustration and measurements (pages 49, 51).

If everything checks out you make the five dollar purchase and move on. This is a real deal for you since an "identified" distributor cap for a D24 Dodge at a show or on the internet usually costs $15–$30. The Field Guide should pay for itself at the first good sized flea market or swap meet you attend.

One of the questions you may ask yourself is what make, model and year of car do the other distributor caps fit. You really don't care. Why should you care that the cap in the box beside yours fits a 1953 Pontiac. Time at a flea market is important and valuable to you. What the Field Guide allows is a quick identification of aftermarket parts for your D24 Dodge and a quick purchase of those parts to allow you to quickly move to the next table.

You were lucky this time. You actually found a part to fit your car. Most tables, banana boxes and tarps will not have parts for your car and you will turn up empty. Let me remind you again what was pointed out in the beginning of the book. The value of the Field Guide to you is that it not only informs you what to buy, it informs you **What Not to Buy.** You used the information in the Field Guide not to buy the other five NOS Echlin distributor caps in the banana box.

What Not to Buy

You walk up to a table and locate in the middle a set of bonded brake shoes (not in a box but tied together with a piece of string) with a label that reads 1946–1948 Dodge—25 dollars. No aftermarket manufacturer, no number, just 1946–1948 Dodge—25 dollars. What do you do?

Step 1.   Look up brake shoes and lining in the **What to Look For** section.
Step 2.   See if the brake shoes match the silhouette illustration in the **What to Look For** section of the Field Guide (page 31). They do!
Step 3.   Place the brake shoes in a circle as if they were inside the brake drum of your car and measure the diameter. 12 inches.
Step 4.   The brake shoes fit a seven passenger D24 Dodge and not your 5–6 passenger four-door Custom (page 30).
Step 5.   You pass on the sale. Again, the Field Guide informed you **What Not to Buy.**

You walk up to a table and see a part in an NOS Toledo Steel aftermarket box numbered ES-180 and labeled 1946–1948 Dodge tie rod ends—30 dollars. What do you do?

Step 1.   Look up the Toledo page (200) in the list of Field Guide catalogs. Information is given about the company: **Toledo Steel.** Toledo Steel advertised their parts "Make Good Engines Better." Toledo engineers kept pace with the new demands of higher speed and higher powered engines through continued research and improved manufacturing methods. The Toledo Steel Products Manufacturing Company was located in Cleveland, Ohio. The Field Guide divides the Toledo Steel information into Engine and Suspension.
Step 2.   Look down the consecutive number and letter column on the left for ES-180. These numbers are not to be found. The Field Guide informs you that the box is mismarked for your D24 Dodge.
Step 3.   Ask permission from the dealer to open the box and inspect the contents.
Step 4.   Check the **What to Look For** section to match the tie rod ends with the illustration (page 36). They do not match. The Field Guide confirms that the box is mismarked for your D24 Dodge.
Step 5.   You pass on the sale. Again the Field Guide informed you **What Not to Buy.**

A Quick Field Guide Test

What follows is a series of nine lists of aftermarket parts that could be found at a flea market or swap meet. Check the Field Guide aftermarket catalog list to see if one or more of the parts fits the D24 Dodge. Remember not all or any of the parts found at a vendor table must fit your D24 Dodge.*

1. Soundmaster Muffler
- A. 71
- B. 68
- C. 156
- D. 69
- E. 28
- F. 343

2. Monmouth Clutch Cover Assembly
- A. CA-3840
- B. CA-371
- C. CA-988
- D. CA-952
- E. CA-369
- F. CA-370A

3. Federal—Clutch Throwout Bearing
- A. 1055
- B. 1086
- C. 1069
- D. 995
- E. 1148
- F. 1030

4. Perfect Circle Piston Rings
- A. 512
- B. 5689
- C. 539
- D. 7763
- E. 8780
- F. 5168

5. McCord Head Gasket
- A. 6134
- B. 5887
- C. 5962
- D. 6213
- E. 5250
- F. 6032

6. Echlin Stoplight Switch
- A. SL-134
- B. SL-127
- C. SL-111
- D. SL-120
- E. SL-113
- F. SL-133

7. Raylock Fuel Pump
- A. 543
- B. 429
- C. 524
- D. 574
- E. 588
- F. 527

8. Thompson Thermostat
- A. 124
- B. 113-C
- C. 24
- D. 3-A
- E. 103-A
- F. 114

9. Allied Raymond Valve Spring
- A. V-486
- B. V-415
- C. V-370
- D. V-338
- E. V-440
- F. V-447

*Answers: (1) C; (2) D; (3) A; (4) C; (5) D; (6) F; (7) E; (8) B; (9) B

4

What to Look For

This section provides an illustration or silhouette of the major original parts found in the D24 Dodge and is used to verify if the NOS aftermarket parts found at a swap meet actually fit your D24 Dodge. Be aware that this section identifies many of the major parts but not all of the parts listed in the aftermarket **Field Guide** section.

What to Look For Example

You search a table at a flea market and find five NOS aftermarket boxes labeled "Morse" and the numbers TC-305, TC-315, TC-401, TC-411 and TC-422. The vendor states they are timing chains but has no idea what they fit and has a "$10 each" sign next to the boxes.

Step 1.   You look up Morse in the aftermarket catalog section and read the following: Morse specialized in the production of front-end-drive timing chains. They maintained a leadership position in the field of supplying manufacturers with chains that provided dependable operation and smooth performance. Morse engineers always searched for improvements in design and construction. Morse was located in Ithaca, New York, and Detroit, Michigan—TC-401 6 cylinder timing chain; 48 links; all models.

The Morse timing chain box TC-401 fits your D24 Dodge. But wait a minute. The boxes look like they have been opened many times and the timing chains probably taken out of the boxes and viewed dozens of times by prospective customers wondering if any of these timing chains fit their car. There is a high probability that a person looking simultaneously at two or three chains could place a chain in the wrong box. Also you have never had your engine apart and you have no idea what the timing chain of a D24 Dodge looks like. You will probably have to rebuild your engine someday and it will be nice to have a NOS timing chain ready on the shelf for that day. You don't know when you will come across one again at a flea market.

Step 2.   Look at the timing chain page under the "**Engine**" section in the **What to Look For Index** (pages 27, 58). The timing chain is illustrated and then described as: center guide type, ½" pitch (distance from center to center of the chain joint in inches), 1" wide and 48 links. A quick measurement (with the tools in the Field Kit) and a count of the chain links verifies that the TC-401 chain is indeed a D24 Dodge timing chain.

What to Look For Index

Bearings

tapered roller bearings (Figures 4-1A-B)
ball roller bearings (Figure 4-1C)

Brakes

brake lining measurements
brake shoe silhouette (Figures 4-2A-B)
hand/emergency brake (Figures 4-3A-B)
master and wheel hydraulic brake cylinders (Figures 4-4A-F)
hydraulic brake hose (Figures 4-5A-C)

Chassis

exploded view of front wheel suspension parts (Figure 4-6A)
upper, inner control arm assembly (Figure 4-6B)
upper, outer control arm assembly (Figure 4-6C)
steering knuckle support (Figure 4-6D)
lower, outer control arm assembly (Figure 4-6E)
lower, inner control arm assembly (Figure 4-6F)
front wheel coil spring (Figure 4-6G)
tie rod ends (Figure 4-7)
front wheel spindle steering knuckle (Figure 4-8)
king pin package (Figures 4-9A-C)
rear spring shackle (Figures 4-10A-B)
shock absorbers (Figure 4-11)
exhaust system (Figures 4-12A-F)

Drive Train

CLUTCH

clutch disc assembly (Figure 4-13A)
clutch pressure plate assembly (Figure 4-13B)
clutch release (throw-out) bearing assembly (Figure 4-13C)

UNIVERSAL JOINT

ball and trunnion (pin) universal joint (Figures 4-14A-C)
cross ball universal joint (Figure 4-14D)
cross-block-bearing universal joint (Figure 4-14E)

Electrical

GENERATOR AND VOLTAGE REGULATOR

  generator assembly (Figure 4-15A)
  generator identification tag (Figure 4-15B)
  generator armature (Figure 4-15C)
  generator brush set (Figure 4-15D)
  generator commutator bushing (Figure 4-15E)
  generator drive end bearing (Figure 4-15F)
  generator voltage regulator (Figure 4-15-G)

STARTER

  starter assembly (Figure 4-16A)
  starter Auto-Lite identification tag (Figure 4-16B)
  starter armature (Figure 4-16C)
  starter solenoid (Figure 4-16D)
  starter drive assembly (Figure 4-16E)
  starter push-button switch (Figure 4-16F)
  starter brushes (Figure 4-16G)
  starter drive end bushing (Figure 4-16H)
  starter commutator end bushing (Figure 4-16I)

BATTERY CABLES

  solenoid to starter cable (Figure 4-17A)
  battery cable to solenoid (Figure 4-17B)
  battery cable to ground (Figure 4-17C)

IGNITION

  distributor IGS-4207A assembly (Figure 4-18A)
  Auto-Lite distributor identification tag (Figure 4-18B)
  distributor cap (Figure 4-18C)
  distributor contact set (Figure 4-18D)
  distributor rotor (Figure 4-18E)
  distributor condenser (Figure 4-18F)
  distributor vacuum chamber (Figure 4-18G)
  distributor lead wires (Figure 4-18H)

COIL

  Auto-Lite coil (Figure 4-19)

SPARK PLUG

  Auto-Lite spark plug (Figure 4-20A)
  spark plug wires (Figure 4-20B)

Engine

PISTON

    piston (Figure 4-21A)
    piston rings (Figure 4-21B)
    piston pin (Figure 4-21C)
    piston expander (Figure 4-21D)

BEARINGS

    crankshaft bearing—position #1 (Figure 4-22A)
    crankshaft bearing—position #2, #3 (Figure 4-22B)
    crankshaft bearing—position #4 (Figure 4-22C)
    connecting rod insert bearing (Figure 4-22D)
    camshaft bearings (Figure 4-22E)

VALVES

    exhaust valve (Figure 4-23A)
    intake valve (Figure 4-23B)
    valve lifter (Figure 4-23C)
    valve spring (Figure 4-23D)
    valve guide (Figure 4-23E)

MOTOR (ENGINE) MOUNTS

    front support motor mount assembly (Figure 4-24A)
    rear upper motor mount support assembly (Figure 4-24B)
    rear lower motor mount support assembly (Figure 4-24C)

TIMING CHAIN

    timing chain/gears assembly (Figure 4-25A)
    timing chain (Figure 4-25B)

WATER PUMP

    water pump assembly (Figure 4-26A)
    water pump gasket (Figure 4-26B)

THERMOSTAT

    bellows type thermostat (Figure 4-27)

RADIATOR HOSE

    cylinder head to radiator hose (Figure 4-28A)
    water by-pass hose (Figure 4-28B)
    water pump outlet tube hose (Figure 4-28C)
    lower outlet tube to radiator hose (Figure 4-28D)

RADIATOR CAP

    atmospheric radiator cap (Figure 4-29)

FAN/GENERATOR BELT

fan/generator belt (Figure 4-30)

OIL PUMP

oil pump assembly (Figure 4-31A)
oil pump base plate bolt pattern (Figure 4-31B)

OIL FILTER

oil filter element (Figure 4-32)

Fuel

CARBURETOR

Stromberg type fluid drive carburetor (Figure 4-33A)
Stromberg type standard drive carburetor (Figure 4-33B)
Carter type carburetor (Figure 4-33C)

AUTOMATIC CHOKE CONTROL

Sisson type automatic choke control (Figure 4-34)

FUEL PUMP

fuel pump with glass bowl filter (Figure 4-35A)
fuel pump without glass bowl filter (Figure 4-35B)

Gaskets

cylinder head gasket (Figure 4-36A)
manifold gasket set (Figure 4-36B)
single piece manifold gasket (Figure 4-36C)
valve spring cover gasket (Figure 4-36D)
fuel pump gasket (Figure 4-36E)
oil pan gasket set (Figure 4-36F)
water pump gasket (Figure 4-36G)
timing chain plate cover case gasket (Figure 4-36H)
timing chain cover case gasket (Figure 4-36I)
oil pump to cylinder block gasket (Figure 4-36J)
water pump to by-pass elbow gasket (Figure 4-36K)
thermostat gasket (Figure 4-36L)
carburetor flange gasket (Figure 4-36M)

Seals

single-piece type of seal assembly (Figure 4-37A)
two-piece type of seal assembly (Figure 4-37B)

Windshield Wiper

electric windshield wiper arm and blade (Figure 4-38A)
vacuum windshield wiper arm and blade (Figure 4-38B)

Lighting

lamps and bulbs (Table 4-1)

Bearings—Tapered Roller and Ball Roller Bearings (Figures 4-1A–C)

Two kinds of roller bearings are found in the D24 Dodge: (1) tapered roller bearings and (2) ball roller bearings. The tapered roller bearing was first patented by Henry Timken in 1898. The bearing consists of a "cone" (Figure 4-1A) with a single row of rolling cylinders and a "cup" (Figure 4-1B) with a matching taper to reduce friction and distribute the load. Major locations of the tapered roller bearing are: front wheel outer and inner bearing, rear axle drive pinion front and rear bearing, rear axle drive shaft inner and outer bearing, and steering gear upper and lower bearing.

The roller ball roller bearing uses roller "balls" (Figure 4-1C) to reduce friction and distribute the load. Major locations of the roller ball bearing are: transmission drive pinion bearing, transmission main shaft rear bearing and transmission extension bearing.

Figure 4-1A. Illustrates an example of the tapered roller bearing "cone" used in all D24 models.

Figure 4-1B. Illustrates an example the matching tapered "cup" used with all tapered roller bearings.

Figure 4-1C. Illustrates an example of the Ball roller bearing used in all D24 models.

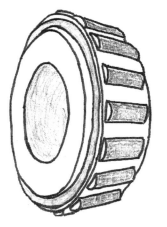 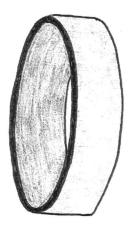 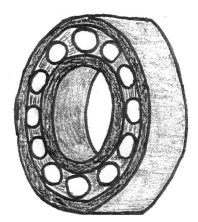

Left: Figure 4-1A. Tapered roller bearing "cone." *Middle:* Figure 4-1B. Tapered roller bearing "cup." *Right:* Figure 4-1C. Ball roller bearing.

Brakes (Figures 4-2A–4-5C)

Brake Lining Measurements

The Friction Materials Standards Institute, Inc. (FMSI) was founded in 1948 and expanded a numbering system for the size and description of brake linings for passenger cars and trucks first used by the Brake Lining Manufacturers' Association, Inc.—the BLMA. Several companies produced and distributed aftermarket replacement brakes for the D24 Dodge. These companies followed the FMSI standards and often incorporated the numbers in their own aftermarket brake numbering system.

Often, brake shoe and brake lining boxes are damaged and the important identifying numbers are missing. The Field Guide supplies measurements for each brake shoe and brake lining. A quick check with a ruler will determine if the part is correct.

Two types of aftermarket brakes are available for the 11" and 12" brake drums for the D24 models: (1) molded and predrilled brake lining to be riveted to front and rear axle shoes and (2) brake lining bonded to the shoe at the factory.

Custom and Deluxe 5–6 Passenger D24 Models

FMSI Number	Location	Drum Diameter	W	T	L	Pieces	Rivets	Size
192A	front	11" drum	2"	³⁄₁₆"	11½"	4	40	4-5
1161A	rear	11" drum	2"	³⁄₁₆"	8⅞"	2	40	4-5
					11½"	2		

Custom 7 Passenger D24 Models

FMSI Number	Location	Drum Diameter	W	T	L	Pieces	Rivets	Size
1105A	front	12" drum	2"	³⁄₁₆"	12⅝"	4	40	4-5
1179	rear	12" drum	2"	³⁄₁₆"	9⅝"	2	36	4-4
					12⅝"	2		

4-5 rivets = ⁹⁄₆₄" shank diameter, ⁵⁄₁₆" head diameter, ⁵⁄₁₆" long
4-4 rivets = ⁹⁄₁₆" shank diameter, ⁵⁄₁₆" head diameter, ¼" long

Often times an aftermarket manufacturer will include both axles in the same box (8 pieces) and the box is then marked with both FMSI numbers such as 192A-1161 for five–six passenger models and with 1105A-1179 for seven passenger models.

Brake Shoe Silhouette—(Figures 4-2A–4-2B)

Observations and measurements that can be carried out in the field to help verify if the brake shoes in hand fits the D24 Dodge.

    1. A silhouette for the front and rear axle brake shoes for the D24 5 and 6 passenger models (Figure 4-2A). A pair of shoes laid flat on the ground to form a circle yields an 11 inch diameter circle.

    2. A silhouette for the front and rear axle brake shoes for the D24 7

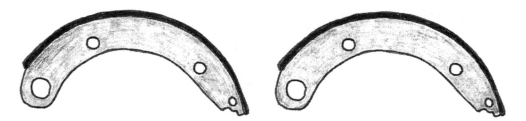

Left: **Figure 4-2A. 5 and 6 passenger brake silhouette.** *Right:* **Figure 4-2B. 7 passenger brake silhouette.**

passenger models (Figure 4-2B). A pair of shoes laid flat on the ground to form a circle yields a 12 inch diameter circle.

Hand/Emergency Brake—(Figure 4-3A–4-3B)

Observations and measurements that can be carried out in the field to help verify if the hand/emergency brake shoe in hand fits the D24 Dodge.

Figure 4-3A. Illustrates an example of the hand/emergency brake lining for all D24 models.

Figure 4-3B. Illustrates an example of the hand/emergency brake lining assembly for all D24 models.

Custom and Deluxe five–six passenger D24 models have a 6" diameter drum that requires a brake lining 2" wide, ⁵⁄₃₂" thick and 16¹¹⁄₁₆" long.

Custom seven passenger D24 models have a 7" diameter drum that requires a brake lining 2" wide, ⁵⁄₃₂" thick and 20" long.

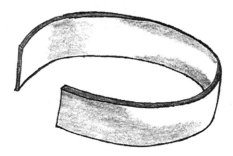

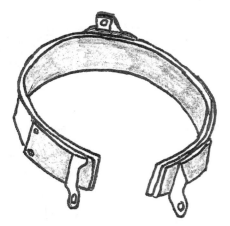

Left: **Figure 4-3A. Hand/emergency brake lining.** *Right:* **Figure 4-3B. Hand/emergency brake assembly.**

Master and Wheel Hydraulic Brake Cylinders— (Figure 4-4A–Figure 4-4F)

Chrysler Corporation first introduced hydraulic brakes on cars in 1924. The first major improvement to the Chrysler brake system occurred with the D24 Dodge when each front wheel increased from one to two cylinders (upper and lower). Each front wheel cylinder now controlled a single front brake shoe. Each of the four front wheel cylinders is different and will not interchange with one another. A touch of the toe on the brake pedal forces equal pressure on all brake cylinders, front and rear.

These wheel cylinders were used on all Dodge and Plymouth models from 1946 to 1952, DeSoto 6-cylinder models from 1946 to 1955, and select Chrysler models from 1946 to 1955.

The master cylinder assembly has a very distinctive silhouette when viewed from the side. Note the position of the three attachment bolt holes on the lower half of the cylinder. This master cylinder was used by Dodge on all models from 1946 to 1952.

Observations of the following silhouette drawings that can be used in the field to help verify if the hydraulic brake cylinders in hand fit the D24 Dodge.

Figure 4-4A. Illustrates the master cylinder used on all D24 models (replaces 1118 284).

Figure 4-4B. Illustrates the upper right front wheel cylinder (replaces 1117 804).

Figure 4-4C. Illustrates the upper left front wheel cylinder (replaces 1117 805).

Figure 4-4D. Illustrates lower right front wheel cylinder (replaces 1117 806).

Figure 4-4E. Illustrates the lower left front wheel cylinder (replaces 1117 807).

Figure 4-4F. Illustrates the right and left rear wheel cylinder (replaces 1117 799).

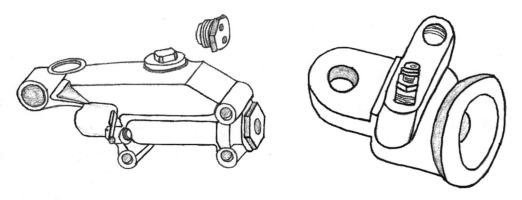

Left: **Figure 4-4A. Master cylinder.** *Right:* **Figure 4-4B. Upper right front wheel cylinder.**

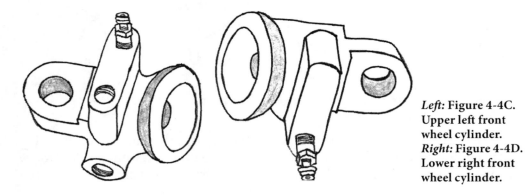

Left: **Figure 4-4C. Upper left front wheel cylinder.** *Right:* **Figure 4-4D. Lower right front wheel cylinder.**

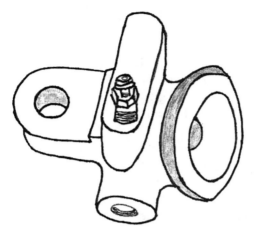

Left: **Figure 4-4E. Lower left front wheel cylinder.** *Right:* **Figure 4-4F. Right/left rear wheel cylinder.**

HYDRAULIC BRAKE HOSE—(FIGURE 4-5A–FIGURE 4-5C)

Flexible brake hoses are required for the up and down motion between the metal brake line on the frame at the rear axle, and the up and down and turning motion between the metal brake line on the frame at each front wheel.

Observations and measurements can be used in the field to help verify if the brake hose in hand fits the D24 Dodge.

Figure 4-5A. Illustrates the front right and left brake hose with $7/16$"–20 threads (for the outer fitting), $3/8$"–24 threads (for the inner fitting), and $10^{29}/_{32}$" long (Replaces 1119 401).

Figure 4-5B. Illustrates the rear brake hose with $7/16$"–20 threads (for the outer fitting), $3/8$"–24 threads (for the inner fitting), and $16^{27}/_{32}$" long (Replaces 1119 402).

Figure 4-5C. Illustrates the hose "U" clips used on all front and rear brake hoses.

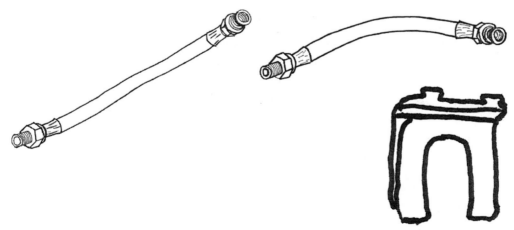

Left: **Figure 4-5A. Front wheel brake hose.** *Right, top:* **Figure 4-5B. Rear wheel brake hose.** *Right, bottom:* **Figure 4-5C. Hose clip.**

Chassis (Figure 4-6A–Figure 4-12F)

FRONT AXLE SUSPENSION (FIGURE 4-6A–FIGURE 4-6G)

Dodge used independent front suspension for the D24 1946–1948 Dodge. Dodge first used this type of suspension in 1935 when Chrysler Corporation replaced the solid front axle that was last used in the 1934 Dodge. Independent front suspension allows the driver side and passenger side wheel on the front axle to move up and down independently from each other over rough roads.

Bumps and potholes on one side of the car do not affect the wheel on the other side of the car as with a solid axle. Passengers notice a smoother ride and drivers notice easier handling.

Figure 4-6A. Illustrates an exploded view of the front axle with the six major parts that are often available as aftermarket assemblies at a swap meet: (A) upper, inner control arm assembly, (B) upper, outer control arm assembly, (C) steering knuckle support, (D) lower, outer control arm assembly, (E) lower, inner control arm assembly and (F) front wheel coil spring.

Figure 4-6B. Illustrates the parts of the upper, inner control arm assembly. The assembly includes one pivot arm, 7⅛" long, two threaded bushings and two dust seals.

Figure 4-6C. Illustrates the parts of the upper outer control arm assembly (also may be listed as upper steering knuckle support pin assembly). The assembly includes: one threaded pin, 3⅞" long, one steering alignment bushing, two dust seals and one castle lock nut and washers.

Figure 4-6D. Illustrates a single steering knuckle support that is used on the right and/or left side. Replaces 856 164 on 5 passenger models and 856 162 on 7 passenger models.

Figure 4-6E. Illustrates the parts of the lower, outer control arm assembly. The assembly includes: one threaded pin, one threaded bushing, two dust seals and one castle lock nut and washer.

Figure 4-6F. Illustrates the parts of the lower, inner control arm assembly. The assembly includes: one pivot arm, 11⅞" long, two threaded bushings and two dust seals.

Figure 4-6G. Illustrates a D24 front wheel coil spring with flat ends. Not shown are the rubber spacers and metal shims found on the top and bottom of the springs when installed into cars. Measurements: (1) 4" inside diameter—all 5 and 7 passenger models, (2) 13¼" free height, .687" wire size—all 5 passenger regular duty, (3) 13¹³⁄₁₆" free height, .719" wire size—all 5 passenger heavy duty, (4) 13¹³⁄₁₆" free height, .719" wire size—all 7 passenger regular duty, and (5) 13⅝" free height, .765" wire size—all 7 passenger heavy duty.

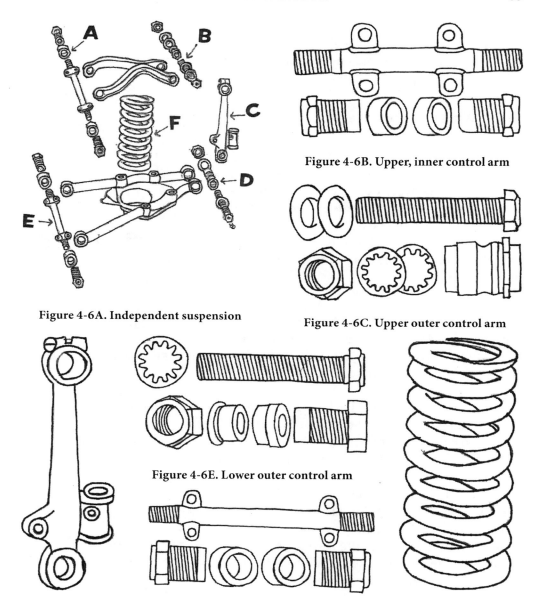

Figure 4-6B. Upper, inner control arm

Figure 4-6C. Upper outer control arm

Figure 4-6A. Independent suspension

Figure 4-6E. Lower outer control arm

Left: Figure 4-6D. Steering knuckle support. *Middle:* Figure 4-6F. Lower inner control arm. *Right:* Figure 4-6G. Front coil spring

TIE ROD ENDS (FIGURE 4-7)

There are four tie rod ends (two each) on the long and short rods used in the steering to push and pull the wheels to the right and left on the D24 Dodge. Figure 4-7 illustrates the basic shape and assembly attachments found on the four tie rod ends.

1. Inner tie rod end on the long rod—right hand thread (replaces 951 302)
2. Outer tie rod end on the long rod—left hand thread (replaces 951 303)

3. Inner tie rod end on the short rod—right hand thread (replaces 951 302)

4. Outer tie rod end on the short rod—left hand thread (replaces 951 305)

Front Wheel Spindle Steering Knuckle (Figure 4-8)

Figure 4-8 illustrates the general shape of both the right and left steering knuckles. Three steering knuckle (spindle) types were used for the 5 passenger D24 models and all three were offered by aftermarket companies. Each type had a right and left identification number and each spindle must be matched to the correct MoPar factory king pin number and build number.

1. MoPar steering number right side 1118 122 and left side 118 123 used MoPar king pin package 933 435 containing four Steering knuckle bushings on cars up to serial number 31006517 (Detroit built) and up to serial number 45022935 (Los Angeles built).

Figure 4-7. Tie rod end

2. MoPar steering knuckle right side 870 920 and left side 870 920 used MoPar king pin package 947 557 containing two steering knuckle bushings and two bearings on cars from serial number 31006517 to 31057047 and after 3184245 (Detroit built) and from serial number 45022935 to 45029117 (Los Angeles built).

3. MoPar steering knuckle right side 1140 451 and left side 1140 452 used MoPar king pin package 1243 731 containing four bearings on cars from serial number 31057047 to 31084245 (Detroit built) and after serial number 45029117 (Los Angeles built).

(Circle the number and description that matches your 5 passenger car.)

There was not enough demand for 7 passenger and limousine model steering knuckle packages and therefore no aftermarket packages were produced. Steering knuckles at the time were ordered and sold separately by MoPar and can still be found at swap meets and on the internet in a MoPar box marked 886 818 (right side) or 886 819 (left side).

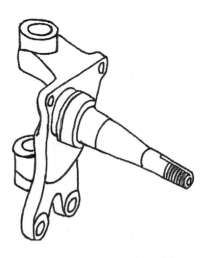

Figure 4-8. Steering knuckle

King Pin Package (Figure 4-9A–Figure 4-9C)

Three king pin packages were used for the 5 passenger models of the D24 Dodge and all three packages were produced by aftermarket companies:

    1. MoPar package 933 435 used four steering knuckle bushings on cars up to serial number 31006517 (Detroit built) and up to serial number 45022935 (Los Angeles built).

    2. MoPar package 947 557 used two steering knuckle bushings and two bearings on cars from serial number 31006517 to 31057047 and after 31084245 (Detroit built) and from serial number 45022935 to 45029117 (Los Angeles built).

    3. MoPar package 1243 731 used four bearings on cars from serial number 31057047 to 31084245 (Detroit built) and after serial number 45029117 (Los Angeles built).

    (Circle the number and description that matches your 5 passenger car.)

Depending on what part needs replaced there is some interchange available to you in repairing a 5 passenger car. All three packages used the same king pin, the same lock pin, the same shim, the same thrust bearing. Bushings and oil seal plugs were interchangeable between packages 1 and 2, and bearings and oil seal plugs were interchangeable between packages 2 and 3.

Figure 4-9A. Illustrates the contents of package number 1 with four bushings and two thrust bearings and what to look for in an aftermarket or factory box.

Figure 4-9B. Illustrates the needle type bearings found in packages 2 and 3.

Figure 4-9C. Illustrates the thrust bearing that was the same for all three king pin packages

Figure 4-9A. King pin package 933 435

Left: **Figure 4-9B. Steering knuckle bushing.** *Right:* **Figure 4-9C. Thrust bearing.**

There was not enough demand for 7 passenger and limousine model king pin packages and therefore no aftermarket packages were produced. King pins at the time were ordered and sold separately by MoPar and can still be found at swap meets and on the internet in a MoPar box marked 634 036.

Rear Spring Shackle (Figure 4-10A–Figure 4-10B)

The shackle is a very simple design feature of the suspension, between the back of the rear spring and the frame, that plays a very important role in the riding comfort of both the front and rear seat passengers. It allows the rear spring and axle to move up and down as the car travels over a rough or bumpy road. If the wheel and axle go up, the leaf spring becomes longer and the spring arc flattens out. If the spring and axle go down, the leaf spring becomes shorter and the spring arc increases. The pivot action of the top and bottom bolt of the shackle allows for these spring length changes.

Figure 4-10A. Illustrates the rear spring shackle package available as an aftermarket replacement for the D24 Dodge. The package should include four rubber bushings, two castle nuts and two metal side shackles with bolts (Replaces 1238 412).

Figure 4-10B. Illustrates the rubber bushings that are the part of the shackle that "wears-out" the most and are available as a bushing replacement kit (replaces 857 836).

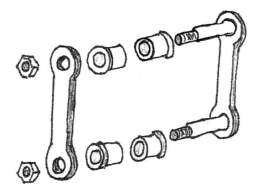

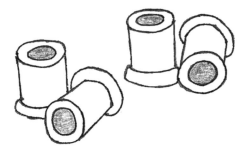

Figure 4-10B. Rear shackle bushing kit

Figure 4-10A. D24 rear shackle

Shock Absorbers (Figure 4-11)

The Houdaille type lever arm shock absorber used by Chrysler in the 1930s was replaced after the war with the "airplane-type" shock absorber on the front and rear wheels of all D24 models (Figure 4-11). Airplane-type shock absorbers provide a smoother ride by reducing the two way up-and-down motion of the springs on rough roads. A piston is located within the shock absorber between upper and lower chambers of oil. Small holes in the piston greatly resist compression and flow of oil between the chambers on bumpy roads. Hence the term "shock" absorber.

Note the method of attachment of the shock absorber to the car. An upper eye bolt with bushings attaches to the frame and a lower eye bolt with bushings attaches to the spring. Bushing kits are available from most aftermarket shock absorber suppliers and also from MoPar. Note also how the top cylinder body of the shock absorber fits over the lower cylinder body to prevent accumulation of water and dirt within the shock absorber.

Do not buy any shock absorber, new or used, that shows signs of leaking oil.

Three front MoPar and aftermarket shock absorber assemblies are available:

1. 1" diameter piston regular duty assembly (replaces 1135 541).
2. 1" diameter piston commercial duty assembly (replaces 1121 207).
3. 1⅜" diameter piston heavy duty assembly (replaces 1122 763).

Three rear MoPar and aftermarket shock absorber assemblies are available:

1. 1" diameter piston regular duty assembly (replaces 1119 876).
2. 1" diameter piston commercial duty assembly (replaces 1135 545).
3. 1⅜" diameter piston heavy duty assembly (replaces 1122 764).

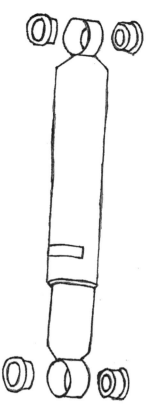

Figure 4-11. Front and rear shock absorber

Exhaust System (Figure 4-12A–Figure 4-12F)

Figure 4-12A. Illustrates the exhaust pipe assembly with flange for all D24 models. The flange is permanently welded into position ¾" from the end of the pipe. The short extension above the fixed flange fits into the exhaust manifold and the two bolts and an exhaust gasket provide a gas tight seal. The D24 exhaust pipe is unique and easy to spot in that it drops straight down from the manifold before curving 90 degrees into the muffler. Very few exhaust pipes are shaped like this (replaces 958 122).

Figure 4-12B. Illustrates the muffler used on all D24 models. The muffler body is oval shaped and measures 17" L × 19¼" around the oval × 3¾" thick and the words "inlet," "outlet" or both imprinted into the metal. Some aftermarket mufflers may not be imprinted with inlet and outlet but they are easy to identify. The inlet pipe is expanded or swollen to fit over the exhaust pipe while the outlet pipe is not expanded or swollen so as to fit into the expanded inlet of the tail pipe. The muffler fits flat under the car with the outlet pipe closest to the outside of the passenger side. The convertible coupe and the 7 passenger exhaust pipe and muffler are often welded together and sold as a single unit.

Figure 4-12C. Illustrates the shape of the tail pipe used for all D24 models. The 5 passenger pipe (1122 759) length is 92¾" long, the convertible coupe (1122 757) is 83¾" long and the 7 passenger pipe (1122 755) is 106³⁄₁₆" long. The outlet on the muffler fits into the tail pipe about 2½" to give a smooth flow and reduce exhaust leaks. The tail pipe passed over the rear axle on the passenger side and exited behind the right rear wheel.

Figure 4-12D. Illustrates the muffler tailpipe and exhaust pipe clamps used on all D24 Dodge models. The exhaust pipe (106 458) and the tail pipe (1064 459) clamps are identical, including hardware, but have different MoPar numbers because of the different location at the front or rear of the muffler.

Figure 4-12E. Illustrates the front tailpipe support assembly used on all D24 models (replaces 861 392).

Figure 4-12F. Illustrates the rear tailpipe support assembly with grommet used on all D24 models. The grommet insulator was prone to wear out before the metal part of the hanger so that replacement insulators were sold separately (replaces 681 934).

Note that the factory hardware used in 1946–1948 was much different than the "universal hangers" available in modern parts stores today. Modern universal hangers will work for a daily driver but will not pass inspection at an AACA or MoPar judging event. Factory type supports are getting harder to find, but original MoPar and aftermarket copies of originals can still be found.

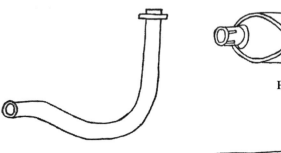

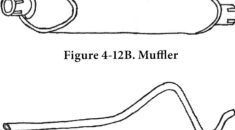

Figure 4-12B. Muffler

Figure 4-12A. Exhaust pipe

Figure 4-12C. Tail pipe

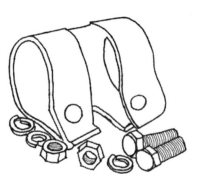

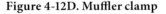

Figure 4-12D. Muffler clamp

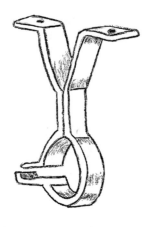

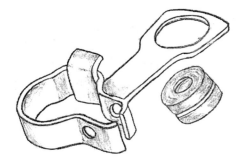

Figure 4-12F. Rear tail pipe support

Figure 4-12E. Front tail pipe support

Drive Train (Figure 4-13A–4-14E)

Clutch (Figure 4-13A–Figure 4-13C)

Figures 4-13A–4-13C illustrate the single dry-plate clutch system used on the D24 Dodge. The system consists of a clutch disc assembly with center hub springs to reduce vibration when the clutch is engaged, a clutch cover/pressure plate assembly, and a clutch release bearing assembly. Both the standard drive and Fluid Drive models have identical looking parts but differ in size and number of pre-drilled holes. The drawings illustrate the parts of the more common Fluid Drive D24 dry plate clutch system.

The Standard drive clutch is 10" with 18 pre-drilled holes while the Fluid Drive clutch is 9¼" with 32 pre-drilled holes. The Fluid Drive 9¼" clutch was used in six cylinder models up to 1954 and the standard 10" clutch was used in six cylinder models up to 1959. Replacement clutch disc assemblies with 9¼" and 10" diameter facings produced after 1948 may have a different number of pre-drilled holes but are still interchangeable with the D24. Rarely found in cars and at swap meets is the 11" diameter clutch that was available to police, taxis and emergency vehicles as a factory option.

Figure 4-13A. Illustrates the clutch disc assembly. The Fluid Drive clutch plate can be found as an assembly that includes a 9¼" friction facing, hub plate and springs (replaces Friction Materials Standards Institute Number 993A). The standard clutch plate can be found as an assembly that includes a 10" friction facing, hub plate and springs (replaces Friction Materials Standards Institute Number 1008A). Clutch facing discs with 9¼" (32 hole—FMSI 993A) and 10" (18 hole—FMSI 1008A) diameters without the hub and springs are available for both the standard and Fluid Drive clutch systems.

Figure 4-13B. Illustrates the clutch cover/pressure plate assembly. The Fluid drive pressure plate in the clutch cover/pressure plate assembly has a 9¼" diameter plate (855 519) and the standard pressure plate in the clutch cover/pressure plate assembly has a 10" diameter plate (670 103).

Figure 4-13C. Illustrates the clutch release (throw-out) bearing assembly found in the D24 Fluid Drive Dodge. Fluid Drive and standard clutch release bearings are not interchangeable. The clutch release bearing assembly of the Fluid Drive (658 948) in the illustration is noticeably longer than the standard drive (658 998) clutch release bearing assembly.

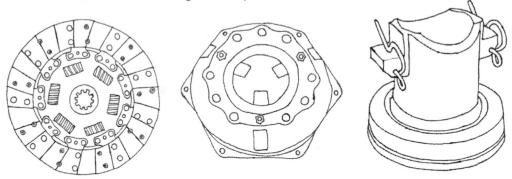

Figure 4-13A. Clutch disc assembly. *Middle:* **Figure 4-13B. Clutch cover/pressure plate assembly.** *Right:* **Figure 4-13C. Clutch release bearing.**

Universal Joint (Figure 4-14A–Figure 4-14E)

Dodge used three different universal joints (U-joints) on the 1946–1948 D24 models: (1) ball and trunnion, (2) cross-ball and (3) cross-block bearing. Aftermarket catalogs, parts books and even Dodge Service Manuals are often unclear as to which model used which of the three U-joints. Also any one car might use one type of U-joint in the front and a second type in the rear. U-joint identification often depended on the answer to questions such as "early or late" in the production year, Detroit or Los Angeles serial number, or even the gear ratio of the rear axle. The Field Guide solution to this dilemma is to simply crawl under the car with a flashlight, identify the U-joint used in the front and rear of your automobile, and then circle the universal joint found, front and back, on the list below.

Front:

1. ball and trunnion
2. cross-ball
3. cross-block bearing

Rear:

1. ball and trunnion
2. cross-ball
3. cross-block bearing

At the flea market or swap meet, carefully compare the contents of the universal joint repair kit against the illustrations below to make sure the needed parts are inside and that it is the correct kit for your car.

Figures 4-14A. Illustrates the ball and trunnion (pin) type universal joint that was used in many models by Chrysler Corporation from the 1930s through the 1960s. This type was commonly used on 5 passenger models and is easily identified by the heavy metal "body" that houses the trunnion (pin) and needle bearings and a flexible protective "boot" that prevents dirt and water damage to the inner working parts. The boot could be of leather or rubber (replaces 939 700). Aftermarket ball and trunnion U-joints are generally found at swap meets in one of four "kits": (1) complete with body and lace type leather boot assembly, (2) complete with body and rubber boot assembly, (3) without body but with lace type leather boot assembly, (4) without body but with rubber boot assembly.

Figure 4-14B. Illustrates a repair kit for the ball and trunnion universal joint without body and with lace type leather boot assembly.

Figure 4-14C. Illustrates a repair kit for the ball and trunnion universal joint without body and with a rubber type boot assembly.

Figure 4-14D. Illustrates a "cross-ball" type U-joint that was commonly used on 5 passenger models. The center "cross" has needle bearing "balls" that are held in place with bolted-down caps. There is no boot. A cross-ball kit contains all the parts necessary to replace a single U-joint (replaces 1134 579).

Figure 4-14E. Illustrates the "cross-block bearing" type of U-joint that was used exclusively on the 7 passenger models. The center cross has needle bearing cups that are held in place with blocks and retainer springs. There is no boot. A cross-block bearing kit contains all the parts necessary to replace a single U-joint (replaces 947 550).

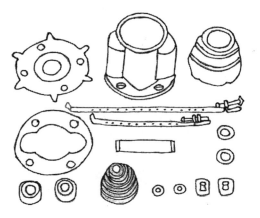

Figure 4-14A. Ball and trunnion U-joint

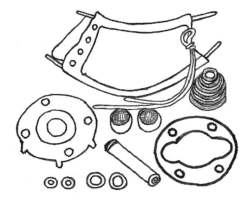

Figure 4-14B. Ball and trunnion U-joint

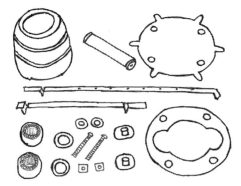

Figure 4-14C. Ball and trunnion U-joint

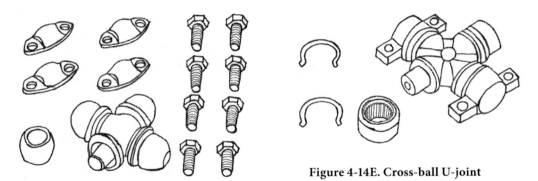

Figure 4-14E. Cross-ball U-joint

Figure 4-14D. Cross-block-bearing U-joint

Electrical (Figure 4-15A–4-20B)

GENERATOR AND GENERATOR VOLTAGE REGULATOR
(FIGURE 4-15A–FIGURE 4-15G)

The D24 Dodge was equipped with a 6 volt shunt type DC generator. In this generator the armature supplies both the field current and load current and therefore permanent magnets are not used. Shunt generators have only two brushes. The advantage of the shunt generator is that it reaches maximum electrical output at a low speed and maintains a constant output throughout an increased speed range.

The increased electrical load for additional accessories and higher operating speeds after the war required the use of a shunt type generator.

Figure 4-15A. Illustrates the Auto-Lite GDZ 4801A generator assembly used as standard equipment on the D24 Dodge (replaces 853 770).

Figure 4-15B. Illustrates the identification tag found on the GDZ 4801A generator.

Figure 4-15C. Illustrates the Auto-Lite generator armature GDZ 2006F used as standard equipment on the D24 GDZ 4801A generator (replaces 859 900).

Figure 4-15D. Illustrates the original Auto-Lite GCE-2012S generator brush set used in the D24 Dodge generator. It is essential to use the correct brushes for size, shape and number embossed on the brush and not just one that "looks like" the D24 brush. Brushes are made of different materials for hardness and conductivity to match the hardness and speed of the generator commutator for which they are intended. Note the insulation on the wire and how the wire is attached to the brush (replaces 673 032).

Figure 4-15E. Illustrates the Auto-Lite shaft bushing (GBF-79) located on the commutator end of the armature (replaces 636 804).

Figure 4-15F. Illustrates the Auto-Lite roller bearing (X-295) located on the drive (pulley) end of the armature (replaces 602 454).

Figure 4-15G. Illustrates the voltage regulator used on the D24 Dodge as standard equipment. The purpose of the voltage regulator is to control or regulate the charging rate within the shunt type generator to the battery circuit. The voltage regulator on the D24 Dodge contains three separate units inside the assembly:

1. A circuit breaker—The circuit breaker, also called a "cut-out," is a simple automatic magnetic switch that closes when the engine is running and the generator charging, and opens when the engine is stopped and the generator not charging. The cut-out relay prevents the battery from discharging to ground whenever the engine is stopped.

2. A current regulator—The current-regulator controls the maximum amperage output of the generator by controlling the current flow to the field windings. Increased flow increases the strength of the magnetic field and produces greater amperage. Lower flow reduces the strength of the magnetic field and yields lower amperage.

3. Voltage regulator—The voltage regulator will automatically increase the charging rate to a low battery until the battery becomes fully charged, and then reduce the charging rate. An example would be when the regulator allows higher voltage to the battery when the car first starts and the battery is lowered, then lower voltage to the battery when it again reaches charge. The voltage regulator also protects the battery from overcharging and the electrical system throughout the car from high voltage.

There are no quick "field tests" that can be applied at a swap meet to determine the condition of a voltage regulator. Buying a used voltage regulator at a flea market is definitely an example of "buyer-beware."

The voltage regulator is sealed at the factory. A broken seal indicates a regulator that was disassembled for adjustments or repairs. Beware. Even a slight error in the settings of a D24 voltage regulator may cause either a low or overcharged battery and damage to the generator.

The critical information about the voltage regulator is always printed on the outside of the NOS box and/or on the underside of the voltage regulator itself. Markings to look for on an aftermarket voltage regulator for the D24 Dodge: (1) positive ground, (2) 6 volts, (3) 35 amps, (4) three terminals marked B-battery, F-field and A-armature.

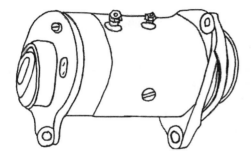

Figure 4-15A. Generator assembly

Figure 4-15B. Generator identification tag

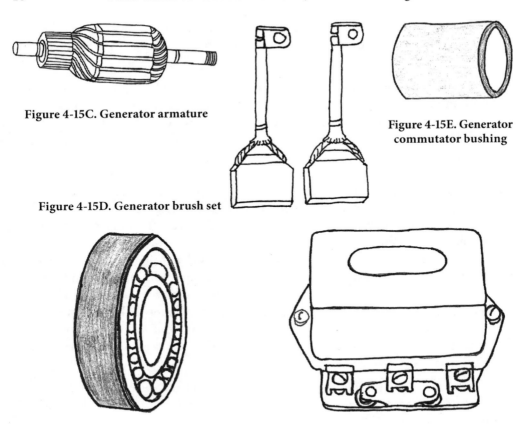

Figure 4-15C. Generator armature

Figure 4-15E. Generator commutator bushing

Figure 4-15D. Generator brush set

Figure 4-15F. Generator drive end bearing

Figure 4-15G. Generator voltage regulator

Starter (Figure 4-16A–Figure 4-16I)

The D24 starter is 6 volt, positive ground, two pole, four brush with a barrel type drive and operated with a pushbutton switch located on the driver's side of the instrument panel. As the button is pushed, the starter solenoid, which is mounted on the left front fender inner shield, causes the starter to engage. The ignition key must be turned on before the solenoid starter will operate.

Figure 4-16A. Illustrates the Auto-Lite MAW-4041 starter assembly used as original equipment on all D24 models (replaces 1113 121).

Figure 4-16B. Illustrates the Auto-Lite identification tag found on the MAW-4041 starter.

Figure 4-16C. Illustrates the Auto-Lite starter armature MAW-2128 used as original equipment on all MAW-4041 starters (replaces 927 079).

Figure 4-16D. Illustrates the Auto-Lite starter solenoid SST-4001 found as original equipment on all D24 models (replaces 1120 518).

Figure 4-16E. Illustrates the Auto-Lite EBA-39/EBB-8 barrel type drive used on all MAW-4041 starters (replaces 927 920).

Figure 4-16F. Illustrates the pushbutton switch used on all D24 models (replaces 903 437 up to serial No. 30867232 or replaces 1237 123 after serial No. 30867232).

Figure 4-16G. Illustrates the MAW-12 insulated brushes (2 used) and the MAW-13 grounded brushes (2 used) as original equipment in all MAW-4041 starters. It is essential to use the correct brushes for size, shape and number embossed on the brush and not just one that "looks like" the D24 brush. Brushes are made of different materials for hardness and conductivity to match the hardness and speed of the starter commutator for which they are intended. Brushes were generally found as an Auto-Lite boxed set MAW-2012S (replaces 2—MoPar 636 838—insulated and 2—MoPar 626 820—grounded brushes in the MoPar 927 902 brush set).

Figure 4-16H. Illustrates the drive end bushing used in the MAW-4041 starter (replaces 652 115).

Figure 4-16I. Illustrates the commutator end bushing used in the MAW-4041 starter (replaces 927 093).

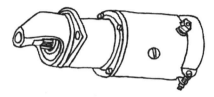

Figure 4-16A. Starter assembly

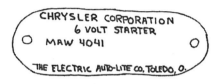

Figure 4-16B. Starter identification tag

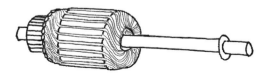

Figure 4-16C. Starter armature

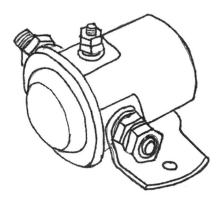

Figure 4-16D. Starter solenoid

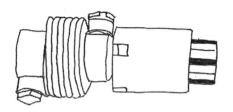

Figure 4-16E. Starter barrel drive

Figure 4-16F. Pushbutton starter switch

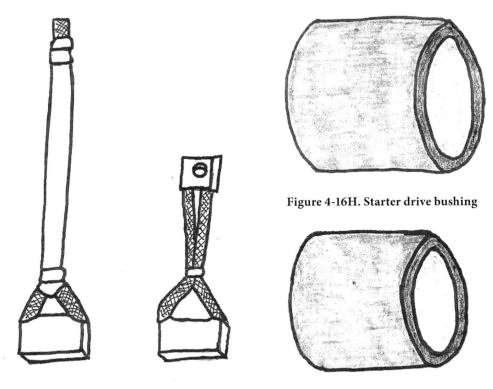

Figure 4-16H. Starter drive bushing

Figure 4-16G. Starter brushes

Figure 4-16I. Starter commutator bushing

Battery Cables (Figure 4-17A–Figure 4-17C)

Insulated No. 1 (heavy) gauge battery cables were used on all D24 models. Gauge of a battery cable is a measure of the total cross-section area of the separate copper strands in the cable. The No. 1 gauge used for all 1946–1948 Dodge models is a relatively thick battery cable that easily carries the current needed for the starter and all the accessories such as radio, heater, defroster, wipers, headlights, turn signals and cigar lighter that may all be running at the same time. The lower the gauge number the greater is the cross-section area and the greater is the current carrying capacity. The higher the gauge number, the less is the cross-section area and the less is the current carrying capacity. The diameter of the copper wire in the No 1 cable is .2895". Cables were not color coded "Red—Positive" and "Black—Negative" as is found with the newer 12 volt systems.

Observations and measurements can be carried out in the field to help verify if the battery cables in hand fit the D24 Dodge. Note the difference in length and the difference on the ends of the cables in the illustrations.

Figure 4-17A. Illustrates the starter solenoid to starter battery cable; No. 1 gauge; insulated; 16" long; bolt down strap ends at each end (replaces 1123 049).

Figure 4-17B. Illustrates the negative battery terminal to solenoid switch battery cable; No. 1 gauge; insulated; 16" long; battery terminal attachment at one end, bolt down strap end at the other (replaces 687 780).

Figure 4-17C. Positive battery terminal to engine ground battery cable; No. 1 gauge; insulated; 24" long; battery terminal attachment at on end, bolt down strap end at the other (replaces 687 782).

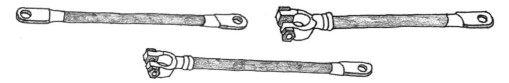

Left: **Figure 4-17A. Solenoid to starter cable.** **Right:** **Figure 4-17B. Negative terminal, cable to solenoid.** **Middle:** **Figure 4-17C. Positive terminal, cable to ground.**

DISTRIBUTOR AND IGNITION (FIGURE 4-18A–FIGURE 4-18H)

The Auto-Lite IGS-4207A-1 distributor assembly was original equipment on all D24 Dodge models. The distributor is easily removed from the engine and it was a common practice at junk yards to remove the distributor before scrapping the car. Therefore, many complete distributors for the D24 can be found at large and small swap meets across the nation. The Dodge distributor has both automatic and vacuum advance methods to control the advance or retard of the spark according to the speed or load of the engine. The automatic method consists of governor operated centrifugal weights located in the base of the distributor that regulate the timing according to speed when there is no vacuum present or when at idle or under rapid acceleration. When driving under normal load and speed there is sufficient vacuum for the "vacuum advance control" to advance the breaker point plate for maximum efficient engine operation.

Figure 4-18A. Illustrates the Auto-Lite "Solar Spark" IGS-4207-A1 distributor assembly used on the D24 Dodge. A metal tag with "SOLAR SPARK" and IGS-4207-A1 is permanently riveted to the side of the distributor. Note the "slot" type of attachment on the base of the shaft rather than a gear as with many distributors (replaces 1120 569).

Figure 4-18B. Illustrates the metal tag riveted to the distributor with the important information that is embossed and stamped onto the tag.

Figure 4-18C. Illustrates the 6 cylinder Auto-Lite distributor cap IGC-1107S used on all D24 Dodge models. Measurements to look for: (1) distance from center of spark plug tower to center of opposite spark plug tower—2¼", (2) outside diameter of distributor cap base—3⅜", (3) height of coil tower from base of cap to top of coil tower—3", and (4) height of spark plug tower from base of the cap to top of the tower—2½" (replaces 1120 569).

Figure 4-18D. Illustrates the two parts of the Auto-Lite contact point set (IGP-3028ES) located under the D24 distributor cap. The set consists of two pieces: (1) the arm with a steel spring and a copper electrical connection (IGP-3028 that replaces 643 912) and (2) the fixed bar (IGS-1086 RM that replaces 643 908). Aftermarket companies in the 1950s also supplied "assembled" contact point sets with the arm and bar assembled into a single unit to assure perfect alignment of the two pieces within the distributor at all times.

Figure 4-18E. Illustrates the Auto-Lite rotor (IGS-1016B) located within the D24 distributor. A metal insert located in the base of the rotor aligns the rotor in the correct position onto the shaft inside the distributor (replaces 869 095).

Figure 4-18F. Illustrates the Auto-Lite condenser located within the D24 distributor. The condenser is a waterproof metal cylinder with a single wire coming out of one end and the whole unit is located under the distributor cap. The function of the condenser is to instantly absorb the current from the primary winding of the coil when the points open. The action of the condenser prevents arcing (spark) at the points and therefore prevents the points from "burning" and at the same time increases the spark at the gap in the spark plug. The capacity (capacitance) of a condenser is measured in microfarads. Three "universal condensers" developed during the 1950s covered the condenser requirements for most cars and light trucks on the road at the time. A "universal condenser" measuring .20–.25 microfarads will meet the needs of most driving conditions for the D24 Dodge and may be used to replace an original D24 condenser (replaces 624 095). Most NOS aftermarket condensers found at swap meets that were made in the U.S.A. are still good. In fact a condenser found in a used distributor will still work and will work either as your primary or back-up condenser. There is no easy field test for a condenser.

Figure 4-18G. Illustrates the Auto-Lite vacuum chamber (VC-2082R) that is attached to the outside of the distributor and controls the advance of the breaker point plate within the D24 distributor (replaces 1135 576).

Figure 4-18H. Illustrates the flexible Auto-Lite "lead wires" that are located within the D24 distributor. The 1⅞" long primary (terminal) lead wire on the left (IGS-59A) replaces 699 309, and the 1¹⁵⁄₁₆" ground lead wire with the small circular clips on the right (IGS 89) replaces 677 193.

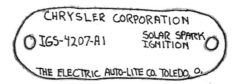

Figure 4-18A. D24 distributor assembly   **Figure 4-18B. Distributor information tag**

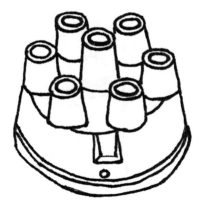

Figure 4-18C. Distributor cap

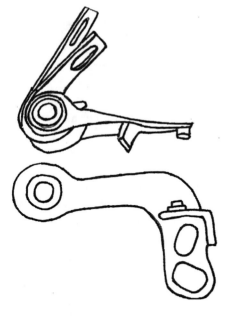

Figure 4-18D. D24 distributor contact set

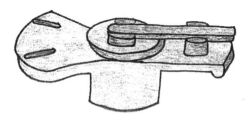

Figure 4-18E. Distributor rotor

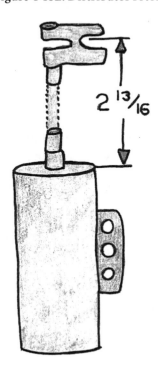

Figure 4-18F. Distributor condenser

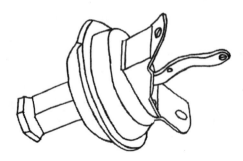

Figure 4-18G. D24 distributor vacuum chamber

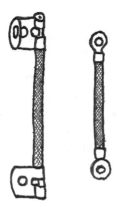

Figure 4-18H. Distributor lead wires

Coil (Figure 4-19)

The function of the coil is to transform low-voltage current from the battery or generator into high-voltage current that has enough electrical pressure to jump across the spark plug gap. Inside the D24 coil is a primary winding that operates on 6 volts and induces a secondary winding to produce the 15,000 volts needed to force the current across the air gap between the spark plug point and ground.

Two coils were used on the D24 Dodge: (1) Auto-Lite IG 4806—1946–1947, and (2) Auto-lite IG 4808—1947–1948. Both coils appear the same on the outside.

Figure 4-19. Illustrates the Auto-Lite IG 4806 coil.

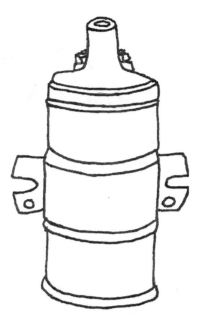

Figure 4-19. Coil

Spark Plug (Figure 4-20A–Figure 4-20B)

The original Auto-Lite A-5 and A-7 spark plugs for the D24 Dodge were mid-heat-range plugs between "cold and hot." Spark plugs were made in several "heat ranges" so that a plug with a suitable heat range for the 230 engine and a given set of driving conditions were available to the driver. The lower the number the colder the plug, the higher the number the hotter the plug. A cold plug is recommended for continuous high speed driving and a hot plug if the car is operated at low speed or in an older engine where the tip of the plug tends to foul. The A-5 and A-7 plugs were designed as "compromise plugs" for new cars to cover a mix of highway and/or city driving conditions.

Figure 4-20A. Illustrates an A-5 spark plug with a thread diameter of 14 mm (0.55") and a hex nut shoulder of $^{11}/_{16}$". Auto-Lite and A5 were printed in capital (block) letters on the porcelain. A copper washer is required to properly seat each plug with an air-tight seal at a torque of 25 ft. lbs. and a gap setting of .025" (replaces 926 101).

Figure 4-20B. Illustrates the ignition wire assembly used on the D24 distributor. The wire has a 90 degree large metal clip on one end for the spark plug and a small metal clip on the other end for the spark plug tower on the distributor cap. A short wire with small metal clips on each end connects the distributor to the coil. Eight rubber dust cups are included in each wire set.

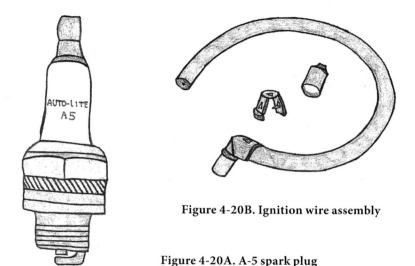

Figure 4-20B. Ignition wire assembly

Figure 4-20A. A-5 spark plug

Engine (Figure 4-21A–Figure 4-32A)

Piston—(Figure 4-21A–Figure 4-21D)

The D24 Dodge aluminum alloy piston is tapered and in a slight oval or "cam-ground." Aluminum pistons expand more than cast iron pistons and all areas of an aluminum piston do not expand at the same rate. The top of the piston gets more heat from the very start of the engine and under driving conditions and therefore expands the most. The skirt at the bottom of the piston runs the coolest and therefore expands the least. In addition, the piston does not expand the same amount around its circumference. MoPar engineers made allowances for this in the piston design of the 230 engine using the "cam-ground" process. The skirt is tapered by a .0005"–.0015" smaller diameter at the top of the piston than at the bottom. Pistons have a .010"–.012" smaller diameter across the piston pin. The piston becomes round and cylindrical when the engine reaches operating temperature.

Figure 4-21A. Illustrates the D24 Dodge aluminum piston. The piston has 4 piston rings and measures $3^{11}/_{16}$" in height and pistons are available in standard to .060" oversize.

Figure 4-21B. Illustrates the piston ring package for the D24 Dodge. MoPar and aftermarket piston rings were packaged 4 rings to an envelope and 6 envelopes to a box. The size of each ring is printed on the outside of the envelope. Each envelope contained: #1 groove top compression ring—$3^1/_4$" × $^3/_{32}$", #2 groove second compression ring—$3^1/_4$" × $^3/_{32}$", #3 groove upper oil control ring—$3^1/_4$" × $^5/_{32}$", and #4 groove lower control ring—$3^1/_4$" × $^5/_{32}$". Ring packages were marked standard to .060" oversize in increments of .010". Each size of piston ring had a different MoPar number.

Figure 4-21C. Illustrates the piston pin. The piston pin has a diameter of $^{55}/_{64}$" and a length of $2^3/_4$". Found in packages of six in standard to .008" oversize.

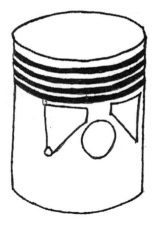

Figure 4-21A. Piston

Figure 4-21B. Piston rings

Figure 4-21C. Piston pin

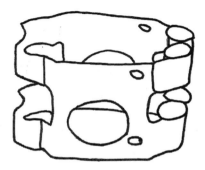

Figure 4-21D. Piston expander

Figure 4-21D. Illustrates the D24 Dodge piston expander. A piston expander was often placed inside a worn piston to expand the piston skirt and reduce piston slap. Unopened packages contain six (853 980) expanders (replaces the 951 330 package of 6 expanders).

ENGINE BEARINGS (FIGURE 4-22A–FIGURE 4-22E)

Crankshaft (main bearings), connecting rod bearings and camshaft bearings are the three types of aftermarket engine bearings often found at swap meets. Crankshaft bearings and connecting rod bearings are measured in standard size and "undersize" which means the diameter of the bearing is decreased to make up for the amount of metal removed if a crankshaft is "reground."

Bearing size is written or printed on the box as standard or undersize. Bearings should always be replaced in pairs (upper and lower). Never use a new bearing half with an old bearing half. Aftermarket main bearings are often found in the following sizes: standard, .001", .002", .003", .005", .010", .012", .020", .022", .030", .040" and .060" undersize. Aftermarket bearing size for crankshaft and connecting rod bearings were available in more sizes than MoPar offered as replacement bearings.

All were steel backed and thin Babbitt lined, not adjustable and precision shell type (divided into two equal halves).

Figure 4-22A. Illustrates the #1 front bearing that has a width of 1¹⁵⁄₆₄".

Figure 4-22B. Illustrates the interchangeable # 2 and #3 bearing that has a width of 1⅓₂".

Figure 4-22C. Illustrates the #4 rear bearing that has a width of 1⅞". Bearing #4 is the only flanged bearing and the one that may be found .010" oversize in width so that it may be fitted to a crankshaft with reground "cheeks."

Figure 4-22D. Illustrates the connecting rod insert bearings found in all models of the D24 engine. All bearings are steel backed and thin Babbitt lined, not adjustable and precision shell type. Bearing inside standard diameter is 2.0625" with a bearing width of 1". Aftermarket bearings are often found in the following sizes: standard, .001", .002", .003", .005", .010", .012", .020", .022", .030", .040" and .060" undersize.

Figure 4-22E. Illustrates the camshaft bearings found in all models of the D24 engine. All are steel backed and thin Babbitt lined, not adjustable, not shell type and not found in pairs as with the crankshaft and connecting rod bearings. Camshaft bearings are either split across the bearing or solid (like a pipe) and in standard and .010" oversize. Camshaft bearings may be labeled on the box as "oversize" so as to replace the space in the engine block from wear or reaming during a regrinding. Camshaft diameter journal No. 1 = 2", No. 2 = 1³¹⁄₃₂", No. 3 = 1¹⁵⁄₁₆" and No. 4 = 1¼". Bearings #1, #2 and #3 are easily replaceable but bearing #4 must be machined into the block.

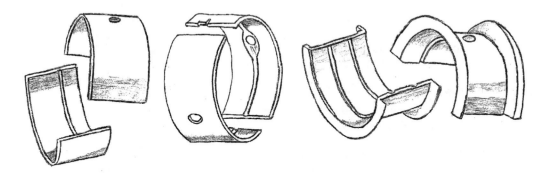

Left: **Figure 4-22A. Position #1.** *Middle:* **Figure 4-22B. Position #2 and #3. Figure 4-22C. Position #4.**

Left: **Figure 4-22D. Connecting rod bearing**

Right: **Figure 4-22E. Camshaft bearing**

Valves and Valve Parts (Figure 4-23A–Figure 4-23E)

The intake and exhaust valves of the 230 D24 Dodge engine were known as "poppet" valves because they "pop" open and shut when the engine is turning. Both the intake and exhaust valves are located in the engine block on the same side of the cylinder in what is known as the "L-Head" arrangement.

Figure 4-23A. Illustrates the exhaust valve used in the Dodge D24 230 engine. What to look for: (1) the valve head is forged with the stem in one piece of high grade heat resisting steel, (2) the beveled face of the head is an angle of 45 degrees, (3) the bottom of the head where it meets the stem is curved downward to direct the exhaust gas away from the cylinder and into the exhaust manifold. (4) two grooves are located at the base of the stem for the "keeper" that holds the working valve in place.

Three measurements can be quickly carried out in the field to verify if the valve in hand fits the D24 Dodge (replaces 954 302).

1. Valve head diameter: $1^{13}/_{32}$"
2. Stem diameter: .340–.341"
3. Length of valve: $4^{25}/_{32}$"

Figure 4-23B. Illustrates the intake valve used in the Dodge D24 230 engine. What to look for: (1) the valve head is forged with the stem in one piece of high grade heat resisting steel, (2) the beveled face of the head is an angle of 45 degrees, (3) the bottom of the head where it meets the stem is curved upward to direct the flow of the air/gas mixture into the cylinder, (4) two grooves are located at the base of the stem for the "keeper" that holds the working valve in place, (5) the stem is slightly thinner just above the top keeper groove.

Three measurements can be quickly carried out in the field to verify if the valve in hand fits the D24 Dodge (replaces 868 886).

1. Valve head diameter: $1^{17}/_{32}$"
2. Stem diameter: .340–.341"
3. Length of valve: $4^{25}/_{32}$"

Figure 4-23C. Illustrates the solid valve lifter of the D24 engine. The lifter is adjusted using two tappet wrenches through the valve cover opening on the side of the engine. Seldom will a valve lifter need to be replaced due to wear. Wear to the lifter is prevented in two ways in the Dodge 230 engine: (1) the valve lifter is well lubricated with oil to prevent wear with the up and down motion that occurs with the opening and closing of the valve, (2) The cam is located off center to the valve lifter so as to turn the lifter to a new spot each time it contacts the cam and thus reduce wear (replaces 670 508).

Figure 4-23D. Illustrates the valve spring used in the D24 Dodge. The function of the valve spring is to hold the valve closed until the valve is pushed upward and off its seat by the valve lifter and cam. Valve springs are designed for size and "strength" for each and every automobile engine and it is no different for the Dodge 230 engine. The correct valve spring must be used in the D24 Dodge. Too strong a spring causes excess wear and friction to the lifter and cam, while too weak a spring causes the valve not to seat firmly and on time. The valve spring is 2" long in the relaxed position and is the same on both the intake and exhaust valves for the 230 engine. Intake and exhaust valve springs are interchangeable (replaces 869 449).

Figure 4-23E. Illustrates the valve guide used in the D24 Dodge 230 engine. The valve guide is located within the cylinder block and holds the stem of the valve in a central position in relation to the seat so that the valve will seat tightly when closing (replaces 1121 490).

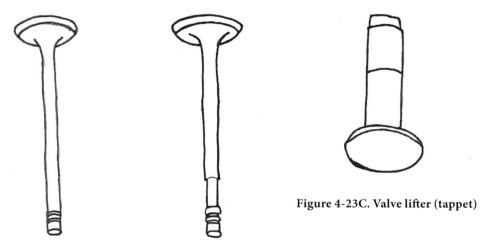

Figure 4-23C. Valve lifter (tappet)

Figure 4-23A. Exhaust valve   Figure 4-23B. Intake valve

Figure 4-23D. Valve spring   Figure 4-23E. Valve guide

Motor Mounts (Figure 4-24A–Figure 4-24C)

Three motor mounts were used to balance the weight of the engine in the engine-bay. The front motor mount assembly was located at the water pump. It was made of two metal plates separated by a center of "live-rubber" and held in position with four hex-nuts. The rear motor mount assembly was located at the bottom of the bell-housing and each assembly consisted of two "live-rubber" upper and lower bushings. When the motor mounts are positioned in the engine-bay there is no metal-metal contact of the engine with the frame. Vibration from the engine to the frame and body is eliminated.

Figure 4-24A. Illustrates the front support insulator assembly (1115 744).

Figure 4-24B. Illustrates the rear upper (right and/or left) support assembly (866 050).

Figure 4-24C. Illustrates the rear lower (right and/or left) support assembly (854 877).

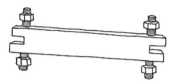  

Left: Figure 4-24A. Engine front support. *Middle:* Figure 4-24B. Rear upper support. *Right:* Figure 4-24C. Rear lower support.

TIMING CHAIN (FIGURE 4-25A–FIGURE 4-25B)

The D24 Dodge uses a timing chain rather than timing gears to regulate the timing of valves and ignition. The chain driven camshaft has several times more contact area than a gear-driven camshaft which means less wear. Additional benefits include silent and dependable performance.

Figure 4-25A. Illustrates the position of the timing chain, camshaft sprocket (38 teeth—610 757) and crankshaft sprocket (19 teeth—601 760) assembly used in the D24.

Figure 4-25B. Illustrates the center guide, no back bend, silent type timing chain used in the D24 Dodge. Measurements: (1) ½" pitch (distance from center to center of the chain joint in inches), (2) 1" wide × 48 links (replaces 1075 001).

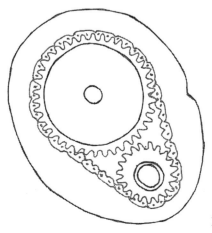

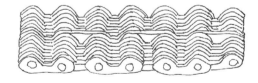

Figure 4-25B. Timing chain

Figure 4-25A. Timing chain and sprockets

Water Pump (Figure 4-26A–Figure 4-26B)

Figure 4-26A. Illustrates the water pump assembly used on all D24 Dodge models. Only three bolts attach the water pump to the engine block (replaces 1064 750).

Figure 4-26B. Illustrates the water pump gasket used on all D24 Dodge models. Note the "half-moon" design on the gasket that is also found on the back of the water pump. The half-moon is used as an identifying characteristic for the 1946–1948 Dodge water pump by most aftermarket companies (replaces 637 440).

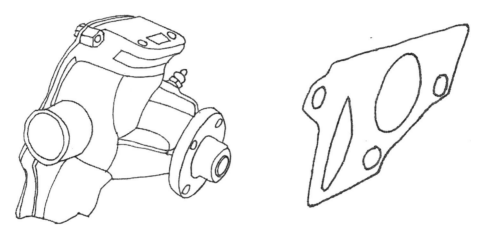

Left: Figure 4-26A. Water pump with "half-moon" on the back. *Right:* Figure 4-26B. Water pump gasket with "half-moon"

Thermostat (Figure 4-27)

The D24 Dodge uses a "bellows" type of thermostat to regulate the coolant in the engine. The coolant in the engine and the radiator is a closed system with the thermostat acting as a "go-no-go" device to regulate coolant flow and maintain a pre-set optimum engine working temperature. If the engine and coolant are cold the thermostat remains closed. If the coolant in the engine is hot the thermostat opens to allow the hot coolant to circulate through the radiator and then return to the engine. Two pre-set thermostat temperatures were available by Dodge for all D24 models: (1) 160 degree (867 040) and (2) 180 degree (1124 989). In addition to the "bellows" type thermostat many aftermarket companies offered a "butterfly" thermostat which works just as well.

Figure 4-27. Illustrates the "bellows" type thermostat used as original in all D24 models

Figure 4-27. Bellows thermostat

RADIATOR HOSE (FIGURE 4-28A–FIGURE 4-28D)

Four straight radiator hose sections were used on the D24 Dodge. Each section was cut to the required length from a 3 foot MoPar hose of the correct diameter. Some aftermarket companies combined hose 4-28C and 4-28D into a single curved hose.

Figure 4-28A. Illustrates the radiator inlet hose from the cylinder head to the radiator. The hose is 6" L × 1¾" inside diameter and cut from a 3 foot long MoPar hose number 734 749.

Figure 4-28B. Illustrates the water bypass hose located above the water pump. The hose is 1⅝" L × 1" inside diameter and cut from a 3 foot long MoPar hose number 734 748.

Figure 4-28C. Illustrates the water outlet hose from the water pump to the outlet tube. The hose is 3½" L × 1½" inside diameter and cut from a 3 foot long MoPar hose 734 737.

Figure 4-28D. Illustrates the lower radiator outlet hose from the lower outlet tube to the radiator. The hose is 5¾" L × 1½" inside diameter and cut from a 3 foot long MoPar hose 734 737.

  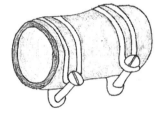

Left: **Figure 4-28A. Radiator inlet hose.** *Middle:* **Figure 4-28B. Bypass hose.** *Right:* **Figure 4-28C. Water pump outlet hose.**

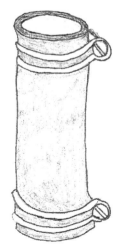

Figure 4-28D. Radiator outlet hose

RADIATOR CAP (FIGURE 4-29)

Two kinds of radiator caps can be found at swap meets: (1) the Atmospheric Radiator Cap, and (2) the Pressure Radiator Cap.

Figure 4-29. Illustrates the Atmospheric Radiator Cap used on all D24 Dodge models. The overflow pipe of the radiator is open to the atmosphere and the cooling system operates under atmospheric air pressure. There is a slow but constant evaporation of water and that is why the gas stations in 1946–1948 always had a water can next to the gas pumps to top off the radiator (replaces 837 237).

Pressure radiator caps were standard for cars starting in the 1950s and can be identified by the pressure release information written on the top center of the cap. As car designs changed and radiators under the hood became smaller, pressure caps allowed for less coolant and higher boiling temperatures. The pressure cap seals the coolant from the overflow pipe until a radiator pressure of 7–15 pounds is reached and the excess pressure is then released through the overflow pipe.

Figure 4-29. Atmospheric radiator cap

Both types of aftermarket radiator caps can be found that will "fit" the D24 Dodge radiator. The pressure cap will seal the radiator opening but it will not pass judging standards and will not work as intended since it will not seal the coolant from the overflow pipe.

Fan/Generator Belt (Figure 4-30)

Almost every gas station before and after the war had a supply of aftermarket fan/generator belts that could be easily replaced in a few minutes' time. It was commonplace for a fan belt to fray or break on 1940s automobiles. The D24 Dodge had a single belt to run the fan, water pump and generator off the crankshaft pulley located on the bottom front of the engine. Belts were designed wide at the top and narrow at the bottom to contact the sides of the fan and generator pulleys and not touch the bottom of the pulley groove.

outside circumference: $49^{1}/_{16}$"
inside circumference: $46^{5}/_{16}$"
top width: $^{47}/_{64}$"
angle: 40 degrees
thickness: $^{7}/_{16}$"

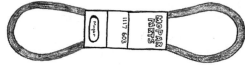

Figure 4-30. Fan/generator belt

Figure 4-30. Illustrates the fan/generator packaging to look for at a swap meet. Note the center cardboard wrapper that identifies the MoPar number or aftermarket company and company number (replaces 1117 603).

Oil Pump (Figure 4-31A–Figure 4-31B)

The prewar 230 engine "gear-type" oil pump was replaced with a postwar "Roto-Pressure" oil pump. The high capacity Roto-Pressure oil pump provides increased oil pressure when idling and a more uniform distribution of increased oil pressure at all engine speeds and temperatures. Gear replacement with a four-lobe inner rotor and a five-lobe outer rotor created 40-45 pounds of oil pressure at driving speeds. Both oil pumps are similar in outer appearance but the D24 230 engine roto-pressure oil pump is easily identified by a five-bolt pattern base plate verses a six-bolt pattern base plate used on the prewar 230 Dodge gear oil pump.

Figure 4-31A. Cut-away illustration of the "Roto-Pressure" oil pump showing the location of the four-lobe inner rotor and the five-lobe outer rotor at the base of the oil pump assembly (replaces 1124 735).

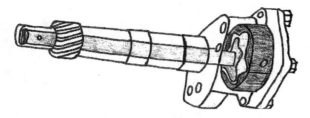
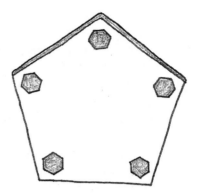

Left: **Figure 4-31A. D24 oil pump.** *Right:* **Figure 4-31B. D24 oil pump base plate bolt pattern.**

Figure 4-31B. Illustration of the 5-bolt pattern base of the D24 post-war roto-pressure oil pump

OIL FILTER ELEMENT (FIGURE 4-32)

The replaceable cartridge (element) type "Micronic Filtration" oil filter was developed during World War II for use in Army and Navy planes and was offered in 1946 for use on the New Dodge. Replacement with the new type filter reduced costs by one-third over that of the older type canister used in the 1930s and early 1940s.

The factory oil filter was not a precision fit within the oil filter housing and this is reflected in a slight size difference with many of the aftermarket replacement oil filters you may find in the field. The reason for the slight size difference is in the end cap of the filter. The end cap (top and bottom) of the aftermarket filter may be paper or metal and the end cap attachment seam may be folded or crimped. This may give a diameter difference up to $3/16$" and a height difference up to $1/8$". The center holes, top and bottom, may also have a diameter difference of $1/8$". Gaskets are unchanged from originals and included with aftermarket filters (replaces 1121 694).

Figure 4-32. Illustrates the oil filter element and gasket used in the D24 Dodge.

filter diameter—$3^{5}/_{16}$"
filter height—$4^{1}/_{8}$"
top hole diameter—$^{9}/_{16}$"
bottom hole diameter—$^{3}/_{4}$"
gasket I.D.—$4^{1}/_{8}$"
gasket O.D.—$4^{1}/_{2}$"

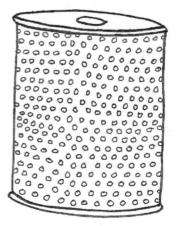

Fuel (Figure 4-33A–4-35B)

CARBURETOR (FIGURE 4-33A–FIGURE 4-33C)

Three carburetors are found as original equipment on all D24 Dodge models: (1) Stromberg BXVD-3, (2) Stromberg BXV-3

Figure 4-32. Oil filter element and gasket

and Carter Ball & Ball D6J1. Complete carburetors were easily removed from engines at garages and junk yards and therefore intact, complete and often working examples are plentiful and affordable at swap meets and flea markets. Most, however, require a rebuild kit before mounting on the intake manifold of your 230 engine. Rebuild kits are readily available online. Each carburetor has a top, middle and bottom section bolted together to form a single barrel, down-draft carburetor.

Figure 4-33A. Illustrates the Stromberg BXVD-3 carburetor. The BXVD-3 identification number is embossed on the bottom section of the carburetor. This carburetor is found on Dodge models that have fluid drive and the D stands for "dash-pot." The dash-pot is an additional feature found in the fluid drive carburetor that offers a slow throttle return valve that prevents the engine from stalling on a fast return to idle.

Figure 4-33B. Illustrates the Stromberg BXV-3 carburetor. The BXV-3 identification number is embossed on the bottom section of the carburetor. The dash-pot feature (D) is absent and this carburetor is found on D24 models that have standard transmission without fluid drive.

Figure 4-33C. Illustrates the Carter Ball and Ball D6J1 carburetor. The D6J1 identification number is stamped into the top section of the carburetor. The dash-pot feature is present on the D6J1 carburetor.

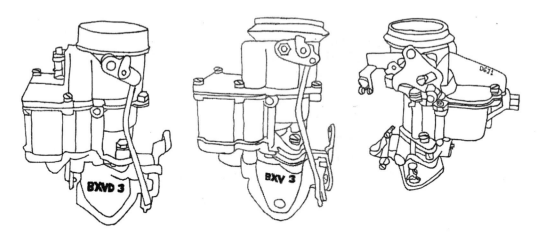

Left: **Figure 4-33A. Stromberg BXVD-3.** *Middle:* **Figure 4-33B. Stromberg BXV-3.** *Right:* **Figure 4-33C. Carter Ball and Ball D6J1.**

Automatic Choke Control (Figure 4-34)

The choke unit is mounted on the exhaust manifold and controls the position of the choke valve in the carburetor using an electromagnet and a thermostat. When the starter is engaged, a connecting wire energizes an electromagnet connection in the unit that closes the choke valve. When the engine starts, the electromagnet connection is broken and then the thermostat controls the choke valve using engine manifold temperature.

Figure 4-34. Illustrates the Sisson Type AC-7588 automatic choke control assembly used on all D24 Dodge models (replaces 667 179).

Fuel Pump (Figure 4-35A–Figure 4-35B)

Two types of AC fuel pumps were used as original on the D24 Dodge:

Figure 4-34. Automatic choke control assembly

Figure 4-35A. Illustrates the fuel pump with a glass sediment bowl filter that was used by Dodge in 1939 and continued through early 1946. Note the sediment bowl is directly below the fuel pump body. It is AC series AT and factory number 3647 or 1523647 with a rebuilt AC number of 505 or 505X.

Figure 4-35B. Illustrates a fuel pump without a glass bowl filter that was used from 1946 to 1948. During the war a fuel filter was developed and located in the gas tank that made the glass bowl sediment filter unnecessary. Note that a cover plate with bolt is located directly below the diaphragm on the fuel pump body. It is AC series BQ factory number 9042 or 1539042 with a rebuilt AC number of 577 or 577X.

The most common aftermarket fuel pump replacement for the D24 Dodge is with a glass bowl sediment filter bowl (looks like figure 4-35A) and numbered 588 or 588X.

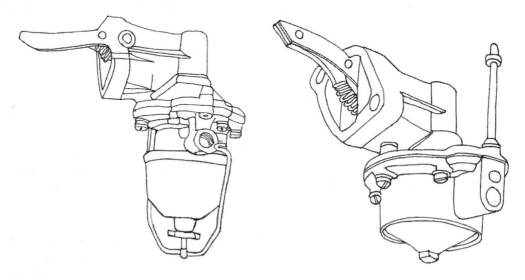

Figure 4-35A. With glass sediment bowl   **Figure 4-35B. Without glass sediment bowl**

Gaskets and Seals (Figure 4-36A–Figure 4-37B)

GASKETS (FIGURE 4-36A–FIGURE 4-36M)

It doesn't take very long at a flea market or swap meet to realize that there are thousands of vintage NOS gaskets available for engines, transmissions and rear axles for vintage automobiles. You will quickly realize that a six cylinder head gasket for a 1946–1948 Chevrolet is not interchangeable with a D24 Dodge. Even six cylinder gaskets from the same company may not be interchangeable. A six cylinder head gasket from a 1946–1948 DeSoto will not fit a D24 Dodge.

Gaskets were generally packaged in a heavy paper envelope or box with the company name and part number clearly printed on the outside. Rarely was the car that the gasket fits printed on the outside of the package along with the part number. A company head gasket number, for instance, was specific for one and only one engine. As an example the Victor 924 head gasket fits the 3¼" six cylinder Dodge 230 while the Victor 1029 head gasket fits the 3⅜" six cylinder DeSoto 237.

Unfortunately after these many years, the gasket is generally now out of the clearly printed and part numbered envelope or box and appears to be impossible to identify. All is not lost. Most gasket companies, but not all, stamped their company name and part number into the gasket itself before packaging. The **What to Look For** section offers silhouette drawings to illustrate the shape and visual features for the most common gaskets to be found at swap meets that fit the D24 Dodge. All the drawings in this section are slightly shaded to enhance the outline and location of the holes in the gasket. Remember that the gasket drawings are not drawn to scale.

Figure 4-36A. Illustrates a replacement six cylinder head gasket that may be found as steel or copper (replaces 1117 542).

Figure 4-36B. Illustrates the 4 piece intake and exhaust manifold gasket set. The set includes a single center gasket (601 275) and four end gaskets (318 042) (replaces 780 460).

Figure 4-36C. Illustrates a single piece intake and exhaust manifold gasket that was available from MoPar and aftermarket companies for the D24 Dodge (replaces 854 395).

Figure 4-36D. Illustrates the valve spring cover gasket set that includes (600 882—2 required per car, and a pair of valve spring cover stud gaskets 693 539—4 required per car) (replaces gasket set 780 469).

Figure 4-36E. Illustrates the fuel pump gasket (replaces 688 482).

Figure 4-36F. Illustrates the 4 piece oil pan gasket set (one right side gasket—600 758, one left side gasket—600 759, and front and rear gaskets—866 680) used on the D24 Dodge (replaces gasket set 933 438).

Figure 4-36G. Illustrates the water pump to cylinder block gasket with the "half-moon" cut-out in the gasket (replaces 637 440).

Figure 4-36H. Illustrates the timing chain plate cover gasket (replaces 695 441).

Figure 4-36I. Illustrates the timing chain case cover gasket (replaces 600 752).

Figure 4-36J. Illustrates the oil pump to cylinder block gasket (replaces 695 4420).

Figure 4-36K. Illustrates the water pump bypass elbow gasket (replaces 622 772).

Figure 4-36L. Illustrates the thermostat gasket (replaces 50 082).

Figure 4-36M. Illustrates the carburetor flange gasket (replaces 637 191).

Left: Figure 4-36A. Cylinder head gasket. *Middle:* Figure 4-36B. Manifold gasket. *Right:* Figure 4-36C. Manifold gasket.

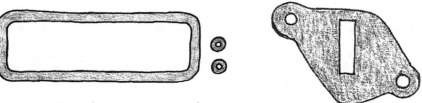

Figure 4-36D. Valve spring cover gasket

Figure 4-36E. Fuel pump gasket

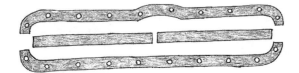

Figure 4-36F. Oil pan gasket

Left: Figure 4-36G. Water pump gasket. *Middle:* Figure 4-36H. Timing plate gasket. *Right:* Figure 4-36I. Timing gasket.

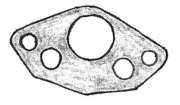
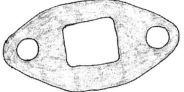

Left: **Figure 4-36J. Oil pump gasket.** *Middle:* **Figure 4-36K. Bypass gasket.** *Right:* **Figure 4-36L. Thermostat gasket**

SEALS (FIGURE 4-37A–FIGURE 4-37B)

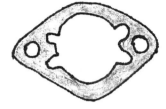

**Figure 4-36M.
Carburetor flange gasket**

Automobile seals were designed to seal the close spaces between rotating and stationary components of wheels, axles, transmissions and engines to prevent lubricants such as oil and grease from escaping and at the same time prevent dust, dirt and moisture from entering. Seals are a metal ring with a flexible inner lining of rubber, leather or cork. Dodge factory and aftermarket seals can be found as a single unit that fits over most shafts and axles (Figure 4-37A) or in two pieces to fit over an engine crankshaft (Figure 4-37B).

Figure 4-37A. Illustrates a single piece type of seal assembly.

Figure 4-37B. Illustrates a two piece type of seal assembly.

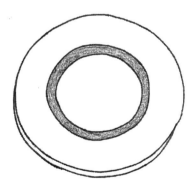

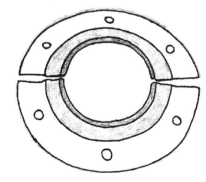

Figure 4-37A.   Figure 4-37B.

Windshield Wipers (Figure 4-38A–Figure 4-38B)

WINDSHIELD WIPERS (FIGURE 4-38A–FIGURE 4-38B)

Two different windshield wiper arms and blades were used on the D24 Dodge: (1) wiper arms and blades for electric wiper motors and (2) wiper arms and blades for vacuum wiper motors. Wiper arms can be found for both type motors as "straight or bent" or "chrome or stainless." All D24 wiper blades have a straight rubber edge, are 10" long and designed for flat windshields.

Figure 4-38A. Illustrates a "straight" windshield wiper arm and matching blade for the D24 electric motor windshield wiper. The arm is attached to the wiper shaft with a nut and washer (replaces 863 814, 815 arm and 830 237 blade).

Figure 4-38B. Illustrates a "bent" windshield wiper and matching blade for the D24 vacuum motor windshield wiper. The arm is "press-fit" onto the knurled wiper shaft and is not held in place with a nut and washer (replaces 935 639-640 arm and 830 237 blade).

Left: **Figure 4-38A. Electric motor arm and blade.** *Right:* **Figure 4-38B. Vacuum motor arm and blade**

Lighting (Table 4-1)

Lamps and Bulbs (Table 4-1)

Table 4-1 lists the Mazda type lamps and sizes that were used in all D24 models. Mazda was the 1909 registered trademark name for the General Electric (GE) patented filament light bulb. The newly developed tungsten filament bulbs for home and auto were more efficient, brighter, and gave greater life expectancy than carbon filament bulbs. GE licensed the Mazda name, socket sizes and production technology to additional manufacturers and that soon established a standard numbering system for bulbs and socket sizes throughout the automobile industry. Mazda was the name for the ancient Persian god of "light/wisdom."

Location	Candlepower	Mazda Number
headlamp	45–35 watts	sealed beam
parking	3	63
front signal & park	21-3	1158
instruments	1½	55
speedometer	6	81
map light	6	81
beam/signal indicator	1	51
tail, license	3	63
rear signal & tail	21-3	1158
stop, back up	21	1129
hand brake	21	1129
Dome	15	87

Table 4-1

5

MoPar Field Guide Numbers

It doesn't take very long at a swap meet to notice all the Chrysler Corporation MoPar boxes on tables, under tables and scattered out on tarps on the ground. You may see dozens of colorful red, blue and tan NOS boxes, most unopened. Close inspection identifies the same problem encountered with the aftermarket NOS boxes: no information on what year or model of MoPar car or truck it fits. One feature about the packaging that catches the eye is that the part may be in a box, a carton, or an envelope. They always have at least two of the following three images: (1) the Chrysler MoPar logo (Figure 5-1), (2) the name MoPar clearly printed in block letters, and (3) the words Chrysler Corporation, Detroit Michigan. In addition the part contains the MoPar number printed somewhere on the outside and maybe even a name for the part inside the packaging.

In the Field Guide the MoPar numbers for the D24 Dodge have been added to help you identify if a NOS MoPar part at a flea market fits a 1946–1948 Dodge. The numbers do not identify what model the part fits, only that it fits a D24 Dodge. Identifying every part number with that information would be a book unto itself since there are over 5,000 pieces to the D24 automobiles.

Five figures are shown to illustrate the diversity of parts and packaging that I have found at flea markets. When I got home and checked the parts I found each one fit my D24 Dodge.

Figure 5-2 MoPar Part Number 1115 838; oil seal assembly

Figure 5-3 MoPar Part Number 951 305; tie rod end package

Figure 5-4 MoPar Part Number 990 547 switch assembly

Figure 5-5 MoPar Part Number
1149 367 tail lamp lens

Figure 5-6 MoPar Part Number
698 415 bearing cone

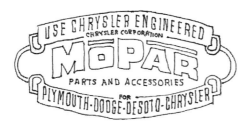

Figure 5-1. Chrysler MoPar logo

Figure 5-2

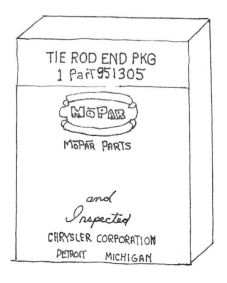

Figure 5-3

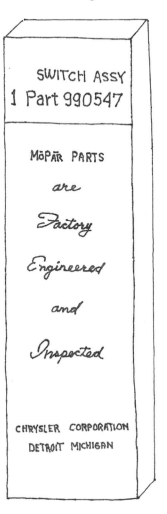

Figure 5-4

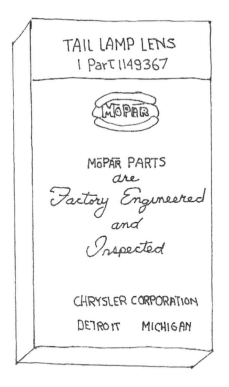

Figure 5-5

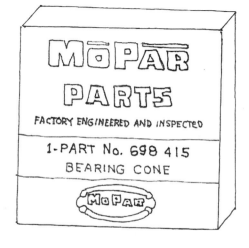

Figure 5-6

32 881	142 306	320 053	466 410	600 801
33 208	142 308	320 055	466 411	600 803
40 654	142 449	320 057	472 473	600 804
41 928	142 756	320 058	478 660	600 805
43 761	144 497	320 059	480 215	600 810
44 650	147 685	320 060	485 289	600 811
44 758	147 925	320 691	488 550	600 817
50 082	150 189	327 072	490 254	600 881
50 291	152 781	327 706	491 605	601 014
50 342	200 434	342 885	492 365	601 108
50 368	201 848	343 570	492 424	601 127
50 652	208 483	344 624	494 153	601 128
50 722	208 485	345 431	494 796	601 129
51 019	211 318	356 513	494 861	601 130
51 094	300 853	364 848	512 530	601 131
51 561	300 934	366 975	522 295	601 268
51 680	301 034	366 978	525 009	601 275
51 921	303 856	376 505	536 249	601 420
52 570	303 857	376 751	537 820	601 757
52 833	306 458	379 621	537-821	601 760
52 855	307 555	384 982	561 133	601 766
53 298	308 246	385 386	567 226	601 859
53 372	308 247	385 532	567 331	601 864
53 553	308 279	385 571	579 445	602 007
55 985	308 282	385 573	581 523	602 454
56 382	308 466	386 162	581 524	602 819
58 149	308 618	386 699	582 880	602 820
66 853	308 619	386 701	583 801	603 480
74 664	309 472	386 718	592 236	604 504
76 390	312 773	386 801	593 804	604 505
76 547	312 941	386 985	594 785	604 509
77 041	313 073	388 302	594 804	604 868
79 783	314 293	389 070	595 371	605 004
89 796	314 332	389 413	597 129	606 345
100 033	314 898	391 888	599 633	608 138
100 035	314 926	392 911	600 183	608 473
115 273	314 957	395 930	600 194	608 804
120 647	314 965	395 931	600 365	610 136
120 668	316 767	398 323	600 472	611 511
120 669	317 180	404 194	600 473	611 828
120 677	317 814	443 524	600 752	611 898
121 615	317 942	456 654	600 758	612 492
125 588	318 042	456 655	600 759	617 115
142 303	320 031	456 656	600 786	618 307
142 304	320 051	456 664	600 787	618 308

618 311	631 456	636 841	640 715	650 038
618 621	631 457	636 899	641 252	650 043
618 622	631 495	637 191	641 446	650 194
619 084	631 794	637 347	641 454	650 328
619 129	631 809	637 438	641 457	651 183
619 166	631 810	637 439	642 440	651 184
619 167	631 823	637 440	642 911	651 185
619 319	631 824	637 539	643 629	651 186
619 354	631 825	638 669	643 691	651 197
619 355	631 869	639 090	643 822	651 205
619 395	631 877	639 091	643 835	651 208
619 463	632 258	639 093	643 892	651 251
619 466	632 381	639 095	643 893	651 401
619 716	632 465	639 097	643 896	651 402
620 178	632 466	639 099	643 897	651 403
620 180	632 467	639 101	643 899	651 678
620 181	632 586	639 102	643 902	652 115
620 371	632 587	639 104	643 903	652 213
622 111	632 685	639 107	643 906	652 840
622 355	633 238	639 108	643 907	652 841
622 772	633 298	639 109	643 908	652 842
622 783	633 405	639 110	643 912	652 845
622 915	633 672	639 111	643 917	652 846
623 302	633 733	639 113	644 620	652 848
623 368	633 734	639 115	644 818	652 970
623 369	633 897	639 116	644 876	653 194
623 370	634 036	639 122	645 411	653 414
623 764	634 753	639 123	645 412	653 466
626 220	635 704	639 126	645 635	655 116
626 248	635 884	639 130	645 636	655 466
626 503	635 885	639 133	645 639	655 498
626 870	636 207	639 138	645 642	655 769
626 871	636 345	639 142	645 669	657 039
626 975	636 796	639 145	645 678	657 047
627 045	636 800	639 146	646 059	657 054
627 488	636 804	639 147	647 070	657 413
627 659	636 810	639 148	647 093	657 417
629 635	636 812	639 174	647 120	657 560
629 768	636 813	639 837	647 123	657 572
629 769	636 815	639 973	647 834	657 583
629 770	636 818	640 038	648 029	657 625
629 792	636 820	640 086	648 246	657 722
630 476	636 821	640 280	648 387	657 723
630 477	636 838	640 331	648 392	657 770
631 122	636 840	640 332	649 123	658 606

658 685	666 143	671 490	677 179	683 003
658 948	666 246	671 673	677 193	683 050
658 998	666 538	671 674	677 204	683 056
660 146	666 867	671 724	677 534	683 057
661 116	666 868	671 729	677 540	683 230
661 117	666 924	671 915	677 541	683 357
661 118	666 927	672 641	677 610	683 358
661 119	667 379	672 969	677 701	683 365
661 120	667 515	672 970	677 702	683 854
661 772	667 516	673 014	677 703	683 858
661 780	667 725	673 031	677 860	683 861
661 825	667 751	673 032	677 861	683 995
662 431	667 774	673 294	678 104	684 140
662 598	668 043	673 418	678 495	684 363
663 790	668 146	673 520	678 576	684 387
662 811	668 147	673 521	678 606	684 389
663 219	668 149	673 523	678 722	684 748
663 220	668 153	673 579	678 844	684 775
663 227	668 154	673 581	679 023	684 943
663 445	668 164	673 587	679 329	684 980
663 446	668 265	673 588	679 498	684 981
663 472	668 479	673 596	680 177	684 982
663 476	668 504	674 292	680 183	685 334
663 479	668 509	674 311	680 184	685 503
663 480	668 555	674 575	680 185	685 624
663 481	668 575	674 608	680 186	685 625
663 482	668 920	674 955	680 191	685 670
663 483	668 963	675 177	680 194	685 817
663 580	669 077	675 501	680 195	686 626
663 602	669 412	675 594	681 307	687 364
663 604	670 103	675 665	681 318	687 391
663 607	670 109	675 666	681 319	687 484
663 647	670 110	675 877	681 320	687 667
663 648	670 111	675 966	681 321	687 669
664 543	670 463	675 115	681 322	687 766
664 604	670 519	675 290	681 349	687 780
664 689	670 583	676 372	681 378	687 782
664 690	670 647	676 515	681 544	687 901
665 140	670 752	676 575	681 934	687 902
665 151	670 945	676 872	682 198	687 975
665 237	670 946	676 949	682 875	688 007
665 270	671 152	676 955	682 904	688 080
665 454	671 477	677 112	682 905	688 102
665 806	671 481	677 153	683 906	688 105
666 014	671 487	677 175	682 907	688 106

688 149	691 211	695 629	698 606	728 694
688 240	691 315	695 857	698 841	734 737
688 311	691 706	695 859	698 842	734 748
688 482	691 707	695 923	698 845	734 749
688 703	691 708	696 043	698 847	739 293
688 710	691 709	696 092	698 848	714 923
688 716	691 710	696 150	698 850	742 879
688 738	691 715	696 226	698 853	744 140
688 739	691 912	697 159	698 855	744 142
688 741	692 039	697 263	698 857	744 721
688 900	692 040	697 313	698 858	744 722
689 062	692 604	697 314	698 863	744 724
689 420	692 791	697 316	698 864	746 722
689 421	692 792	697 321	698 869	747 877
689 467	693 268	697 497	698 870	748 108
689 468	693 958	697 498	698 872	749 702
689 484	693 959	697 574	698 884	715 287
689 485	694 185	697 697	698 891	751 305
689 488	694 499	697 704	698 920	751 308
689 489	694 523	697 709	699 165	751 309
689 493	694 660	697 710	699 291	751 591
689 501	694 770	697 711	699 309	751 789
689 504	694 771	697 717	699 793	754 492
689 505	694 773	697 812	699 795	757 932
689 506	694 890	697 814	699 808	760 075
689 507	694 891	697 823	699 811	760 423
689 508	694 895	698 157	699 813	760 734
689 510	695 068	698 388	699 814	761 907
689 520	695 249	698 389	699 815	761 987
689 775	695 315	698 390	699 816	763 057
689 784	695 349	698 391	699 839	763 705
689 785	695 350	698 394	702 837	764 211
689 786	695 351	698 395	704 063	766 651
689 787	695 352	698 399	704 105	766 748
689 790	695 353	698 400	712 609	766 780
689 792	695 441	698 401	717 053	767 693
689 793	695 442	698 402	719 378	767 969
689 794	695 445	698 403	719 379	770 024
689 867	695 536	698 404	719 380	779 288
689 869	695 537	698 413	719 778	780 182
690 676	695 539	698 414	723 218	780 460
690 939	695 564	698 415	723 900	780 469
691 144	695 626	698 491	724 797	780 482
691 200	695 627	698 508	724 099	782 673
691 209	695 628	698 566	726 119	783 769

786 659	830 821	852 271	854 022	855 240
787 810	830 822	852 274	854 038	855 274
787 918	830 823	852 334	854 049	855 275
787 919	830 824	852 346	854 059	855 452
787 920	830 825	852 414	854 061	855 518
787 921	834 696	852 429	854 072	855 519
787 922	837 237	852 430	854 082	855 524
789 720	837 247	852 431	854 085	855 646
789 721	837 999	852 454	854 105	855 694
790 032	842 000	852 455	854 140	855 872
790 562	843 885	852 456	854 356	855 888
790 828	844 929	852 473	854 362	855 890
791 025	844 941	852 623	854 395	855 891
791 026	845 434	852 633	854 400	855 917
792 276	845 481	852 750	854 401	855 943
792 416	845 488	852 777	854 403	856 013
793 597	845 892	852 829	854 407	856 108
793 884	846 797	852 978	854 413	856 162
793 885	848 446	853 156	854 420	856 164
795 230	848 469	853 271	854 472	856 177
795 231	848 611	853 282	854 529	856 178
795 528	848 647	853 284	854 630	856 197
795 529	848 690	853 369	854 674	856 206
799 220	848 869	853 459	854 798	856 220
830 056	848 926	853 462	854 801	856 332
830 096	848 933	853 488	854 872	856 339
830 197	849 005	853 489	854 876	856 350
830 237	849 065	853 562	854 877	856 351
830 253	849 196	853 563	854 894	856 396
830 660	849 321	853 748	854 896	856 464
830 661	849 517	853 770	854 897	856 469
830 663	849 735	853 853	854 910	856 520
830 667	849 765	853 855	854 911	856 612
830 668	850 183	853 857	854 933	856 777
830 670	850 184	853 858	854 939	856 842
830 672	850 665	853 863	854 940	856 957
830 673	850 762	853 864	855 004	856 965
830 809	850 771	853 867	855 033	856 982
830 810	850 867	853 876	855 034	857 040
830 812	850 897	853 877	855 035	857 076
830 813	851 667	853 880	855 036	857 286
830 814	852 000	853 886	855 071	857 309
830 816	852 007	853 895	855 192	857 310
830 819	852 026	853 980	855 200	857 419
830 820	852 075	854 011	855 201	857 420

857 443	859 796	861 537	863 388	864 396
857 477	859 805	861 540	863 390	864 479
857 630	859 882	861 547	863 392	864 703
857 642	859 896	861 555	863 393	864 818
857 679	859 897	861 558	863 401	864 845
857 687	859 898	861 559	863 413	864 897
857 695	859 899	861 574	863 419	864 912
857 706	859 900	861 618	863 424	864 927
857 759	859 901	861 621	863 425	864 930
857 766	859 903	861 829	863 481	865 170
857 825	859 974	861 830	863 487	865 180
857 636	860 001	861 848	863 724	865 181
857 994	860 002	861 946	863 727	865 276
857 997	860 070	861 948	863 728	865 315
857 999	860 240	862 053	863 741	865 316
858 000	860 241	862 175	863 742	865 336
858 001	860 253	862 322	863 756	865 343
858 002	860 255	862 392	863 775	865 413
858 006	860 309	862 496	863 776	865 414
858 007	860 491	862 529	863 814	865 415
858 012	860 492	862 546	863 815	865 491
858 021	860 493	862 669	863 816	865 492
858 156	860 552	862 692	863 849	865 498
858 213	860 573	862 693	863 905	865 547
858 214	860 671	862 705	863 916	865 548
858 245	860 701	862 707	863 986	865 551
858 269	860 919	862 772	863 987	865 599
858 270	860 932	862 773	864 003	865 688
858 271	860 933	862 775	864 004	865 689
858 566	860 939	862 831	864 054	865 690
858 628	861 128	862 832	864 168	865 724
858 851	861 131	862 849	864 148	865 760
859 054	861 132	862 850	864 250	865 844
859 164	861 212	862 851	864 172	865 891
859 196	861 213	862 852	864 173	865 892
859 197	861 214	862 853	864 217	865 902
859 228	861 217	862 859	864 218	865 905
859 763	861 248	862 892	864 275	865 953
859 764	861 296	862 898	864 281	866 050
859 765	861 392	862 899	864 287	866 069
859 783	861 508	862 909	864 290	866 132
859 791	861 525	863 096	864 321	866 162
859 793	861 526	863 105	864 322	866 241
859 794	861 535	863 141	864 337	866 244
859 795	861 536	863 220	864 372	856 245

866 246	866 898	868 258	870 062	871 358
866 247	866 905	868 262	870 137	871 388
866 248	866 908	868 381	870 238	871 414
866 250	866 923	868 382	870 273	871 416
866 259	866 929	868 454	870 275	871 418
866 260	867 014	868 530	870 276	871 425
866 265	867 015	868 532	870 277	871 426
866 271	867 016	868 555	870 302	871 429
866 361	867 017	868 556	870 311	871 430
866 395	867 018	868 558	870 469	871 437
866 419	867 019	868 715	870 499	871 438
866 559	867 026	868 748	870 500	871 441
866 561	867 040	868 886	870 538	871 442
866 569	867 077	868 888	870 539	871 456
866 571	867 150	868 889	870 540	871 477
866 586	867 151	868 921	870 562	871 524
866 587	867 152	869 018	870 598	871 525
866 589	867 173	869 135	870 772	871 589
866 591	867 204	869 185	870 821	871 596
866 600	867 386	869 187	870 900	871 661
866 601	867 519	869 189	870 902	871 662
866 621	867 526	869 198	870 904	871 666
866 624	867 592	869 281	870 917	871 667
866 640	867 593	869 323	870 919	871 685
866 680	867 711	869 325	870 920	871 752
866 731	867 712	869 328	870 926	871 767
866 732	867 735	869 329	871 049	871 824
866 734	867 800	869 331	871 108	871 829
866 735	867 809	869 357	871 168	871 836
866 739	867 811	869 431	871 169	871 863
866 740	867 815	869 449	871 216	871 907
866 747	867 853	869 571	871 217	871 917
866 749	867 854	869 572	871 218	871 918
866 771	867 856	869 659	871 219	871 919
866 772	867 857	869 668	871 235	871 928
866 773	867 935	869 684	871 237	871 934
866 774	867 940	869 685	871 251	871 975
866 775	867 945	869 688	871 252	871 977
866 811	867 949	869 693	871 259	871 991
866 818	867 956	869 728	871 262	871 992
866 819	868 031	869 732	871 271	871 993
866 890	868 095	869 848	871 272	871 996
866 892	868 097	869 997	871 281	871 998
866 896	868 156	869 998	871 297	871 999
866 897	868 254	870 001	871 357	872 008

872 039	884 161	892 673	893 144	893 517
872 142	884 162	892 683	893 145	893 519
872 176	884 163	892 696	893 223	893 521
872 231	884 164	892 697	893 224	893 522
872 232	884 169	892 698	893 252	893 548
872 244	885 064	892 699	893 253	893 585
872 297	885 078	892 759	893 254	893 607
872 397	885 238	892 760	893 262	893 609
872 400	888 129	892 784	893 267	893 610
872 675	889 648	892 785	893 268	893 618
872 924	889 696	892 819	893 296	893 619
873 012	889 698	892 820	893 350	893 620
873 183	890 074	892 836	893 351	893 668
873 278	890 854	892 837	893 355	893 669
874 585	891 011	892 869	893 356	893 670
874 870	891 401	892 872	893 357	893 671
874 920	892 189	892 873	893 358	893 672
875 135	892 195	892 874	893 359	893 697
875 331	892 197	892 875	893 360	893 707
875 408	892 224	892 876	893 361	893 708
875 409	892 232	892 877	893 362	893 709
875 410	892 240	892 878	893 363	893 710
875 411	892 248	892 879	893 366	893 711
875 412	892 252	892 880	893 367	893 712
875 413	892 269	892 885	893 400	893 713
876 128	892 270	892 886	893 401	893 714
876 134	892 273	892 905	893 406	893 715
876 296	892 274	892 906	893 407	893 716
877 038	892 277	892 911	893 453	893 717
877 994	892 285	892 912	893 460	893 718
878 253	892 286	892 932	893 461	893 805
878 256	892 305	892 933	893 477	893 816
878 374	892 313	892 936	893 478	893 817
880 822	892 380	892 967	893 479	893 818
881 870	892 381	892 968	893 488	893 840
882 926	892 435	892 971	893 489	893 844
882 936	892 436	893 031	893 493	893 857
882 943	892 448	893 032	893 501	893 866
883 084	892 532	893 056	893 510	893 882
883 086	892 533	893 057	893 511	893 912
883 090	892 546	893 058	893 512	893 913
883 091	892 570	893 059	893 513	893 923
883 092	892 668	893 065	893 514	894 012
884 057	892 669	893 066	893 515	894 040
884 111	892 672	893 143	893 516	894 085

894 086	895 131	895 818	900 356	903 717
894 087	895 139	895 819	900 445	903 718
894 093	895 143	895 841	900 451	903 721
894 185	895 144	895 842	901 721	903 723
894 303	895 145	895 860	901 722	903 739
894 323	895 146	895 864	901 723	903 766
894 324	895 147	895 982	901 724	903 772
894 325	895 148	896 118	901 746	903 790
894 326	895 149	896 242	901 817	903 792
894 327	895 218	896 644	901 818	903 799
894 518	895 230	896 656	901 819	903 836
894 520	895 231	896 657	901 822	903 899
894 587	895 232	896 811	901 823	903 900
894 588	895 234	896 812	901 949	903 901
894 683	895 290	896 817	901 963	903 902
894 689	895 302	896 818	902 034	903 906
894 690	895 303	896 899	902 036	903 907
894 713	895 304	896 908	902 037	903 960
894 769	895 305	896 913	902 038	903 965
894 770	895 306	896 961	902 056	904 925
894 781	895 307	898 409	902 057	905 020
894 782	895 314	898 447	902 126	905 021
894 783	895 315	898 504	902 163	905 050
894 784	895 364	898 545	902 264	905 051
894 810	895 365	898 546	902 265	905 144
894 870	895 366	898 551	902 266	905 159
894 871	895 410	898 552	902 411	905 206
894 879	895 411	898 571	902 415	905 209
894 880	895 546	898 572	902 543	905 218
894 883	895 547	898 576	902 592	905 288
894 907	895 549	898 577	902 614	905 292
894 908	895 550	898 754	902 615	905 293
894 939	895 592	899 085	902 616	905 328
894 956	895 593	899 458	902 617	905 329
894 957	895 594	899 459	902 780	905 378
894 958	895 595	899 473	902 781	905 378
894 959	895 605	899 514	902 782	905 383
895 029	895 606	899 536	902 785	905 481
895 030	895 611	899 545	902 786	905 482
895 069	895 635	899 874	902 791	905 483
895 076	895 636	899 875	902 792	905 484
895 085	895 751	900 334	903 409	905 485
895 086	895 752	900 335	903 437	905 506
895 089	895 782	900 350	903 558	905 574
895 103	895 783	900 351	903 716	905 626

905 628	909 765	932 138	935 902	941 807
905 629	909 768	932 434	935 903	942 008
905 649	909 769	932 977	935 905	942 013
905 989	910 484	933 435	935 921	942 014
906 300	910 521	933 438	935 922	942 018
906 401	910 522	933 612	936 146	942 021
906 576	910 523	933 613	936 147	942 022
906 577	910 597	933 614	936 148	942 037
906 640	910 691	933 615	936 149	942 038
906 641	910 741	933 616	936 213	942 192
906 806	910 752	933 617	936 221	942 221
906 807	911 231	933 758	936 227	942 222
906 808	911 267	933 759	936 230	942 223
906 810	911 515	933 762	936 231	942 233
906 811	911 516	933 763	936 326	942 235
906 817	911 517	933 766	936 365	942 245
907 002	911 533	933 767	936 366	942 246
907 229	911 832	933 870	937 226	942 254
907 230	913 297	933 871	937 347	942 266
907 232	916 592	933 874	937 556	942 389
907 324	920 355	933 875	937 689	942 833
907 382	920 402	934 341	937 690	942 873
907 470	921 276	934 345	937 831	942 878
907 471	925 525	934 460	937 888	942 884
907 502	926 025	934 683	938 964	942 885
907 530	926 026	934 804	938 987	943 050
907 531	926 101	934 805	939 527	943 051
907 553	927 079	934 815	939 548	943 131
907 595	927 082	935 175	939 572	943 147
907 596	927 083	935 432	939 700	943 148
907 782	927 084	935 433	939 720	943 230
907 838	927 085	935 434	939 794	943 231
907 839	927 086	935 455	939 797	943 768
907 840	927 087	935 456	939 860	943 983
907 841	927 088	935 457	941 254	944 105
907 875	927 089	935 508	941 409	944 106
908 505	927 090	935 583	941 511	944 123
908 506	927 091	935 639	941 512	944 124
908 784	927 092	935 640	941 560	944 148
908 798	927 093	935 647	941 724	944 149
908 814	927 096	935 883	941 747	944 150
908 815	927 909	935 884	941 748	944 151
909 760	927 960	935 887	941 750	944 156
909 761	930 304	935 895	941 796	944 157
909 764	932 066	935 901	941 806	944 220

944 221	945 430	946 754	951 495	952 686
944 244	945 431	946 755	951 583	952 687
944 245	945 442	946 779	951 715	952 874
944 304	945 472	946 780	951 717	952 875
944 313	945 473	946 783	951 724	952 905
944 314	945 514	946 784	951 726	952 906
944 503	945 534	946 933	951 881	952 913
944 513	945 536	946 940	951 882	952 941
944 528	945 537	946 942	951 886	952 948
944 612	945 538	947 065	951 887	952 950
944 613	945 539	947 066	951 981	952 955
944 668	945 582	947 119	952 002	952 956
944 669	945 594	947 132	952 007	952 982
944 682	945 595	947 159	952 038	952 983
944 683	945 596	947 177	952 039	953 064
944 688	945 597	947 483	952 041	953 070
944 738	945 602	947 550	952 042	953 074
944 739	945 603	947 557	952 062	953 075
944 742	945 634	947 580	952 222	953 114
944 743	945 635	947 582	952 244	953 123
944 762	945 679	947 597	952 273	953 124
944 763	945 770	947 613	952 295	953 128
944 893	945 771	947 847	952 360	953 129
944 894	945 776	949 118	952 365	953 144
945 192	945 777	949 119	952 368	953 191
945 193	945 778	949 120	952 369	953 192
945 194	945 779	949 284	952 407	953 193
945 195	945 780	949 285	952 431	953 197
945 270	945 781	949 372	952 538	953 198
945 271	945 848	949 374	952 539	953 200
945 291	945 849	949 477	952 544	953 205
945 348	945 893	949 478	952 545	953 222
945 349	945 894	949 575	952 547	953 240
945 350	945 895	949 576	952 555	953 255
945 351	945 896	949 593	952 576	953 278
945 353	945 897	949 594	952 581	953 366
945 354	945 912	950 205	952 582	953 369
945 386	945 913	950 206	952 583	953 392
945 387	945 916	951 302	952 584	953 483
945 420	945 917	951 303	952 585	953 493
945 421	945 954	951 304	952 603	953 494
945 424	945 955	951 305	952 622	953 583
945 425	945 962	951 327	952 628	953 584
945 428	946 017	951 330	952 633	953 591
945 429	946 192	951 494	952 635	953 592

953 627	954 913	958 162	959 346	975 871
953 628	954 916	958 163	959 881	975 872
953 638	954 999	958 164	959 889	975 921
953 640	955 046	958 165	960 003	975 924
953 645	955 142	958 166	960 011	975 925
953 647	955 143	958 167	960 077	976 056
953 654	955 343	958 168	960 107	976 148
953 684	955 576	958 170	967 055	976 211
953 714	955 621	958 171	967 056	976 433
953 717	955 642	958 172	972 251	976 434
953 755	955 646	958 173	972 724	976 435
953 756	955 983	958 174	972 800	976 776
953 761	956 052	958 175	972 801	976 777
953 762	956 138	958 176	972 973	976 790
953 764	956 406	958 183	972 974	976 791
953 769	956 442	958 184	973 148	976 870
953 780	956 561	958 213	973 155	976 871
953 823	956 767	958 214	973 158	976 879
953 824	956 784	958 216	973 187	976 898
953 825	956 791	958 217	973 218	976 899
953 831	956 814	958 221	973 221	976 900
953 832	957 002	958 229	973 511	976 901
953 864	957 321	958 246	973 557	976 902
953 875	957 322	958 248	973 561	976 903
954 157	957 323	958 249	973 614	976 904
954 241	957 324	958 297	973 618	976 905
954 302	957 329	958 303	973 695	976 937
954 376	957 330	958 314	974 409	976 938
954 377	957 331	958 348	974 467	976 939
954 392	957 344	958 353	974 505	976 940
954 393	957 458	958 375	974 511	976 961
954 529	957 591	958 376	974 677	977 004
954 600	957 593	958 659	974 678	977 005
954 688	957 777	958 665	974 679	977 006
954 689	957 778	958 666	974 682	977 007
954 719	957 783	958 681	974 862	977 010
954 723	957 798	958 716	974 934	977 146
954 724	957 801	958 827	974 936	977 147
954 729	957 802	959 134	974 966	977 154
954 730	957 803	959 232	974 978	977 155
954 761	957 859	959 238	975 002	977 156
954 871	958 122	959 239	975 003	977 157
954 873	958 148	959 280	975 397	977 232
954 874	958 160	959 319	975 779	977 233
954 912	958 161	959 321	975 870	977 234

977 235	979 994	981 626	984 600	987 087
977 311	979 995	981 688	984 907	987 294
977 352	979 996	981 689	984 956	987 295
977 353	979 997	981 865	984 957	987 317
977 380	979 999	982 108	985 468	987 318
977 381	980 001	982 109	985 782	987 343
977 382	980 002	982 117	985 783	987 347
977 383	980 003	982 118	985 784	988 059
977 384	980 445	982 119	985 785	988 098
977 385	980 446	982 120	985 786	989 165
977 418	980 681	982 123	985 787	989 382
977 419	980 682	982 127	985 789	989 513
977 484	980 685	982 185	985 790	989 900
977 485	980 686	982 192	985 972	989 901
977 597	980 687	982 253	985 973	989 902
977 718	980 688	982 255	985 974	989 903
977 851	980 691	982 257	985 989	989 906
977 972	980 692	982 259	985 990	989 907
977 973	980 695	982 297	985 997	989 908
978 011	980 696	982 298	985 998	989 909
978 012	980 698	983 090	986 007	989 910
978 126	980 791	983 398	986 008	989 911
978 147	980 792	983 399	986 012	989 912
978 218	980 849	983 400	986 013	989 913
978 569	980 984	983 462	986 047	989 934
978 570	981 105	983 466	986 048	989 935
978 571	981 106	983 468	986 049	989 936
978 572	981 109	983 496	986 050	989 940
978 942	981 110	983 497	986 322	989 941
978 943	981 370	983 498	986 323	989 942
979 037	981 374	983 499	986 324	989 943
979 087	981 381	983 500	986 325	989 944
979 113	981 484	983 501	986 326	989 950
979 117	981 485	983 568	986 327	989 951
979 133	981 486	983 574	986 332	989 954
979 135	981 487	983 580	986 337	989 955
979 160	981 488	983 586	986 383	989 960
979 765	981 489	983 592	986 398	989 961
979 871	981 490	983 596	986 399	989 971
979 872	981 491	983 600	986 448	989 972
979 982	981 492	983 604	986 449	989 973
979 983	981 496	983 617	986 450	989 974
979 986	981 498	983 618	986 451	990 106
979 990	981 514	984 097	986 452	990 107
979 992	981 515	984 594	986 453	990 108

990 109	994 714	1064 580	1064 891	1115 445
990 110	994 715	1064 675	1064 940	1115 462
990 111	994 716	1064 676	1065 511	1115 576
990 138	994 717	1064 677	1065 512	1115 577
990 139	994 718	1064 678	1065 754	1115 595
990 140	994 719	1064 685	1065 783	1115 744
990 141	994 720	1064 686	1065 792	1115 768
990 142	994 721	1064 687	1065 801	1115 780
990 143	994 722	1064 688	1065 897	1115 783
990 144	994 723	1064 704	1066 873	1115 926
990 145	994 724	1064 705	1070 933	1115 938
990 158	994 725	1064 706	1070 934	1115 945
990 159	994 742	1064 707	1072 816	1116 160
990 160	994 743	1064 728	1072 839	1116 232
990 161	994 744	1064 730	1072 840	1116 246
990 547	944 745	1064 733	1072 842	1116 266
992 041	994 748	1064 740	1072 843	1116 267
992 093	944 749	1064 743	1075 001	1116 697
992 164	994 758	1064 745	1088 101	1117 171
992 168	994 759	1064 749	1088 603	1117 181
992 473	994 760	1064 750	1089 084	1117 270
992 586	994 761	1064 754	1089 626	1117 281
992 587	944 762	1064 756	1092 826	1117 301
992 862	994 767	1064 761	1092 861	1117 380
993 381	994 769	1064 762	1112 341	1117 381
993 382	995 069	1064 763	1112 754	1117 382
993 818	995 889	1064 764	1113 072	1117 383
993 819	996 378	1064 768	1113 073	1117 384
994 130	996 817	1064 769	1113 074	1117 429
994 510	997 686	1064 770	1113 075	1117 430
994 511	998 664	1064 816	1113 076	1117 482
994 512	1057 794	1064 817	1113 081	1117 542
994 517	1057 840	1064 818	1113 082	1117 603
994 518	1061 157	1064 819	1113 083	1117 661
994 519	1061 168	1064 820	1113 099	1117 666
994 520	1063 642	1064 821	1113 121	1117 667
994 524	1063 655	1064 822	1113 774	1117 703
994 525	1063 656	1064 823	1113 777	1117 712
994 526	1063 681	1064 824	1113 778	1117 713
994 527	1063 700	1064 825	1115 100	1117 723
994 528	1063 857	1064 826	1115 165	1117 725
994 532	1064 458	1064 827	1115 166	1117 727
994 555	1064 459	1064 841	1115 185	1117 729
994 636	1065 520	1064 861	1115 433	1117 748
994 713	1064 536	1064 890	1115 443	1117 750

1117 771	1118 882	1120 550	1121 977	1122 763
1117 797	1118 883	1120 551	1121 983	1122 764
1117 799	1118 884	1120 552	1121 984	1122 920
1117 800	1119 223	1120 569	1121 985	1122 964
1117 801	1119 401	1120 632	1121 990	1122 965
1117 802	1119 402	1120 648	1121 991	1122 982
1117 803	1119 410	1120 652	1121 992	1122 989
1117 804	1119 422	1120 672	1121 993	1123 005
1117 805	1119 423	1120 742	1122 013	1123 010
1117 806	1119 439	1120 755	1122 026	1123 011
1117 807	1119 624	1120 756	1122 027	1123 012
1117 808	1119 674	1120 795	1122 028	1123 049
1117 810	1119 717	1120 834	1122 037	1123 087
1117 814	1119 854	1120 837	1122 038	1123 152
1118 109	1119 876	1120 839	1122 058	1123 293
1118 110	1119 993	1120 841	1122 061	1123 294
1118 111	1119 994	1120 844	1122 063	1123 305
1118 112	1119 995	1120 845	1122 134	1123 311
1118 115	1119 996	1120 847	1122 177	1123 313
1118 116	1119 997	1120 853	1122 178	1123 316
1118 122	1120 003	1120 854	1122 218	1123 319
1118 123	1120 004	1120 860	1122 219	1123 332
1118 130	1120 409	1120 861	1122 220	1123 340
1118 131	1120 427	1120 883	1122 221	1123 367
1118 133	1120 458	1120 885	1122 238	1123 371
1118 135	1120 515	1120 901	1122 239	1123 372
1118 136	1120 518	1121 121	1122 344	1123 383
1118 137	1120 552	1121 122	1122 350	1123 489
1118 149	1120 525	1121 207	1122 359	1123 755
1118 161	1120 532	1121 262	1122 361	1123 856
1118 282	1120 533	1121 490	1122 374	1123 922
1118 284	1120 534	1121 500	1122 375	1124 001
1118 316	1120 537	1121 520	1122 420	1124 002
1118 402	1120 538	1121 652	1122 448	1124 003
1118 838	1120 539	1121 694	1122 450	1124 004
1118 839	1120 540	1121 695	1122 532	1124 157
1118 850	1120 541	1121 742	1122 602	1124 182
1118 851	1120 542	1121 743	1122 610	1124 394
1118 854	1120 543	1121 774	1122 736	1124 462
1118 855	1120 544	1121 781	1122 737	1124 463
1118 866	1120 545	1121 843	1122 746	1124 470
1118 867	1120 546	1121 845	1122 747	1124 503
1118 872	1120 547	1121 848	1122 755	1124 550
1118 873	1120 548	1121 939	1122 757	1124 551
1118 881	1120 549	1121 940	1122 759	1124 552

1124 555	1134 486	1139 156	1149 065	1149 893
1124 558	1134 579	1139 203	1149 066	1149 940
1124 561	1134 903	1139 316	1149 067	1149 941
1124 564	1134 949	1139 317	1149 069	1149 956
1124 570	1135 197	1139 896	1149 073	1149 957
1124 677	1135 201	1139 899	1149 076	1149 958
1124 678	1135 245	1140 084	1149 078	1149 959
1124 679	1135 282	1140 451	1149 089	1149 960
1124 680	1135 541	1140 452	1149 090	1149 961
1124 724	1135 545	1140 679	1149 097	1149 962
1124 725	1135 576	1140 708	1149 146	1149 963
1124 735	1135 883	1140 773	1149 304	1150 928
1124 736	1135 896	1141 914	1149 360	1151 546
1124 795	1136 488	1141 925	1149 363	1151 547
1124 802	1136 489	1142 473	1149 364	1151 577
1124 803	1136 530	1148 019	1149 367	1151 789
1124 959	1136 609	1148 100	1149 368	1151 790
1124 984	1136 765	1148 101	1149 390	1151 796
1124 989	1136 766	1148 108	1149 392	1151 797
1125 093	1136 872	1148 119	1149 393	1151 798
1125 131	1136 895	1148 120	1149 394	1151 799
1125 140	1136 896	1148 427	1149 395	1151 804
1125 167	1137 606	1148 500	1149 439	1151 805
1125 168	1137 607	1148 501	1149 581	1151 812
1125 171	1137 634	1148 540	1149 582	1151 813
1125 172	1137 635	1148 641	1149 583	1151 818
1125 179	1137 646	1148 642	1149 584	1151 819
1125 209	1137 647	1148 647	1149 585	1151 820
1125 392	1137 669	1148 648	1149 586	1151 821
1125 581	1137 684	1148 651	1149 604	1151 833
1125 585	1137 720	1148 652	1149 613	1151 834
1125 816	1137 743	1148 779	1149 616	1151 835
1125 817	1137 744	1148 784	1149 667	1151 836
1126 527	1137 824	1148 785	1149 672	1151 852
1126 729	1138 050	1148 788	1149 674	1151 853
1126 955	1138 246	1148 789	1149 684	1151 856
1127 041	1138 247	1148 867	1149 685	1151 857
1127 173	1138 251	1148 868	1149 743	1151 862
1127 216	1138 694	1148 869	1149 744	1151 875
1127 794	1138 695	1148 870	1149 745	1151 876
1127 823	1138 696	1148 874	1149 801	1151 877
1127 836	1138 697	1148 880	1149 823	1151 878
1134 464	1138 698	1148 892	1149 844	1151 902
1134 465	1138 699	1148 896	1149 857	1151 903
1134 466	1138 990	1148 956	1149 877	1151 904

1151 905	1152 630	1152 962	1154 216	1154 469
1151 932	1152 631	1152 964	1154 217	1154 471
1151 933	1152 661	1152 967	1154 219	1154 476
1151 934	1152 662	1152 968	1154 220	1154 477
1151 935	1152 704	1152 989	1154 221	1154 478
1151 936	1152 709	1152 990	1154 222	1154 492
1151 937	1152 712	1152 993	1154 223	1154 493
1151 938	1152 725	1152 994	1154 224	1154 641
1151 939	1152 726	1153 279	1154 225	1154 642
1151 940	1152 737	1153 280	1154 226	1154 644
1151 941	1152 738	1153 981	1154 229	1154 645
1151 942	1152 747	1153 982	1154 231	1154 646
1151 943	1152 748	1154 026	1154 234	1154 647
1151 944	1152 751	1154 027	1154 240	1155 043
1151 945	1152 752	1154 039	1154 244	1155 045
1151 946	1152 753	1154 041	1154 245	1155 048
1151 947	1152 766	1154 042	1154 247	1155 167
1151 948	1152 767	1154 051	1154 248	1155 176
1151 949	1152 780	1154 052	1154 253	1155 188
1151 950	1152 786	1154 053	1154 255	1155 189
1151 951	1152 787	1154 095	1154 256	1155 190
1152 243	1152 789	1154 108	1154 257	1155 191
1152 244	1152 796	1154 110	1154 258	1155 204
1152 251	1152 797	1154 113	1154 259	1155 205
1152 252	1152 804	1154 115	1154 260	1155 207
1152 263	1152 805	1154 116	1154 261	1155 208
1152 264	1152 812	1154 117	1154 270	1155 316
1152 279	1152 813	1154 118	1154 277	1155 317
1152 280	1152 816	1154 119	1154 287	1155 359
1152 283	1152 829	1154 121	1154 288	1155 360
1152 284	1152 830	1154 122	1154 372	1155 361
1152 437	1152 841	1154 123	1154 373	1155 362
1152 439	1152 842	1154 124	1154 374	1155 363
1152 441	1152 857	1154 140	1154 375	1155 364
1152 476	1152 858	1154 141	1154 376	1155 380
1152 477	1152 897	1154 194	1154 377	1155 403
1152 491	1152 898	1154 195	1154 380	1155 404
1152 492	1152 909	1154 200	1154 382	1155 460
1152 583	1152 910	1154 202	1154 387	1155 512
1152 606	1152 925	1154 205	1154 407	1155 513
1152 607	1152 926	1154 207	1154 412	1155 535
1152 626	1152 941	1154 208	1154 417	1155 536
1152 627	1152 942	1154 212	1154 457	1155 838
1152 628	1152 951	1154 214	1154 459	1155 841
1152 629	1152 952	1154 215	1154 466	1155 842

1155 843	1157 956	1161 149	1161 586	1162 438
1155 915	1157 962	1161 150	1161 587	1162 439
1155 922	1157 963	1161 182	1161 588	1162 440
1155 923	1158 228	1161 183	1161 591	1162 441
1156 245	1158 280	1161 195	1161 592	1162 442
1156 246	1158 317	1161 196	1161 597	1162 444
1156 247	1158 349	1161 197	1161 606	1162 445
1156 324	1158 371	1161 275	1161 607	1162 446
1156 325	1158 400	1161 294	1161 618	1163 173
1156 337	1158 401	1161 295	1161 619	1163 174
1156 338	1158 408	1161 296	1161 714	1163 190
1156 347	1158 409	1161 297	1161 715	1163 191
1156 351	1158 414	1161 298	1161 734	1163 197
1156 352	1158 430	1161 299	1161 735	1163 229
1156 390	1158 431	1161 300	1161 776	1163 230
1156 459	1158 539	1161 301	1161 788	1163 231
1156 464	1158 540	1161 304	1162 096	1163 232
1156 693	1158 541	1161 305	1162 105	1163 233
1156 695	1158 542	1161 306	1162 192	1163 271
1156 949	1158 543	1161 307	1162 193	1163 272
1156 950	1158 544	1161 368	1162 194	1163 363
1157 212	1158 545	1161 373	1162 262	1163 364
1157 318	1158 546	1161 374	1162 263	1163 438
1157 319	1158 547	1161 375	1162 282	1163 439
1157 388	1158 548	1161 376	1162 283	1163 440
1157 401	1158 550	1161 407	1162 296	1163 441
1157 407	1158 551	1161 424	1162 297	1163 442
1157 432	1158 552	1161 428	1162 308	1163 443
1157 491	1158 623	1161 430	1162 309	1163 444
1157 492	1158 976	1161 453	1162 318	1163 445
1157 699	1158 977	1161 462	1162 386	1163 446
1157 832	1159 226	1161 480	1162 405	1163 447
1157 848	1159 621	1161 500	1162 413	1163 489
1157 855	1159 622	1161 525	1162 414	1163 490
1157 865	1160 000	1161 528	1162 427	1163 497
1157 896	1161 034	1161 529	1162 428	1163 498
1157 897	1161 035	1161 530	1162 429	1163 499
1157 898	1161 036	1161 531	1162 430	1163 516
1157 905	1161 037	1161 532	1162 431	1163 555
1157 908	1161 038	1161 534	1162 432	1163 563
1157 916	1161 039	1161 566	1162 433	1163 564
1157 932	1161 084	1161 568	1162 434	1163 569
1157 937	1161 085	1161 571	1162 435	1163 575
1157 946	1161 095	1161 583	1162 436	1163 583
1157 947	1161 146	1161 584	1162 437	1163 603

1163 607	1164 386	1164 529	1164 586	1164 661
1163 608	1164 387	1164 530	1164 587	1164 662
1163 612	1164 388	1164 531	1164 588	1164 665
1163 614	1164 394	1164 536	1164 589	1164 666
1163 617	1164 395	1164 537	1164 590	1164 667
1163 619	1164 396	1164 540	1164 591	1164 668
1163 640	1164 397	1164 541	1164 592	1164 669
1163 663	1164 398	1164 544	1164 593	1164 670
1163 664	1164 400	1164 545	1164 594	1164 671
1163 669	1164 401	1164 546	1164 595	1164 672
1163 672	1164 403	1164 547	1164 596	1164 673
1163 682	1164 404	1164 548	1164 597	1164 674
1163 683	1164 405	1164 549	1164 603	1164 675
1163 772	1164 431	1164 550	1164 607	1164 676
1163 774	1164 432	1164 551	1164 608	1164 678
1163 808	1164 490	1164 552	1164 609	1164 689
1163 822	1164 491	1164 553	1164 610	1164 690
1163 824	1164 492	1164 554	1164 622	1164 691
1163 841	1164 493	1164 555	1164 623	1164 692
1163 850	1164 497	1164 556	1164 624	1164 693
1163 851	1164 498	1164 557	1164 625	1164 694
1163 853	1164 499	1164 558	1164 626	1164 695
1163 854	1164 500	1164 560	1164 627	1164 696
1163 855	1164 501	1164 561	1164 628	1164 697
1163 881	1164 502	1164 562	1164 629	1164 700
1163 891	1164 503	1164 563	1164 630	1164 701
1163 893	1164 504	1164 564	1164 631	1164 702
1163 895	1164 505	1164 565	1164 632	1164 703
1163 906	1164 506	1164 566	1164 636	1164 704
1163 911	1164 507	1164 567	1164 637	1164 705
1163 918	1164 508	1164 568	1164 638	1164 706
1163 923	1164 509	1164 569	1164 639	1164 707
1163 929	1164 510	1164 570	1164 640	1164 708
1163 979	1164 511	1164 571	1164 641	1164 709
1163 982	1164 514	1164 572	1164 644	1164 710
1163 990	1164 515	1164 573	1164 645	1164 711
1163 991	1164 516	1164 574	1164 648	1164 712
1163 992	1164 517	1164 575	1164 649	1164 713
1163 996	1164 522	1164 576	1164 652	1164 714
1164 295	1164 523	1164 578	1164 653	1164 715
1164 296	1164 524	1164 579	1164 654	1164 716
1164 307	1164 525	1164 580	1164 655	1164 717
1164 308	1164 526	1164 581	1164 656	1164 718
1164 380	1164 527	1164 582	1164 657	1164 719
1164 381	1164 528	1164 583	1164 658	1164 720

1164 721	1164 779	1164 833	1164 902	1165 567
1164 722	1164 780	1164 834	1164 903	1165 568
1164 723	1164 781	1164 835	1164 904	1165 578
1164 724	1164 782	1164 836	1164 905	1165 579
1164 725	1164 783	1164 837	1164 906	1165 581
1164 726	1164 784	1164 838	1164 907	1165 582
1164 727	1164 786	1164 839	1164 908	1165 585
1164 728	1164 787	1164 850	1164 909	1165 586
1164 729	1164 788	1164 851	1164 910	1165 587
1164 730	1164 789	1164 852	1164 911	1165 588
1164 732	1164 790	1164 853	1164 912	1165 597
1164 733	1164 791	1164 854	1164 961	1165 598
1164 734	1164 794	1164 855	1164 962	1165 603
1164 735	1164 795	1164 856	1164 963	1165 604
1164 736	1164 797	1164 857	1164 964	1165 605
1164 737	1164 798	1164 858	1164 965	1165 607
1164 738	1164 799	1164 859	1164 966	1165 608
1164 739	1164 800	1164 860	1164 967	1165 627
1164 740	1164 801	1164 864	1164 968	1165 647
1164 741	1164 804	1164 865	1164 973	1165 648
1164 742	1164 805	1164 866	1164 974	1165 649
1164 743	1164 806	1164 867	1164 977	1165 650
1164 744	1164 807	1164 868	1164 978	1165 651
1164 745	1164 808	1164 869	1164 979	1165 654
1164 746	1164 809	1164 870	1164 980	1165 674
1164 747	1164 810	1164 871	1164 981	1165 675
1164 748	1164 811	1164 872	1164 982	1165 676
1164 749	1164 812	1164 873	1164 983	1165 677
1164 753	1164 813	1164 874	1164 984	1165 678
1164 754	1164 814	1164 875	1164 985	1165 679
1164 755	1164 815	1164 876	1164 986	1165 683
1164 756	1164 816	1164 877	1164 987	1165 684
1164 757	1164 817	1164 878	1164 988	1165 685
1164 758	1164 818	1164 879	1164 991	1165 686
1164 759	1164 819	1164 880	1164 992	1165 688
1164 760	1164 820	1164 881	1164 993	1165 695
1164 761	1164 821	1164 882	1165 354	1165 696
1164 769	1164 822	1164 883	1165 355	1165 698
1164 770	1164 823	1164 884	1165 500	1165 699
1164 771	1164 824	1164 885	1165 502	1165 701
1164 772	1164 827	1164 886	1165 503	1165 702
1164 773	1164 828	1164 887	1165 508	1165 873
1164 774	1164 829	1164 892	1165 509	1165 874
1164 775	1164 830	1164 893	1165 555	1165 876
1164 778	1164 832	1164 901	1165 556	1165 878

1165 879	1166 892	1188 417	1233 114	1236 142
1165 882	1166 893	1188 452	1233 116	1236 143
1165 884	1166 894	1188 456	1233 161	1236 244
1165 885	1166 895	1188 502	1233 180	1236 245
1165 887	1166 912	1188 716	1233 508	1236 262
1165 888	1166 913	1188 971	1233 562	1236 288
1165 893	1166 914	1189 547	1233 586	1236 521
1165 894	1166 979	1192 362	1233 655	1236 522
1166 523	1166 982	1192 363	1233 657	1236 523
1166 524	1166 983	1192 364	1233 659	1236 524
1166 525	1166 984	1192 365	1233 809	1236 574
1166 526	1166 985	1192 393	1233 813	1236 575
1166 527	1166 986	1192 394	1233 870	1236 576
1166 528	1166 987	1192 395	1233 871	1236 577
1166 529	1166 989	1195 113	1233 872	1236 578
1166 530	1166 990	1232 514	1233 873	1236 579
1166 534	1166 991	1232 556	1233 874	1236 598
1166 535	1166 992	1232 561	1233 875	1237 013
1166 549	1167 002	1232 562	1233 876	1237 123
1166 550	1167 003	1232 590	1233 877	1237 130
1166 551	1167 004	1232 594	1233 878	1237 131
1166 552	1167 005	1232 608	1233 879	1237 137
1166 553	1167 006	1232 610	1233 880	1237 198
1166 554	1167 007	1232 627	1233 881	1237 241
1166 586	1167 009	1232 628	1233 882	1237 242
1166 587	1167 013	1232 629	1233 883	1237 243
1166 608	1167 014	1232 630	1233 884	1237 244
1166 609	1167 015	1232 631	1233 896	1237 300
1166 610	1167 016	1232 632	1233 897	1237 316
1166 612	1167 017	1232 639	1234 188	1237 379
1166 613	1167 018	1232 663	1234 202	1237 380
1166 614	1167 019	1232 664	1234 203	1237 451
1166 615	1167 020	1232 665	1234 369	1238 182
1166 616	1167 021	1232 666	1235 424	1238 387
1166 617	1167 507	1232 670	1235 426	1238 388
1166 618	1188 220	1232 683	1235 427	1238 409
1166 619	1188 407	1232 684	1235 503	1238 412
1166 620	1188 408	1232 686	1235 513	1238 432
1166 869	1188 409	1232 695	1235 517	1238 433
1166 885	1188 411	1232 720	1235 543	1238 434
1166 887	1188 412	1243 748	1235 559	1238 435
1166 888	1188 413	1232 947	1235 595	1238 436
1166 889	1188 414	1232 948	1236 139	1238 437
1166 890	1188 415	1233 112	1236 140	1238 438
1166 891	1188 416	1233 113	1236 141	1238 439

1238 440	1239 703	1240 994	1241 698	1244 218
1238 441	1239 710	1240 999	1243 532	1244 323
1238 442	1239 711	1241 004	1243 618	1244 397
1238 443	1239 718	1241 005	1243 632	1244 398
1238 444	1239 719	1241 006	1243 667	1244 493
1238 445	1239 728	1241 014	1243 698	1244 497
1238 446	1239 729	1241 058	1243 700	1244 498
1238 516	1239 738	1241 059	1243 703	1244 499
1238 518	1239 739	1241 060	1243 705	1244 505
1238 525	1239 746	1241 063	1243 707	1244 508
1238 553	1239 747	1241 066	1243 709	1244 670
1238 554	1239 756	1241 067	1243 711	1244 710
1238 555	1239 757	1241 068	1243 714	1244 921
1238 556	1239 764	1241 069	1243 716	1244 922
1238 557	1239 765	1241 070	1243 718	1253 041
1238 571	1239 774	1241 071	1243 726	1253 046
1238 695	1239 775	1241 072	1243 727	1253 055
1238 984	1239 794	1241 073	1243 731	1253 056
1238 985	1239 795	1241 074	1243 759	1253 057
1239 259	1239 804	1241 500	1243 761	1253 102
1239 261	1239 805	1241 505	1243 762	1253 103
1239 319	1239 812	1241 508	1243 765	1253 120
1239 335	1239 813	1241 540	1243 767	1253 121
1239 360	1239 822	1241 541	1243 770	1253 122
1239 367	1239 823	1241 542	1243 772	1253 160
1239 369	1239 830	1241 543	1243 773	1254 605
1239 371	1239 831	1241 544	1243 776	1254 606
1239 372	1239 836	1241 545	1243 778	1254 607
1239 418	1239 841	1241 622	1243 781	1254 608
1239 431	1239 842	1241 623	1243 783	1254 631
1239 684	1239 844	1241 624	1243 784	1254 632
1239 685	1240 256	1241 625	1243 787	1254 677
1239 693	1240 257	1241 626	1243 789	1254 751
1239 697	1240 856	1241 627	1243 791	1255 081
1239 699	1240 857	1241 628	1243 792	1260 728
1239 700	1240 961	1241 629	1244 153	1261 466
1239 701	1240 962	1241 691	1244 154	1311 339
1239 702	1240 964	1241 692	1244 155	

The Field Guide

An alphabetical listing of the aftermarket catalogs covered in the Field Guide and information to be noticed within the list when using the Field Guide.

    1. Each catalog in the list is followed by 1–5 key words to give a general idea of the replacement parts manufactured and/or sold by the aftermarket company.

    2. When a MoPar replacement number was included by the company in their catalog, that number is included in the Field Guide.

    3. MoPar replacement numbers reported in an aftermarket catalog published after 1948 may not match the factory numbers in the **What to Look For** section. Remember that the **What to Look For** section reports the 1946–1948 factory numbers while the aftermarket catalog published after 1948 often reported superseded numbers.

    4. The description of the aftermarket replacement part in the Field Guide, exactly or closely, follows the description of the part in the aftermarket catalog for the D24 Dodge.

ABC—Ball and Tapered Roller Bearings

    ABC (The American Ball Bearing Company) was a manufacturer of precision antifriction ball and roller bearings. ABC was the first, in 1908, to use, develop and manufacture the now famous "Radial Ball Bearing" that is used worldwide. At the time the D24 was built (1946–1948) ABC was the only bearing factory in the world that produced the four major types of bearings: (1) ball bearings; (2) tapered roller bearings; (3) cylindrical roller bearings; and (4) clutch-thrust bearings. ABC was located in Brooklyn, New York.

09074	front wheel outer bearing cone; 5 passenger models
09194	front wheel outer bearing cup; 5 passenger models
5-BC	steering gear bearing cone; 5 passenger models
6	steering gear bearing cup; 5 passenger models
6C	steering gear bearing cup; 5 passenger models
11-BC	steering gear bearing cone; 7 passenger models
13-C	steering gear bearing cup; 7 passenger models
14-C	steering gear bearing cup; 7 passenger models
158R	transmission mainshaft front bearing; 5 and 7 passenger models

365R	transmission countershaft front or rear bearing; 5 and 7 passenger models
1729	front wheel outer bearing cup; 7 passenger models
1755	front wheel outer bearing cone; 7 passenger models
2523	front wheel inner bearing cup; 7 passenger models
2585	front wheel inner bearing cone; 7 passenger models
2736	rear wheel inner bearing cup; 7 passenger models
2780	rear wheel inner bearing cone; 7 passenger models
3203	generator bearing; 5 and 7 passenger models
3207	transmission mainshaft rear bearing; 5 and 7 passenger models
3420	front pinion bearing cup; 7 passenger models
3476	front pinion bearing cone; 7 passenger models
3820	rear pinion bearing cup; 7 passenger models
3875	rear pinion bearing cone; 7 passenger models
7507	propeller shaft bearing; 5 and 7 passenger models
14125-A	front wheel inner bearing cone; 5 passenger models
14276	front wheel outer bearing cup; 5 passenger models
25520	differential bearing cup; right or left; 5 and 7 passenger models
25580	differential bearing cone; right or left; 5 and 7 passenger models
25821	rear wheel inner bearing cup; 5 passenger models
25877	rear wheel inner bearing cone; 5 passenger models
31520	front or rear pinion bearing cup; 5 passenger models
31593	front or rear pinion bearing cone; 5 passenger models
47505	drive shaft rear bearing; 5 and 7 passenger models
N-959	steering knuckle bearing; 5 and 7 passenger models
N-1054	clutch release bearing; replaces factory number 658998; models without fluid drive
N-1055	clutch release bearing; replaces factory number 658948; models with fluid drive
N-1310	clutch release bearing and sleeve assembly; replaces factory number 862859; models without fluid drive
N-1312	clutch release bearing and sleeve assembly; replaces factory number 867734; models with fluid drive

AC—Fuel Pump, Oil Filter and Spark Plug

AC produced precisely engineered new replacement fuel pumps with precision made heavy duty parts at the critical wear points to assure long life. AC rebuilt pumps were completely rebuilt, thoroughly checked, strenuously tested and warranted. All rebuilt pumps were equipped with new molded and impregnated diaphragms for more efficiency and longer life. AC was a division of General Motors of Flint, Michigan.

45	spark plug; 14 mm; all models with a cast iron head
505-X	fuel pump; replaces AT series pump with glass bowl; AC pump number 3647; factory number 1523647, all models

577-X   fuel pump; replaces BQ series pump without glass bowl; AC pump number 9042; factory number 1539042; all models

588   fuel pump; all models

2588   rebuilt fuel pump; all models

D-117   diaphragm repair kit for 588 fuel pump

GL-57   flexible gas line; late 1948 D24 models

GL-59   flexible gas line; D24 models 1946—early 1948

PF-316   oil filter

Accurate—Clutch Assemblies, Bearings and Clutch Plates

Accurate Clutch offered a "ReNu Accurate Clutch Set" that included a clutch facing and clutch plate that were individually balanced to assure vibration free performance. The parts were then matched, mated and tested together at the factory to make sure they released freely and engaged smoothly before being shipped to customers. Accurate Clutch was located in Cleveland, Ohio.

700   clutch set with remanufactured plate—includes RE-427, X-1247 and PB-5; models without fluid drive

701   clutch set with remanufactured plate—includes RE-457 and X-1297; models with fluid drive

4700   clutch set with new plate—includes F-427, X-1247 and PB-5; models without fluid drive

4701   clutch set with new plate—includes F-457 and X1297; models with fluid drive

BB-3   clutch release bearing; fluid drive models

BB-7   clutch release bearing; models without fluid drive

BB-8   clutch release bearing; without fluid drive

BB-31A   throwout bearing and sleeve assembly; models without fluid drive

BB-36A   throwout bearing and sleeve assembly; fluid drive models

BB-37A   clutch release bearing; models without fluid drive

BB-45A   clutch release bearing and sleeve assembly; fluid drive models

F-427   new clutch plate—10" O.D.—10 spline—1" spline diameter; models without fluid drive

F-457   new clutch plate—9¼" O.D.—10 spline—1¼" spline diameter; models with fluid drive

PB-5   flywheel pilot bushing

RE-427   remanufactured clutch plate; without fluid drive

RE-457   remanufactured clutch plate; fluid drive models

RS-16A   release collar or bearing sleeve only; without fluid drive

RS-22A   release collar or bearing sleeve only; fluid drive models

TF-25   throwout fork assembly; all models

TK-13   throwout fork assembly repair kit; all models

X-1247   pressure plate (Borg and Beck manufacture); without fluid drive

X-1297   pressure plate (Borg and Beck manufacture); fluid drive models

ACE—Voltage Regulator and Water Pumps

ACE supplied a line of remanufactured automotive products for passenger cars and trucks including voltage regulators, brake cylinders and water pumps. ACE was located in Louisville, Kentucky.

11-85   remanufactured voltage regulator; replaces Auto-Lite 6 volt positive ground; all models

15-53   remanufactured water pump; all models

Aetna—Clutch Release Bearings

The Aetna Bearing Company started in 1916 and produced ball, roller and thrust bearings for passenger cars and trucks. Agriculture, mining, military and industry also use Aetna Bearings. Superior engineering and production techniques, using the most advanced tools, led to anti-friction bearings with optimum bearing life. The Aetna Bearing Company was located in Chicago, Illinois.

A-494   clutch release bearing; fluid drive models

A-625   clutch release bearing; fluid drive models

A-749   clutch release bearing; conventional drive models without fluid drive

A-816   clutch release bearing; fluid drive models

A-856   clutch release bearing; replaces factory number 658998; conventional drive models without fluid drive

A-857   clutch release bearing; replaces factory number 658948; fluid drive models

A-902   clutch release bearing; replaces factory number 658998; conventional drive models without fluid drive

A-903   clutch release bearing; replaces factory number 658948; fluid drive models

A-903-2   clutch release bearing; fluid drive models

A-903-14   clutch release bearing; fluid drive models

A-935   clutch release bearing; conventional drive models without fluid drive

A-935-1   clutch release bearing; replaces factory number 658998; conventional drive models without fluid drive

A-935-2   clutch release bearing; conventional drive models without fluid drive

A-935-4   clutch release bearing; conventional drive models without fluid drive

A-935-14   clutch release bearing; conventional drive models without fluid drive

A-1609   clutch release bearing; replaces factory number 658998; models without fluid drive

A-1963   clutch release bearing; replaces factory number 658948; models with fluid drive

A-2262   clutch release bearing; fluid drive models

Airtex—Fuel Pumps and Water Pumps

Airtex water pumps and fuel pumps were designed, engineered and manufactured in their own plants to assure positive control of each component. This was followed by rigid inspections and rigorous tests that assured a quality of performance that met and surpassed original equipment specifications. Airtex Automotive was located in Fairfield, Illinois.

588	fuel pump; all models with single diaphragm pumps
588AX	fuel pump; replaces AT type fuel pump; all models
706AX	fuel pump; all models
1050	fuel pump repair kit; all 588, 588AX fuel pumps
1276	fuel pump diaphragm repair kit; all 588 and 588AX fuel pumps
AW-11	bushing type replacement water pump; all models
AW-713	water pump; replaces 1064 750; all models

Alco—Universal Joint and Universal Joint Repair Kits

Alco used carefully selected raw materials and maintained high quality through regular checks and analysis in the manufacture process. Each component part is fabricated to proper tolerances and assembled to exact specifications to insure long, dependable service. Alco Automotive Products was located in Chicago, Illinois.

J-72625-2	cross-ball type universal joint; kit less housing; 5 passenger models; front and rear early 1946; late 1946–1948 rear
J-83254-3	cross-ball type universal joint; kit less housing; 5 passenger models; early 1946
JR-52A	ball and trunnion universal joint; kit with body; all 5 passenger models except early 1946
JR-67A	ball and trunnion universal joint; kit without body; early 1946, 5 passenger models
UR-60	ball and trunnion universal joint; all 5 passenger models except early 1946

Allied (A.P.C.)—Water Pump and Engine Rebuild Parts

Allied (A.P.C.—Allied Products Corporation) was always printed in script on the box. A.P.C. of Cincinnati, Ohio, produced the engine parts such as pistons, pins, valves, guides and pumps for the Allied Motor Parts Company of Detroit, Michigan. Allied products were sold through NAPA Stores.

661-A	piston; 3¼" diameter; 6 cylinder models
661-AP	piston; 3¼" diameter; 6 cylinder models
732	replacement type aluminum piston; 3¼" diameter; 2—$\frac{3}{32}$" compression and 2—$\frac{5}{32}$" oil rings
732-A	replacement type aluminum piston; 3¼" diameter; 2—$\frac{3}{32}$" compression and 2—$\frac{5}{32}$" oil rings
751	original type piston; U—slot; 3¼" diameter; 2—$\frac{3}{32}$" compression and 2—$\frac{5}{32}$" oil rings

751-P	piston sleeve; 3¼" diameter; 6 cylinder models
832-AP	piston; 3¼" diameter; 6 cylinder models
996	intake valve
997	exhaust valve
1226	intake valve
2349	piston pin bushing
2459	piston pin bushing; .008" oversize
3337	exhaust valve guide
3338	intake valve guide
BU-294	water pump front bushing
BU-295	water pump rear bushing
CP-157	water pump; factory type bushing pump
CP-157A	water pump; all models
CS-15	water pump repair kit; complete set
CS-225	water pump repair kit
G-31	water pump miscellaneous parts kit
G-46	water pump miscellaneous parts kit
HU-4	water pump fan hub
IS-104	intake valve seat
IS-207	exhaust valve seat
P-101	water pump packing
PC-56	piston pin
U-81	valve lock; intake or exhaust
V-415	valve spring; intake or exhaust
WA-1048	water pump assembly; with seal
WS-57	cylinder sleeve; cut-to-length sleeve

Alloy—Universal Joints and Universal Joint Repair Kits

Alloy produced a line of replacement universal joints and universal joint repair kits for passenger cars and trucks. All raw materials were carefully selected and a high quality of production was maintained through regular checks and analysis. Each component was carefully assembled to exact factory specifications to ensure a perfect fit and long dependable service. Alloy Automotive Co. was located in Chicago, Illinois.

J-72625-2	Cross-Block Bearing type universal joint; 7 passenger models; replaces 947 550
J-83254-3	Cross-Ball type universal joint; rear; 5 passenger models; replaces 1134 579
JR-67A	Ball and Trunnion type universal joint; less body; rubber boot; early 1946 front; 5 passenger models; replaces 939 700
UR-60	Ball and Trunnion type universal joint; early 1946 front; 5 passenger models; replaces 939 700

Allstate (Sears)—Full Line of Popular Replacement Parts

Allstate was the trademark brand for Sears automotive parts. Parts were sold in Sears stores nationwide or through their mail-order catalog. Only the basic number is given below to identify the part number found on the box. Prefix letters or numbers were often added to the packaging to identify if a part was obtained from a store or catalog. Sears was located in Chicago, Illinois.

6	lower flexible radiator hose
8	upper flexible radiator hose
112	front and/or rear wheel cylinder repair kit
143	master cylinder repair kit
679C	custom style fender skirts for outline fit
1337K	GDZ generator
1368	heavy duty starter solenoid
1418	adjustable voltage regulator for GDZ, GGW, and GGU generators
1422C	rebuilt starter
1454	standard type voltage regulator
1787	brake shoe release springs; front only
1788	brake shoe release springs; rear only
1812	Allstate "25" (25K) Ready-Lined bonded front and/or rear axle brake shoe set; 7 passenger
1826	Allstate "25" (25K) Ready-Lined bonded rear axle brake shoe set; 5 passenger
1830	Allstate "25" (25K) Ready-Lined bonded rear axle brake shoe set; 5 passenger
1843	hand brake cable; fluid drive
1890	brake master cylinder
1909	Allstate "35" (35K) Ready-Lined bonded front and/or rear axle brake shoe set; 7 passenger
1913	Allstate "35" (35K) Ready-Lined bonded front axle brake shoe set; 5 passenger
1917	Allstate "35" (35K) Ready-Lined bonded rear axle brake shoe set; 5 passenger
2024L	sports cruiser type fender skirts; all models
2069	brake shoe hold-down kit
2125	carburetor; standard transmission without fluid drive
2216	speedometer cable and assembly
2264	rebuilt carburetor; models with fluid drive
2306	full set connecting rod bearings; .002" undersize
2387	full set connecting rod bearings; standard size
2403	high speed carburetor for high speed manifold
2448	"Good Single" diaphragm fuel pump; all models
2517	timing chain
2581	engine rebuild kit No. 4; connecting rod set
2593	replacement camshaft

2621	tie rod ends; short rod; left
2622	tie rod ends; long rod; right
2635	front and/or rear universal joint; excludes 1946; 5 passenger
2642	"Best Single" diaphragm fuel pump; all models
2656	oil pump
2873N	factory rebuilt 6 cylinder engine
2976	exhaust valve
2977	intake valve
3017N	engine rebuild kit No. 3; crankshaft, rod and main bearings
3055N	engine rebuild kit No. 2; crankshaft, rods and bearings
3102	clutch release bearing; fluid drive models
3193	valve spring set (12)
3201	clutch disc only; fluid drive models
3233	high speed intake manifold
3271C	clutch pressure plate and disc set; fluid drive models
3275C	clutch pressure plate and disc set; models without fluid drive
3281	clutch disc only; models without fluid drive
3435	piston pin set; marked standard, .003" or .005" undersize
3470N	rebuilt transmission; fluid drive up to engine No. 132935
3503	piston without rings; 3¼" diameter
3514	piston with "Chrome Edge" rings
3610	full set "Chrome-Master" piston rings
3670	full set "Steel-Master" piston rings
3711	full set "Chrome-Edge" piston rings
3825	piston with "Chrome-Master" rings
3851	front grease seal; original quality
3860	rear axle outer oil seal; original quality
3862	rear axle inner oil seal; original quality
3920	valve guide set
3975	replacement engine mounts set
4087	manifold gasket
4089	crankshaft full set main bearings; .002" undersize
4090	crankshaft full set main bearings; standard size
4142	front wheel bearing set
4186	oil pan gasket
4198	cylinder head gasket
4263	valve grinding gasket set
4293C	overhead gasket set
4296	exhaust pipe gasket
4558	oil filter refill; heavy duty
5055	complete king bolt set; 5 passenger models
5081N	rebuilt standard transmission; without fluid drive
5240	outer front suspension kit; 5 passenger models
5241	inner front suspension kit; 5 passenger models
5315	steering knuckle support; 5 passenger models

5398	clutch release bearing; models without fluid drive
5404	new water pump
5410	lower, outer front end suspension kit; 5 passenger models
5411	lower, inner front end suspension kit; 5 passenger models
5468	upper, outer front end suspension kit; 5 passenger models
5469	upper, inner front end suspension kit; 5 passenger models
5871	stoplight switch
6011	Allstate regular spark plug
6348	vacuum windshield wiper motor; D24 Deluxe model
7071	spark plug wire set
7101	battery hold down
7317	upper and lower straight radiator hose
7785	standard temperature thermostat
7786	high temperature thermostat
7889	front "Supramatic" (heavy duty) shock absorbers
7906	rear "Supramatic" (heavy duty) shock absorbers
7947	direct action shock absorber bushing
8135	standard voltage regulator
8146	distributor cap
8153	rear "Supramatic" (regular duty) shock absorbers
8155	front "Supramatic" (regular duty) shock absorbers
8156	rear "Supramatic" (regular duty) shock absorbers
8299	heavy duty Allstate distributor tune-up kit
8325	rebuilt distributor
8552C	heavy duty muffler
8619C	standard muffler
8743L	heavy duty tail pipe
8871C	heavy duty exhaust pipe
9174C	glass-packed muffler
9366N	radiator
9816K	rear leaf spring; 5 passenger models
9862K	matched pair of front coil springs; 5 passenger models
9960	rear shackle set; 5 passenger models
10304	rear hydraulic brake hose
10580	upper left front wheel cylinder
10581	upper right front wheel cylinder
10582	lower left front wheel cylinder
10583	lower right front wheel cylinder
10588	right and/or left rear wheel cylinder
10595	front hydraulic brake hose
23060	full set connecting rod bearings; marked .010", .020" or .030" undersize
25007	valve cover gasket set
29301	thermostat gasket
30008N	complete engine rebuild kit No. 1

35014	piston with "Krome King" rings; 3¼" diameter piston
35811	camshaft bearing set
36519	"Krome King" piston rings; 3¼" diameter piston
37858	timing chain sprocket set
38012	front grease seal
38014	rear axle outer oil seal
38016	rear axle inner oil seal
40890	full set main bearings; marked .010", .020" or .030" undersize
41215	piston pin set; .0015"
52070	right side of car right tie rod end
52071	left side of car right tie rod end
52078	right side of car left tie rod end
52079	left side of car left tie rod end
60110	Allstate super spark plug
78604	front "Futuristic" shock absorber
78605	rear "Futuristic" shock absorber
81350	adjustable voltage regulator
82990	deluxe distributor tune-up kit
F2	pre-stretched fan belt
H	coil
J-11	champion spark plug
P-2	fan belt

American Brakeblok—Fan/Generator Belts, Brakes, Clutches and Hoses

American Brakeblok supplied both bonded brake shoes and pre-drilled molded sets as replacement brakes for passenger cars and trucks. Brake lining for emergency brakes was also available. The company also supplied fan belts, hoses and clutch plates. Fan belts were advertised as long lasting because the cords were "Pre-Stretched" before assembly. American Brakeblok was located in Detroit, Michigan.

109	fan/generator V belt; all models
120	fan/generator V belt; all models
124	fan/generator V belt; all models
762	molded and curved lower radiator hose substitution; all models
868	brake shoe lined set; 5 passenger models
AS-62037	brake lining set; axle set; 5 passenger models
B-44	brake shoe set (4 pieces); front and/or rear axle 11" drum; 5 passenger models
B-192A	front wheel bonded brake set; 5 passenger models
B-314	emergency brake; all models with standard transmission; 6" × 2" × ³⁄₁₆"
B-1105A	front wheel bonded brake set; 7 passenger models
B-1161A	rear wheel bonded brake set; 5 passenger models

B-1179	rear wheel bonded brake set; 7 passenger models; can be substituted by 1105A
CS-62037	brake lining set; car set; 5 passenger models; drilled and countersunk; 8 pieces
CS-63027DC	brake lining set; 5 passenger models; replaces 192A-1161A; 8 pieces
STG-993A	clutch facing plate; 9¼" outside diameter; 32 rivet holes; fluid drive transmission; 2 required
STG-1008A	clutch facing plate; 10" outside diameter; 18 rivet holes; standard transmission; 2 required

American Hammered—Piston Rings

American Hammered Piston Ring Company was founded in Baltimore in 1912 and quickly started to supply a full line of replacement piston rings for automobile, truck, marine and industrial applications. They also made available special order piston rings. American Hammered was part of the Piston Ring Division of the Koppers Company, Inc., of Baltimore, Maryland.

149	re-ring piston ring set (6 pistons—high quality)
1049	re-bore piston ring set (6 pistons—high quality)
2049	re-bore piston ring set (6 pistons—economy quality)

Amoco—Fan/Generator Belts

Amoco (brand name) fan/generator belts were sold and serviced at Amoco gas stations across the nation. Amoco started as the American Oil Company in 1922 in Baltimore, Maryland.

2   fan/generator V belt; all models

Ampco—Ignition, Fuel Pump and Electrical Replacement Parts

The Ampco line of electrical products was founded on engineering, fabrication and quality of design. Every step was taken to control quality of manufacture "under one roof." Ampco engineering and manufacturing paralleled the growth of the automotive industry and the "challenge of keeping pace" was accomplished as Ampco enjoyed an ever-increasing volume and distribution of business. Ampco stands for the American Motor Products Corporation that was located in Fond Du Lac, Wisconsin.

588	fuel pump; all models
4258	starter bushing—drive end
4278	generator bushing—commutator end
AL-37	regular point set
AL-522	regular condenser
AL-923	distributor rotor
AL-930	distributor cap
AL-1037	heavy duty point set

AL-1037M	heavy duty matched point set
AL-1037MV	heavy duty matched and ventilated point set
AL-1430	starter switch
AL-1522	heavy duty condenser
AV-105	vacuum chamber
C-807	coil
EX-18	starter brush set
EX-46	generator brush set to be used with GEG generators
EX-57	generator brush set—excludes GEG generators
F-4804	stop light switch
HR-604	horn relay
TK-109MV	visual-pak tune-up kit
UDS-408	dimmer switch
VR-662	voltage regulator to be used with a GEG generator
VR-665	voltage regulator—excludes GEG generator

Andrews Bearing Corp.—Clutch Assemblies and Clutch Release Bearings

The Andrews Bearing Corp. produced precision ball and roller bearings for passenger car and trucks. The company was located in Spartanburg, South Carolina.

CB-956	clutch release bearing; conventional drive models without fluid drive
CB-1054	clutch release bearing; conventional drive models without fluid drive
CB-1054-C	clutch release bearing and carrier assembly; conventional drive models without fluid drive
CB-1055	clutch release bearing; fluid drive models
CB-1055-C	clutch release bearing and carrier assembly; fluid drive models
CB-1070	clutch release bearing; conventional drive models without fluid drive
CB-1097	clutch release bearing; conventional drive models without fluid drive
CB-1116	clutch release bearing; conventional drive models without fluid drive
CB-1148	clutch release bearing; conventional drive models without fluid drive

Andrews Line—Ignition, Voltage Regulator and Electrical Replacement Parts

Andrews Manufacturing Company started in 1921 and advertised "Your Best Electrical Connection" replacement parts for passenger cars and trucks. They offered precision workmanship, engineered for heavy duty service, using the highest quality materials. Andrews was located in St. Louis, Missouri.

AL-52	distributor contact set
AL-100	distributor condenser
AL-201	distributor rotor
AL-251	distributor cap
C-92	standard coil
C-93	regular duty coil
C-94	heavy duty coil
C-95	regular duty coil
DL-180	primary lead for IGS distributor
DL-187	ground lead for IGS distributor
DS-51	dimmer switch; heavy duty; all models
EX-37-38	starter brush set
EX-45-2	generator brush set
LS-174	stoplight switch
SS-32	solenoid starter switch; heavy duty; all models
VR-3	positive ground 3 unit voltage regulator; all models
VR-10	voltage regulator for GEG-4823A,B generator

AP—Exhaust Clamps, Pipes and Mufflers

AP Mufflers were engineered to deliver original equipment performance while correct size and design assured perfect fit with quick and easy installation. AP mufflers met or surpassed the requirements for sound and noise reduction, and at the same time stayed within the allowances for back pressure set by the engine designers. AP was located in Toledo, Ohio.

194	muffler; all models
1175	universal pipe bracket; all models
2029	muffler outlet clamp; all models
2036	muffler inlet clamp; all models
EP-188	exhaust pipe; excludes 7 passenger models and convertible coupe
P-225	tail pipe; excludes 7 passenger models and convertible coupe

Apeco—Remanufactured Water Pumps

Apeco supplied quality remanufactured water pumps for passenger cars, trucks, buses, farm equipment and industrial machinery. They supplied the correct water pump for the D24 Dodge with the half-moon shaped water outlet on the backing plate. Apeco was a unit of Maremont Corporation, located in Los Angeles, California.

88-0053	remanufactured water pump; replaces original factory casting number 637 437 or 642 398

Arco Products Co.—Ignition, Filters, Fuel Pumps and Thermostats

Arco Products Company were distributors of high quality automotive accessories and tools. Arco was located in Brooklyn, New York.

16	bellows type standard temperature thermostat
16-HT	bellows type high temperature thermostat
588-A	single action type fuel pump; all models
3130	stop light switch
AL-30	ignition contact set
AL-430	solenoid switch
AL-522	distributor condenser
AL-923	distributor rotor
AL-930	distributor cap
C-809	6 volt heavy duty coil
L-70	micron type oil filter cartridge

Armor-Flex—Bushings, Motor Mounts and Rubber Replacement Parts

Armor-Flex was the trade name used by the Doan Manufacturing Corp. Doan specialized in automotive rubber replacement parts such as motor mounts, bushings, and mats. Doan Manufacturing was located in Cleveland, Ohio.

6	front and/or rear universal floor mat; all models
32	front fitted floor mat; all models
1003	shock absorber bushing; standard size shocks; all models; replaces 668 164
1009	rear spring shackle bushing; all models; replaces 857 836
1026	shock absorber grommet; oversize shocks; all 5 passenger models; replaces 689 062
1028	rear axle strut bushing; all models; replaces 866 246
1031	tail pipe support spacer grommet; all models; replaces 677 701
1032	rear spring bushing; all models; replaces 306 458
1042	steering gear arm insulator; all models; replaces 694 499
1043	gear shift control rod bushing; all models; replaces 866 586
1053	rear spring and shackle bushing; all models; replaces 1137 704
1054	accelerator stem boot assembly; all models; replaces 498 221
1056	control arm lower rubber bumper; all models; replaces 1124 470
1068	thermostat gasket; all models; replaces 863 220
2015	rear lower motor mount; all models; two required; replaces 854 877
2016	rear upper motor mount; all models; two required; replaces 866 050
2018	front motor mount; all models; replaces 1115 744
3004	brake and clutch pedal pads; all models
6001	brake and clutch weather pad replacement

Arrow—Armature, Clutch, Generators, Starters, Fuel Pumps and Water Pumps

Arrow supplied factory rebuilt generators, starters and armatures for passenger car, truck, industry, farm and marine. Starters and generators were stripped to bare metal and every part was inspected and tested to be perfect or it was replaced. Each armature was rewound on a perfect core with a perfect shaft. Field coils were tested for amperage and dielectric values. Each starter and generator was tested and passed conditions more severe than encountered in actual use. The Arrow Armature Company was located in Boston, Massachusetts, and Spartanburg, South Carolina.

7-1006	water pump; all models
81-505	fuel pump; all models
505	generator armature; replaces armature for GDZ-A,B generators
2069	starter armature; replaces armature for MAW-4041 starter
CA-1854	clutch assembly; 1946–1948 models without fluid drive; 10" O.D., 10 spline, 1" hub.
CD-2289	clutch disc; 1946–1948 models without fluid drive; 10" O.D., 10 spline, 1" hub.
CS-35	starter; replaces MAW-4041 starter; all models
UG-4	"G" line generator; replaces GDZ-4801A,B generator
UR-4	"R" line generator; replaces GDZ-4801A,B generator

ATB—Clutch Release Bearings

ATB (Automotive Thrust Bearing) specialized in clutch release bearings and assemblies for passenger cars and trucks. Bearings were produced with the highest quality materials under rigid inspections. They were a division of Aetna Ball and Roller Bearing Company, Chicago, Illinois.

A-691	clutch release bearing; fluid drive models
A-813	clutch release bearing; conventional drive models without fluid drive
A-826	steering bearing; 5 passenger models
A-838	clutch release bearing; fluid drive models
A-873	clutch release bearing; models without fluid drive
A-873-S	clutch release bearing and carrier assembly; fluid drive models
A-874	clutch release bearing; conventional drive models without fluid drive
A-874-S	clutch release bearing and carrier assembly; conventional drive models without fluid drive
A-899	clutch release bearing; conventional drive models without fluid drive
A-901	clutch release bearing; conventional drive models without fluid drive
A-904	clutch release bearing; fluid drive models
A-927	clutch release bearing; conventional drive models without fluid drive
A-993	steering bearing; 7 passenger models
AT-41	clutch release bearing; conventional drive models without fluid drive
AT-53	clutch release bearing; conventional drive models without fluid drive
AT-67	clutch release bearing; fluid drive models

Atlas—Fan/Generator Belts, Brakes and Chassis Replacement Parts

Atlas was a major supplier of new, rebuilt and replacement parts for passenger cars and trucks. Parts included ignition, brakes, switches, regulators, belts, hoses, fluids and most other supplies needed for quick repairs to "get the vehicle back on the road." Atlas supplies were available at jobbers, garages and repair shops nationwide. Atlas Supply Company was located in Springfield, New Jersey.

192-44	front axle brake shoe package; 5 passenger
588A	fuel pump; all models
628	fan/generator V-belt; all models
651	heavy duty fan/generator V-belt; all models
1013	master cylinder; all models
1161-44	rear axle brake shoe package; 5 passenger
2019	master cylinder repair kit; all models
3025	left and/or right rear wheel cylinder
5011	front and/or rear wheel cylinder repair kit
6000	stop light switch
7016	rear wheel brake hose
7017	front wheel brake hose
ES-60L	left tie rod end; all models
ES-60R	right tie rod end; all models
ES-131L	left tie rod end; all models
ES-131R	right tie rod end; all models
P-70	oil filter; replaces 1121 694; all models
U-3021	left front upper wheel cylinder; all models
U-3022	right front upper wheel cylinder; all models
U-3023	left front lower wheel cylinder; all models
U-3024	right front lower wheel cylinder; all models

Auburn—Spark Plugs

Auburn first manufactured spark plugs in 1910. They engineered the "Triple Concave Ground Electrode" to overcome spark plug difficulties caused by fuel and oil additives required by high speed, high compression engines. Triple electrodes exposed twelve edges on the ground electrode for the spark to jump from the center electrode. This insured complete combustion and greater power from a given quantity of gas, and more miles per gallon. Auburn was located in Auburn, New York.

14	super Auburn spark plug with single electrode and adjustable gap with hotter tip to prevent fouling
14-8	Auburn chrome triple electrode spark plug with non-adjustable gap
14 R	super Auburn spark plug with single electrode and adjustable gap
14-11	Auburn chrome triple electrode spark plug with non-adjustable gap with hotter tip to prevent fouling
145 T	TC-3 Black Triple electrode spark plug with non-adjustable gap
147 T	TC-3 Black Triple electrode spark plug with non-adjustable gap with hotter tip to prevent fouling

Autoline—Master Cylinder, Brake Wheel Cylinders

Autoline supplied "Genuine Remanufactured" brake cylinders, water pumps, voltage regulators and solenoids for passenger cars and trucks. They were a member of the Rebuilders Division of the Automotive Service Industry Association. Autoline was located in Chicago, Illinois.

3241	master cylinder; all models
10588	right and/or left rear wheel brake cylinder; all models
L-10582	lower left front wheel brake cylinder; all models
L-10583	lower right front wheel brake cylinder; all models
U-10580	upper left front wheel brake cylinder; all models
U-10581	upper right front wheel brake cylinder; all models

Auto-Lite—Ignition, Generators, Starters and Electrical Replacement Parts

Auto-Lite started in 1911 as the Electric Auto-Lite Company and produced small generators for the electric lights on early automobiles. They quickly expanded and by 1935 supplied all the major electrical components for passenger cars and trucks for Chrysler Corporation. The starter, generator, ignition, gauges and switches on the D24 Dodge all came from Auto-Lite. Auto-Lite was located in Toledo, Ohio.

100810FC	stop light switch
A-5	spark plug for all cast iron heads 1946–1948
A-7	spark plug; regular cast iron head
AL-7	spark plug; all high compression aluminum heads
CR-4001	ignition coil
EBA-39	starter Bendix
EBA-2105	Bendix drive spring
GBF-79	generator commutator end bearing; for GDZ-4801A, GDZ-4801B generators
GBW-45	generator brush spring (2 required); for GDZ-4801A, GDZ-4801B generators
GCJ-26	brush arm; generators GDZ-4801A,B; 2 required
GDZ-1003	generator drive end head assembly
GDZ-1005	generator field coil assembly; for GDZ-4801A, GDZ-4801B generators
GDZ-2002S	generator commutator end head assembly; for GDZ-4801A, GDZ-4801B generators
GDZ-2006F	generator armature; for GDZ-4801A, GDZ-4801B generators
GDZ-4801A	generator
GDZ-4801B	generator
GGU-2012S	generator brush set; for GDZ-4801A, GDZ-4801B generators
IAT-14	distributor ground lead
IG-579A	distributor bearing (2 required)
IG-636HS	distributor weight spring set
IG-3927G	distributor condenser
IG-4806	service coil 1946; early 1947
IG-4809	service coil
IGC-1107S	distributor cap

IGP-3028ES	distributor contact set
IGS-181	distributor primary lead
IGS-1016B	distributor rotor
IGS-1113R	distributor drive shaft
IGS-2158	distributor base assembly
IGS-3004J	distributor breaker plate assembly
IGS-4207A-1	distributor
MAW-2002F	starter commutator end head assembly
MAW-2012S	starter brush set; for MAW-4041
MAW-2128	starter armature; for MAW-4041
MAW-2129	starter intermediate bearing
MAW-3005S	starter field coil package
MAW-4041	starter motor
MG-77A	starter drive end bearing
MZ-19	starter brush spring; 4 required
PS-1252	starter drive end pinion housing
SP-1299	pulley for GDZ-4801A generator
SP-1310	pulley for GDZ-4801B generator
SST-4001	starter switch
STA-34	ignition kit; includes rotor, contact set, condenser and primary lead
VC-2082R	distributor vacuum chamber
VRP-4001A	voltage regulator
VRP-4401A	voltage regulator
VRP-4501A	voltage regulator
VRP-4503A	voltage regulator; for GDZ-4801A, GDZ-4801B generators; replaces voltage regulators VRP-4001A, VRP-4401A, VRP-4501A
X-295	generator drive end bearing; for GDZ-4801A, GDZ-4801B generators

Automotive—Armatures, Generators, Starters and Electrical Replacement Parts

Automotive supplied remanufactured armatures, generators, starters, regulators and solenoids for passenger cars and trucks. Original factory numbers were always cross-referenced with the remanufactured products. Generators were always bench tested at the factory before shipment and supplied with or without pulleys.

4	generator armature for generator GDZ-4801
1745	starter armature for starter MAW-4041
3246	starter; replaces starter with original number MAW-4041
9413	generator; replaces generator GDZ-4801
17330	voltage regulator; replaces voltage regulator VRP-4501A
FC-203	field coil; replacement field coil for generator GDZ-4801

Autostat—Thermostats

Autostat thermostats often had the names Fulton or Fulton-Sylphon written in large letters on the box. Autostat designed and engineered thermostats that were ideal for pressurized and non-pressurized cooling systems. They supplied attractive counter top displays of standard and high temperature thermostats for automobiles, trucks and tractors for many garages and jobbers.

Autostat was made by Fulton-Sylphon Division of Robertshaw Controls Co., located in Knoxville, Tennessee.

95-F	standard temperature thermostat; all models
95-FHT	high temperature thermostat; all models
96-F	bellows type thermostat; standard temperature; 160 degrees F; all models
96-FHT	bellows type thermostat; high temperature; 180 degrees F; all models
97-F	summer thermostat; all models
97-FHT	winter thermostat; all models

Babcock Thermostats—*See* Bishop and Babcock Thermostats

Badger—Pistons

Badger pistons for the D24 Dodge were produced and sold in sets of 6 pistons. All piston sets were "interchangeable" but some may not be identical to the factory pistons. Badger Manufacturing Company was located in Marinette, Wisconsin.

P-220	piston; 3¼" diameter; 6 cylinder models
P-221	piston; 3¼" diameter; 6 cylinder models

Baldwin—Oil Filters

Baldwin started the manufacture of oil filters in 1936 and advertised "Full-Flow" using cotton or pleated paper for passenger car and truck filters. Baldwin manufacturing Company was located in Kearney, Nebraska.

C-37P	replacement oil filter; all models

Balkamp—General Line of Popular Replacement Parts

Balkamp supplied a wide range of aftermarket replacement parts for passenger cars and light and heavy duty trucks. Parts were sold nationwide through local NAPA stores and most Balkamp products had a NAPA logo on the package. Balkamp was located in Indianapolis, Indiana.

2-144	Stromberg carburetor tune-up kit; all with Stromberg carburetor
2-2040	Stromberg carburetor gasket set; all with Stromberg carburetor
2-3023	Stromberg carburetor needle and seat set; all with Stromberg carburetor
3-566	starter drive; all models
3-735	17" oil line replacement; all models

3-736	12" oil line replacement; all models
3-3310	oil pump; all models
3-3963	steering sector set; all models
3-4112	clutch front pilot bushing; models with fluid drive; replaces 868 381
3-4113	clutch rear pilot bushing; models with fluid drive; replaces 868 382
3-5013	front motor mount all models
3-5016	rear upper motor mount; all models
3-5017	rear lower motor mount; all models
3-5105	rear upper motor mount; all models
3-5209	hinge type accelerator pedal; all models
3-5254	brake and clutch pedal pads; all models
3-5351	front shock absorber bushing; oversize
3-5356	front and rear shock absorber bushing; standard; all models
3-6605	valve tappet; all models
3-7261	flywheel gear; all models
3-7501	heater and defroster small motor; all models
13-1596	cylinder block water distribution tube; steel; all models
13-1598	cylinder block water distribution tube; brass; all models

BCA or Bower or BCA-Bower or Bower-BCA—Bearings

The bearing box may be labeled BCA, Bower, BCA-Bower or Bower-BCA. BCA (Bearing Corporation of America) and Bower were producers of aftermarket anti-friction bearings for passenger cars, trucks, farm machinery and industry. They specialized in clutch release, tapered and cylindrical roller bearings. BCA and Bower used the same bearing numbers and were Divisions of Federal Mogul Corporation, Detroit, Michigan.

09074	front wheel outer bearing cone; 5 passenger models
09194	front wheel outer bearing cup; 5 passenger models
5-BC	steering gear upper and lower bearing cone; 5 passenger models
6	steering gear upper bearing cup; 5 passenger models
6-CE	steering gear lower bearing cup; 5 passenger models
11-BC	steering gear upper and lower bearing cone; 7 passenger models
13-C	steering gear upper bearing cup; 7 passenger models
14-XS	steering gear lower bearing cup; 7 passenger models
203	generator bearing; all models
206	transmission main shaft extension bearing; all models
207	transmission main shaft rear bearing; all models
207-S	propeller shaft bearing; 7 passenger models
207-SL	transmission drive shaft rear bearing; all models
1503	clutch release bearing; models without fluid drive
1505	clutch release bearing; models without fluid drive
1505-1	clutch release bearing; models without fluid drive
1505-14	clutch release bearing; models without fluid drive
1729X	front wheel outer bearing cup; 5 passenger models

1755	front wheel outer bearing cone; 7 passenger models
1872	clutch release bearing; models with fluid drive
1972-C	clutch release bearing and carrier assembly; models with fluid drive
2523	front wheel inner bearing cup; 7 passenger models
2585	front wheel inner bearing cone; 7 passenger models
2736	rear wheel outer bearing cup; 7 passenger models
2780	rear wheel outer bearing cone; 7 passenger models
3420	pinion front bearing cup; 7 passenger models
3476	pinion front bearing cone; 7 passenger models
3820	pinion rear bearing cup; 5 passenger models
3875	pinion rear bearing cone; 5 passenger models
14125A	front wheel inner bearing cone; 5 passenger models
14276	front wheel inner bearing cup; 5 passenger models
25520	rear axle differential cup; all models
25580	rear axle differential cone; all models
25821	rear wheel outer bearing cup; 5 passenger models
25877	rear wheel outer bearing cone; 5 passenger models
31520	pinion front and/or rear bearing cup; 5 passenger models
31590	pinion front bearing cone; 5 passenger models
31593	pinion rear bearing cone; 5 passenger models
C-417Q	transmission main shaft pilot bearing; all models
C-1086Q	countershaft front and rear bearing; reverse idler bearing; all models
CTD-48	clutch release bearing; conventional drive models without fluid drive
CTDS-48	clutch release bearing; conventional drive models without fluid drive
CTS-60	clutch release bearing; fluid drive models
P-1605C	clutch release assembly; models without fluid drive

Bendix—Brake Shoes

Bendix advertised "Super Quality—Super Safety Brakes." Bendix produced new brake shoes that restored "New Car" braking performance to passenger cars and trucks. New brake shoes were made with the same tools and methods as the original shoes in the vehicle when new. The Bendix Corporation was located in South Bend, Indiana.

303691	front axle new lined brake shoes; 2 wheels; replaces F.M.S.I. No. 192-44; 5 passenger models
303692	rear axle new lined brake shoes; 2 wheels; replaces F.M.S.I. No. 1161-44; 5 passenger models
307911	front and/or rear new lined brake shoes; 12" diameter drums; replaces F.M.S.I. No. 1105-45; 7 passenger models

Benson Industries—Armatures, Generators, Starters and Voltage Regulators

Benson Corporation was advertised as New York's largest rebuilder of starters, generators, armatures, voltage regulators and distributors. Rebuilt parts were inspected and bench tested for top performance during the rebuilding process to meet or exceed original factory specifications. The Benson Corporation was located in Brooklyn, New York.

4	rebuilt generator armature; fits all models
606	rebuilt distributor; fits all models
1745	rebuilt starter armature; fits all models
9413	rebuilt generator; fits all models
A-79	rebuilt starter drive; fits all models
ST-601	rebuilt starter; fits all models
VRP-4503	rebuilt voltage regulator; fits all models

Besco—Clutch Bearings

Besco (Buchanan Electric Steel Company) supplied ball and roller bearings for passenger cars and trucks and was advertised as the "Complete Bearing Service." Besco was located in Buchanan, Michigan.

CBA-40	clutch release bearing and carrier assembly; conventional drive models without fluid drive
CBA-44	clutch release bearing and carrier assembly; fluid drive models

B.G. Engineering—Master Cylinder and Wheel Cylinders

B.G. Engineering was "The Original Chrome" company for the remanufacture of chrome sleeve inserts for hydraulic brake and wheel cylinders. They advertised their products as "They're Better Than Brand New." B.G. Engineering was located in Baltimore, Maryland.

3241	master cylinder; all models
10580	front, upper left wheel cylinder; all models
10581	front, upper right wheel cylinder; all models
10582	front, lower left wheel cylinder; all models
10583	front, lower right wheel cylinder; all models
10588	rear wheel cylinder; right or left; all models

B.H.T.—Brake Shoes, Fuel Pumps and Clutch Assemblies

B.H.T. was a major supplier of brake shoes, fuel pumps and clutch cover assemblies for passenger cars and trucks to NAPA. Parts were sold nationwide through local NAPA stores with NAPA headquarters located in Detroit, Michigan.

4505	single type mechanical fuel pump; new; all models
AT-305	single type mechanical fuel pump; rebuilt; all models
AT-588	rebuilt fuel pump; all models
B-192A	front wheel brake shoe set; 5 passenger models
B-1105	front and/or rear wheel brake shoe set; 7 passenger models
B-1161A	rear wheel brake shoe set; 5 passenger models

CA-952 clutch cover assembly; 9¼"; all models with fluid drive
CA-957 clutch cover assembly; 10"; all models without fluid drive

Bishop & Babcock—Thermostats

Bishop and Babcock (B&B) started producing thermostats almost as soon as automobiles needed water temperature control for engine efficiency and the addition of aftermarket and factory installed heaters. In addition to thermostats, B&B produced a water line and a hose line of parts for automobile water heaters. All products were designed and engineered for use with permanent anti-freeze. Thermostats for Chrysler cars were designed to obtain maximum efficiency for by-pass type engine cooling systems. Bishop & Babcock Mfg., Co., was located in Cleveland, Ohio.

S13A   low temperature bellows type thermostat; all models
S13AHT   high temperature bellows type thermostat; all models

Bishop Thermostats—*See* Bishop and Babcock Thermostats

Blackstone—Fuel Pumps

Blackstone fully guaranteed their fuel pumps against defects in material, workmanship and performance. Castings were tested to be absolutely leak proof. The diaphragm was constructed, of a special high grade chemically impregnated cloth, to last under long service. All parts were accurately made and inspected before the fuel pump was assembled. Blackstone Manufacturing Co., Inc., was located in Chicago, Illinois.

588   fuel pump for all 6 cylinder models
GI-51   fuel pump; all models; replaces AC exchange number 505 or 588 fuel
             pumps; replaces factory AT series numbers 1523647 or 1539042
GI-202   fuel pump; all models; replaces AC exchange numbers 505 or 588 fuel
             pumps; replaces factory AT series numbers 1523647 or 1539042
PK-22   fuel pump repair kit; all models

Blue Crown—Spark Plugs

Blue Crown Spark Plugs featured the "X-Citer" spark plug with double-grounded side electrodes. Their design differed from the ordinary two-grounded plug in that the electrodes were at the end of the center tip rather than the side. This resulted in greater resistance to oil and carbon fouling as the ignition spark ionized the entire gap area of the plug to give complete combustion of the fuel. Customers were rewarded with easier starting, better idling, improved acceleration, longer gap life and greater fuel economy. Blue Crown was located in Chicago, Illinois.

M-5X   colder heat range "X-CITER" Blue Crown spark plug; all models
M-7   normal heat range "HUSKY" Blue Crown spark plug; all models
M-7X   normal heat range "X-CITER" Blue Crown spark plug; all models
M-9X   hotter heat range "HUSKY" Blue Crown spark plug; all models

Blue Streak/Standard—Ignition and Electrical Replacement Parts

Blue Streak was known for quality and supplied replacement parts for ignition, starter and generator systems as well as wire and cable. Blue Streak was known for its "Service Bulletins" that supplied practical servicing tips to jobbers and repair shops alike. Standard Motor Products, Inc., of Long Island City, New York, manufactured and supplied the Blue Streak Line of replacement parts.

4264	starter bushing—drive end
4278	generator bushing—commutator end
AL-3 J	ignition coil; "Standard"
AL-50	breaker point arm; "Standard"
AL-50X	breaker point arm; "Blue Streak"
AL-57	stationary contact point; "Standard"
AL-57X	stationary contact point; "Blue Streak"
AL-5057	breaker point set; "Standard"
AL-5057X	breaker point set; Blue Streak"
AL-96	distributor cap; "Standard"
AL-98	rotor; "Standard"
AL-101	condenser; "Standard"
AL-101X	condenser; heavy duty; "Blue Streak"
BX-9R	starter drive Bendix spring
DS-47	dimmer switch; "Standard"
DS-47X	dimmer switch; heavy duty; "Blue Streak"
DS-109	headlight switch
E-37	starter brush (needs 2)
E-38	starter brush (needs 2)
E-45	generator main brush; excludes generators GCB-4802A,B or GEB-4801A; 2 brushes required
E-46	generator main brush if generator GCB-4802A,B or GEB-4801A is used; 2 brushes required
EX-37	starter brush set
EX-45	generator brush set, excludes generators GCB-4802A,B or GEB-4801A
EX-46	generator brush set if generator GCB-4802A,B or GEB-4801A is used
HR-112	horn relay
SLS-27	stop light switch
UC-500 R	ignition coil (heavy duty); "Blue Streak"
VR-313	voltage regulator; 6 volt, 30 amp, positive ground; for GEB-4801A generator; "Standard"
VR-313X	voltage regulator; 6 volt; 30 amp, positive ground; for GEB-4801A generator; heavy duty "Blue Streak"
VR-322	voltage regulator; 6 volt. 35-45 amp, positive ground; excludes generator GEB-4801A; "Standard"
VR-322X	voltage regulator; 6 volt, 35-45 amp, positive ground; excludes generator GEB-4801A; heavy duty "Blue Streak"

X-4264	starter bushing—drive end
X-4278	generator bushing—commutator end

Bohnalite—Water Pumps

Bohnalite supplied a line of rebuilt water pumps and water pump repair kits for most U.S. passenger cars, trucks and tractors. Bohnalite water pumps were rebuilt by the Bohn Aluminum & Brass Corporation, formerly Clawson and Bals, and were located in Holland, Michigan.

P-19	rebuilt water pump; factory bushing type pump
PK-218	water pump repair kit; factory bushing type pump
WT-432	water distributing tube

Borg-Warner—Clutch Assemblies, Bearings, Plates and Chassis Replacement Parts

Borg-Warner was founded in 1928 with the merger of Warner Gear and Borg & Beck. The company became best known for passenger car and truck clutches and bearings. All were matched and balanced to vehicle speed before shipping. The company also produced engine, chassis, drive train and ignition parts. Borg-Warner was located in Chicago, Illinois.

26-3301	hinge type accelerator pedal
27-3025	brake or clutch pedal pad
31-2015	left or right hand; rear; lower motor mount
31-2016	left or right hand; rear; lower motor mount; early number
31-2018	front motor mount
31-2105	left or right hand, rear upper motor mount
46-1053	rear spring and shackle bushing; 8 required
47-1026	front shock absorber grommet; oversize
48-1031	tail pipe support insulator; rear
97-160	low temperature (160 F) thermostat; all models
97-180	high temperature (180 F) thermostat; all models
114-52A	front universal joint repair kit; without body; early 1946
114-52R	front and rear universal joint; excludes early 1946; 5 passenger models
114-55	front universal joint repair kit; includes body; early 1946; 5 passenger models
114-225	front and rear universal joint; 7 passenger models
114-235	rear universal joint; early 1946; 5 passenger models
146-XF	flywheel gear; 10" and 11" clutch; all models
931	clutch cover assembly; 11"–1" heavy duty, police and taxi models with standard transmission
952	clutch cover assembly; 9¼"–1¼"; models with fluid drive transmission
993A	clutch facing for 9¼" clutch disc (CD 756); models with fluid drive
1008A	clutch facing for 10"–1" clutch disc (CD 728); models without fluid drive

1169A	clutch facing for 11"–1" clutch disc 381850
150265	clutch release bearing; fluid drive models
150266	clutch release bearing; conventional drive models without fluid drive
150290	clutch release bearing and carrier assembly; conventional drive models without fluid drive
150292	clutch release bearing and carrier assembly; fluid drive models
360957	clutch cover assembly; 10"—1"; standard transmission without fluid drive
381850	clutch disc; 11"–1"; heavy duty police and taxi models with standard transmission
470447	complete clutch; 9¼"; models with fluid drive
470448	complete clutch; 10"; models without fluid drive
CD-728	clutch disc; 10"–1"; standard transmission models without fluid drive
CD-756	clutch disc; 9¼"–1¼"; models with fluid drive
FP-847	fuel pump; new; all models
N-1054	clutch release bearing; standard transmission without fluid drive; all models
N-1055	clutch release bearing; fluid drive; all models
N-1310	clutch release bearing and carrier assembly; conventional drive models without fluid drive
N-1312	clutch release bearing and carrier assembly; fluid drive models
RFP-588	fuel pump; remanufactured
S-126	cam sprocket; 38 teeth; all models
S-127	crank sprocket; 19 teeth; all models
TC-401	timing chain; all models

Bower or Bower Bearings—*See* BCA Bearings

Bower Bearings supplied antifriction clutch release, tapered and cylindrical roller aftermarket bearings for passenger cars, trucks, tractors and industry. Bower was a Division of Federal Mogul Corporation of Detroit, Michigan.

Bowes—Fan/Generator Belts

Bowes supplied fan/generator V-belts and molded or cut-to-fit hoses for most cars, trucks and tractors. Bowes supplied a wide variety of car care products, but was best known for their "Seal Fast" line of tube and tubeless tire repair products. Other products included filters, cables, fluids and spark plugs. The Bowes "Seal Fast" Corporation was located in Indianapolis, Indiana.

262	heavy duty fan/generator V-belt; all models
264	fan and generator V-belt belt; all models

Bridgeport—Thermostats

Bridgeport offered a complete coverage line of thermostats for automobiles, trucks and tractors to duplicate the original equipment specifications. The company produced a design that offered higher flow-through without leakage and was not subject to being held open by dirt or scale. The Bridgeport bellows type thermostats were equipped with a liquid which vaporized when heated and generated pressure to operate the valve. Bridgeport Thermostat was a member of the Robertshaw-Fulton Company located in Knoxville, Tennessee.

16	low temperature bellows type thermostat; all models
16-HT	high temperature bellows type thermostat; all models

Briggs—Shock Absorbers

Briggs advertised a permanent "Leakproof Seal" shock absorber that once installed needed no adjusting or servicing. They provided the "Ride of Your Life—For the Life of Your Car." Briggs shock absorbers were sold through local NAPA stores nationwide. The Briggs Shock Absorber Company was located in Cleveland, Ohio.

4504-B	front shock absorber; regular duty; all models
8038-B	rear shock absorber; regular duty; all models
BR-375B	front shock absorber; heavy duty; all models
BR-725B	rear shock absorber; heavy duty; all models

Buffalo—Oil Filters

Buffalo supplied canister, sock and cartridge type replacement oil filters for passenger cars and trucks. Buffalo Pressed Steel Company was located in Youngstown, Ohio.

K-715	replacement oil filter; all models

Bull Dog—Motor Mounts

Bull Dog produced a variety of small but important aftermarket replacement parts for passenger cars and trucks. Bull Dog was owned by Jambor Tool & Stamping Co., of Milwaukee, Wisconsin.

MM-2000	front engine support motor mount; replaces 1115 744; all models
MM-2006	rear upper engine support motor mount; replaces 866 050; all models
MM-2007	rear lower engine support motor mount; replaces 854 877; all models

Burd—Piston Rings

Burd Piston Rings were specifically engineered for re-ring and re-bore replacement service. All rings were packaged in sets to match the correct ring grooves for original factory equipment pistons. Burd was located in Eau Claire, Wisconsin.

556	re-ring and/or re-bore piston ring set for 3¼" piston diameter; all 6 cylinder models

Caltherm—Thermostats

Caltherm offered low and high temperature "Precision Thermostats" for passenger cars and light trucks. Caltherm Corporation was located in Columbus, Indiana.

VO 756 low temperature (160°F) thermostat; all models
VO 758 high temperature (180°F) thermostat; all models

Camco—Armatures, Generators and Starters

The Carr Automotive Mfg. Corp. (CAMCO) advertised as the "Exchange Specialists" for rebuilt generators, starters and armatures for cars and light trucks. Exchanges for rebuilt water pumps, fuel pumps, distributors, solenoids, regulators, clutches and brake cylinders were also available. The company was located in Tappahannock, Virginia.

4	generator armature; replaces Auto-Lite armature GDZ 2006 in the GDZ 4801 generator
1745	starter armature; replaces Auto-Lite armature MAW 2128 in the MAX 4041 starter
3246	starter; replaces Auto-Lite MAX 4041
9413	generator; replaces Auto-Lite GDZ 4801

CaPaC—Fuel Pumps

The CaPaC logo is derived from the high fuel flow that provides "Capacity" flow to prevent vapor formation and vapor lock. CaPaC fuel pumps are made from high density non-porous zinc that provides strength yet prevents warpage, and a specially treated nylon fabric that is resistant to gasoline, motor oil and alcohol blended fuels. CaPaC fuel pumps are a product of Wells Manufacturing Corporation of Fond du Lac, Wisconsin.

588	fuel pump; all models
CN-2712	fuel pump diaphragm
FD-144	fuel pump diaphragm kit
M-587	fuel pump; all models
R-7	fuel pump repair kit

Capsul-Pac—Carburetor Tune-Up Kits (See Pacco—Carburetor)

Capsul-Pac was the trademark of the Precision Automotive Components Company (Pacco) located in Baldwin, Missouri.

Cardo—Carburetors and Fuel Pumps

Cardo Automotive Products started in 1937 as a part-time rebuilding operation and grew to a company that supplied carburetors and fuel pumps for most U.S. passenger cars and trucks. Cardo insisted on absolute perfection in their products and had an industry-wide reputation for quality, dependability and customer service. They were considered one of the most modern and up-to-date companies in the field. Cardo was located in Philadelphia, Pennsylvania.

588	fuel pump; with glass bowl; all models
9926	fuel pump; with metal bowl; all models
D-15	Stromberg carburetor; BXV-3; 3-83, 3-84; models without fluid drive
D-16	Stromberg carburetor; BXVD-3; 377, 3-82, 3-93; models with fluid drive

Carter—Fuel Pumps and Thermostats

The Carter line of fuel pumps at the time covered all U.S. cars and trucks. Carter engineering advances in aluminum castings, diaphragms and stamped steel assemblies were combined to produce "the finest most dependable fuel pump on the market." Carter was located in St. Louis, Missouri.

30-84	fine grain ceramic fuel filter element; all models
847	fuel pump for all 6 cylinder models
GF-827	gas filter; all models
M-847	fuel pump; all models with single diaphragm pump

Casco—Distributors and Vacuum Controls

Casco supplied replacement distributor vacuum controls for most passenger cars and trucks. Casco Products was located in Bridgeport, Connecticut.

V-105	replacement distributor vacuum chamber assembly; replaces 1135 576

Celoron—Timing Gears

Celoron was advertised as the world's oldest and largest producer of "Silent Timing Gears." They were made of a laminated phenolic condensation material bonded with bakelite that resulted in a noiseless gear that was tough, resilient and non-absorbent. Gears did not warp or swell under extreme driving conditions. Celoron was the product name of the Diamond State Fibre Company of Bridgeport, Pennsylvania, and Chicago, Illinois.

S-126	cam timing chain sprocket
S-127	crank timing chain sprocket

Cepco—Brake Shoes

CEPCO supplied rebuilt bonded brake shoes for passenger cars and trucks. Emergency brake lining for repair of Chrysler Products was also available. Central Products, Inc. (CEPCO) was located in Baltimore, Maryland.

44	front brake lining; 11" drums; 5 passenger models
45	front and or rear brake lining; 12" brake drums; 7 passenger models
CB-2	emergency brake band; all models
CS-192-44	front brake lining; 11" drums; 5 passenger models
CS-1105-45	front and or rear brake lining; 12" drums; 7 passenger models

Champ-Items—Cables, Fasteners and Springs

Champ-Items was best known for counter-top and wall display racks of spring, fastener, stud and screw assortment parts that were easily seen by customers in garages and repair shops. The list below gives an ides of the variety of additional parts that were available. Champ-Items, Inc., was located in St. Louis, Missouri.

404A	speedometer cable and casing assembly; 1948 models
404F	speedometer cable and casing assembly; 1946–1947 models
479	rotary door lock lug shim; all models
484T	inside door lock button; all models
640A	rotary door lock repair kit; left front door; all models
640B	rotary door lock repair kit; right front door; all models
640E	rotary door lock repair kit; right rear door; all models
640F	rotary door lock repair kit; left rear door; all models
642	oil feed line with fittings; all models
646C	water outlet gasket; all models
646D	water by-pass gasket; all models
647C	fuel pump to cylinder gasket
943G	door lock spring
960D	remote control door lock spring

Champion—Spark Plugs

Champion spark plugs were known for the ribbed insulator that reduces "flash-over" under humid conditions, the plated finish for anti-rust protection and the precision standards that maintain a specific gap for longer service. All plugs were designed with close tolerances and leak-proof gaskets. The Champion Spark Plug Company was located in Toledo, Ohio.

H-10	spark plug; all high compression aluminum heads; 14mm
J-8	spark plug; all regular cast iron heads; 14mm

Champion ReNu—Water Pumps

Champion ReNu had seven rebuilding plants in the U.S. to provide the national replacement market with fast, efficient service on a full line of quality rebuilt products. All products were engineered for simplified installation with the best possible original fit. From complete disassembly to final adjustment and pre-testing, Champion remanufactured products met stringent quality-control standards that were the hallmark of the rebuilding industry. Champion was located in Chicago, Illinois.

W-53	factory rebuilt water pump; original factory casting number 637 437 or 642 398

Chefford-Master—Clutch Bearings, Fuel Pumps and Universal Joints

The Chefford company in the 1920s produced auto parts only for Chevrolets and Fords. Chefford-Master was formed with the fusion of Chefford Automotive Parts of Brooklyn, New York, and Master Parts Manufacturing of Chicago. The resulting company expanded and produced assorted parts such as water pumps, fuel pumps and clutch bearings for most passenger cars and trucks. Chefford Master Manufacturing Co., Inc. was located in Fairfield, Illinois.

588-M	fuel pump replacement for all models; replaces original AC pump number 152 3647
CH-16	clutch release bearing; conventional drive models without fluid drive
CH-22	clutch release bearing; fluid drive models
CH-26	clutch release bearing; conventional drive models without fluid drive
CH-30	clutch release bearing; conventional drive models without fluid drive
CH-37	clutch release bearing; conventional drive models without fluid drive
DK-276	fuel pump diaphragm repair kit; repairs original AC pump number 152 3647; all models
MDR-52	replacement universal joint for all models that used the Detroit type universal joint, excludes early 1946 models
RK-50	fuel pump repair kit; repairs original AC pump number 152 3647; all models

Cities Service—Fan/Generator Belts

Cities Service was formed in 1910 and by mid-century had hundreds of service stations and garages across the country. Quality radiator and generator V-belts were always on-hand for quick repairs. Cities Service was located in New York, New York.

V-45	fan and generator belt; all models

Clawson and Bals—Engine Bearings

Clawson and Bals offered replacement bearings for complete motor bearing and connecting rod service for passenger car, truck and industrial engines. Their "Ring-True" line of bearings were engineered to 0.0001" to provide minimum wear and failure, and to assure the utmost efficiency of rebuilt engines. Clawson and Bals was located in Chicago, Illinois.

S-5098	connecting rod bearings; 6 pair required; all models
S-5100	front main engine bearing; 1 pair required; all models
S-5102	intermediate main engine bearings; 2 pair required; all models
S-5104	rear main engine bearing; 1 pair required; all models

Clevite—Engine Bearings

Clevite produced ultra-precision bearings that were exact duplicates of original equipment structure and design. Their steel backed bearings with a fine Babbitt precision lining lasted up to four times longer than thick Babbitt bearings that needed reaming. Clevite Bearings was located in Cleveland, Ohio.

CB-60G	connecting rod bearing
MS-523M	main bearing set
MB-2011M	main bearing; position #1
MB-2012M	main bearing; position #2 and #3
MB-122M	main bearing; position #4
SH-23S	cam bearing set

Cloyes—Timing Gears and Chains

Cloyes supplied new, not rebuilt, timing gears, chains and sprockets for replacement in automobile, truck, bus, tractor and industrial engines. Cloyes products were distributed through independent automotive warehouse distributors throughout the United States. They were a member of the Automotive Warehouse Distributors Association, the Automotive Service Industry Association and the Automotive Engine Rebuilders Association. Cloyes was located in Cleveland, Ohio.

C-401	timing chain; 48 links; replaces factory number 1075 001
C-401 S	matched set; timing chain and gears
S-126	cam gear; 38 teeth; replaces factory number 601 757
S-127	crank gear; 19 teeth; replaces factory number 601 760

Columbus Shock Absorber—Shock Absorbers

The Columbus Parts Corp. "full time" shock absorber widened the inside chamber to increase the working surface of the piston up to two times that of ordinary shock absorbers. Columbus claimed this resulted in a longer lasting shock absorber with faster action, more control and a smoother ride. A heavy duty seal kept vital hydraulic fluid locked in for longer, trouble free service and dependable safety. The company was located in Toledo, Ohio.

411	"Velvet-Ride" front shock absorber; excludes 7 passenger models
641	"Velvet-Ride" rear shock absorber; excludes 7 passenger models
901-B	"Luxury-Ride" front shock absorber; excludes 7 passenger models
1281	"Luxury-Ride" rear shock absorber; excludes 7 passenger models

Crown—Armatures, Generators and Starters

Crown supplied rebuilt generators, starters and armatures for upwards of 98 percent of the passenger cars at the time the 1946–1948 Dodges were on the road. They featured the restoration of original equipment only and did not supply any conversion substitutes. Each generator was assembled with its proper pulley. Every phase of their operation was designed to insure the restoration was back to the original manufacturers' tolerance. Crown was located in Pittsburgh, Pennsylvania.

| **210** | generator armature; replaces GDZ-2006 armature of the GDZ-4801A generator; all models |
| **582** | generator replaces original Auto-Lite number GDZ-4801A; all models |

    MAW 2128   starter armature; all models
    MAW 4041   starter; all models

Crown—Fan/Generator Belts

Crown advertised the "Non-Stretching Cord" fan and generator belt. The Crown Products Co., was located in Omaha, Nebraska.

    147   fan/generator belt

Cyclone—Oil Filters

Cyclone offered three types of oil filters: (1) pleated paper, (2) cotton filled sock, and (3) the Cyclone-Duo with a mixture of paper and cotton. Cyclone Sales, Inc., was located in Longmont, Colorado.

    X-118   replacement oil filter; all models; replaces 1121 694

Dayton—Fan/Generator Belts and Radiator Hoses

Dayton was advertised as "The Original Equipment Belt" and as "The World's Largest Manufacturer of V-Belts." Dayton was the first major company to perfect the first successful V-Type fan belt and offered Interchange Guides, at garages and jobbers, to replace competitive belts with Dayton Belts. Oversized molded and curved radiator hoses were plainly marked as to where to cut-to-fit particular makes and models of cars. The Dayton Rubber Company was located in Dayton, Ohio.

    827-X   heavy duty fan/generator V-belt; all models
    905-M   fan/generator V-belt; all models
    CH-106   single molded and curved lower radiator hose substitution; all models
    CH-118   single molded and curved lower radiator hose substitution; all models
    CH-143   single molded and curved lower radiator hose substitution; all models
    D-8   rear floor mat; all models
    D-2007   front floor mat; contour type with black felt back; all models
    D-3103   front floor mat; all models
    VX-68   fan/generator V-belt; all models
    VX-68M   fan/generator V-belt; all models

Delco—Shock Absorbers

Delco started producing shock absorbers in the 1920s and by 1946–1948 was the largest manufacturer of shock absorbers used as original and replacement equipment in the automobile industry. Their shock absorbers were engineered to give maximum performance and quality materials insured maximum safety, long life and uniform riding qualities. Delco was a General Motors product of Flint, Michigan.

    741   bushing kit; front and rear standard duty shock absorber kit; all models

747	heavy duty bushing kit; front and rear heavy duty shock absorber kit; all models
1030-C	front axle direct-action airplane type hydraulic shock absorber
1031-S	rear axle direct-action airplane type hydraulic shock absorber
1031-T	rear axle direct-action airplane type hydraulic shock absorber
1041-S	rear axle direct-action airplane type hydraulic shock absorber
1050-C	front wheel shock absorber; all models
1051-T	rear wheel shock absorber; all models
D-726	front wheel; "Ride Control" 1⅜" double acting airplane type shock absorber
D-727	rear wheel; "Ride Control" 1⅜" double acting airplane type shock absorber
S-174	front wheel; standard double acting 1" airplane type shock absorber
S-193	rear wheel; standard double acting 1" airplane type shock absorber
H-970-E	front wheel heavy duty shock absorber; all models
H-970-W	rear wheel heavy duty shock absorber; all models

Detroit—Universal Joints

Detroit produced the three different types of universal joints used on the front and rear of the 1946–1948 Dodge. U-joints were offered as complete units or as replacement parts kits. Detroit U-joints were sold nationwide through local NAPA stores and independent jobbers. Universal joints were manufactured by Detroit Universal Division of Dearborn, Michigan.

7225-2	cross-block bearing type U-joint; 1946–1948 7 passenger models
42083	replacement wire tie leather boot for the ball and trunnion type U-joint
72625-2	cross-block bearing type U-joint; 1946–1948 7 passenger models
83254-3	cross-ball type U-joint; rear; early 1946 5 passenger models
420819	replacement clamp type boot for the ball and trunnion type U-joint
420825-1	replacement rubber boot for the ball and trunnion type U-joint
R-52	ball and trunnion type U-joint; complete with body; leather boot; late 1946–1948 5 passenger models
R-52A	ball and trunnion type U-joint; without body; leather boot; late 1946–1948 5 passenger models
R-55	ball and trunnion type U-joint; complete with body; leather boot; early 1946 5 passenger models
R-67A	ball and trunnion type U-joint; without body; leather boot; early 1946 5 passenger models

Dittmer—Transmission Gears

Dittmer produced replacement transmission parts for passenger cars, trucks and buses. Gears and shafts were of the highest quality materials and made in accordance with the best recognized standards in the industry. Replacement transmission parts were sold nationwide through local NAPA stores. Dittmer Automotive Parts was located in Franklin Park, Illinois.

PG-1P	transmission main sliding gear shaft; 18⁵⁄₁₆" long; all models; replaces 853 488
PG-6C	transmission reverse idler gear; all models; replaces 952 244
PG-7B	low and reverse sliding gear; all models; replaces 853 886
PG-8D	second speed gear; all models; replaces 852 456
PG-12B	countershaft cluster gear; all models; replaces 697 823
PG-22K	main drive gear pinion clutch shaft; 11¹⁄₃₂" long; all models; replaces 853 864
PG-70	reverse idler shaft; 2½" long; all models; replaces 631 869
PG-71B	countershaft; 8⁷⁄₃₂" long; all models; 852 473
PG-81	clutch gear synchronizer stop ring; all models; replaces 853 867
PG-83D	clutch gear sliding sleeve; all models; 856 464
PG-84D	clutch gear with sleeve synchronizer assembly; all models; replaces 1115 595
PG-609	transmission small parts kit; all models

Dole—Thermostats and Radiator Caps

Dole advertised "The Most Complete Line of Modern Thermostats." All thermostats accurately controlled desired engine water temperature for quick warm-ups and heater efficiency. Dole products were designed, manufactured and tested to the strictest standards of the Society of Automotive Engineers. All Dole products were designed to be used with permanent antifreeze. The Dole Valve Company was located in Morton Grove, Illinois.

DGL-50	locking gasoline cap; all models
DGL-80	locking gasoline cap; all models
DGS-20	gasoline cap; stainless steel; all models
DO-61	oil cap; all models
DV-3	butterfly type thermostat; summer 160 degree; all models
DV-3H	butterfly type thermostat; winter 180 degree; all models
DV-3XH	butterfly type thermostat; winter 195 degree; all models
DV-5	pellet type thermostat; standard temperature; 160 degree; all models
DV-5H	pellet type thermostat; high temperature; 180 degree; all models
DVN-35	nozzle type thermostat; summer 160 degree; all models
DVN-35H	nozzle type thermostat; winter 160 degree; all models
DVN-35XH	nozzle type thermostat; winter 195 degree; all models
DR-3	standard non-pressure radiator cap; all models
WO-35063	water outlet gasket; all models

Dorman—Clutch Bearings, Fasteners and Hardware

Dorman started in 1918 and soon became a leading supplier of automobile and truck aftermarket replacement parts. They supplied major parts such as clutch bearings, but were best known for the display cabinets, in garages, of small parts such as studs, fasteners, clamps, hoses, nuts, bolts, etc. Dorman was located in Cincinnati, Ohio.

956	clutch release bearing; conventional drive models without fluid drive
1054	clutch release bearing; conventional drive models without fluid drive
1055	clutch release bearing; fluid drive models
1116	clutch release bearing; conventional drive models without fluid drive
1149	clutch release bearing; conventional drive models without fluid drive
CB-77	clutch release bearing; fluid drive models
CB-87	clutch release bearing; conventional drive models without fluid drive
RS-4-A	clutch release bearing and carrier assembly; fluid drive models

Double Diamond—Flywheel Ring Gears

Double Diamond supplied the highest quality metal gear supplies for transmission and rear axle in the passenger car and truck industry. Double Diamond Automotive Gear Works, Inc., was located in Richmond, Indiana.

619	flywheel ring gear; standard transmission with 10" clutch
647	flywheel ring gear; standard transmission with 11" clutch
654	flywheel ring gear; models with fluid drive transmission

Duckworth—Timing Chains

Duckworth started producing quality metal products in 1891. Beginning in the 1920s they produced and advertised a line of "Silent Chain" replacement timing chains for cars and trucks. Their link and pin design allowed greater distribution of lubrication for silent operation, longer mileage and greater wear. Duckworth also produced motorcycle and bicycle chains. The Duckworth Company was located in Springfield, Massachusetts.

9-401	timing chain; all models

Dueco—Clutch Assemblies

DUECO Clutch used specially built balancing equipment to neutralize the unbalance often found in rotating parts that causes vibration, poor performance and excessive wear. The DUECO "Balanced Line" process exceeds the original balance specifications of the manufacturer. DUECO the "Detroit Unit Exchange Co.," was established in 1942 and was located in Detroit, Michigan.

CA-938	clutch cover assembly; 6 cylinder standard transmission models; 10" clutch
CA-952	clutch cover assembly; 6 cylinder fluid drive model; 9¼" clutch
CB-1310 C	release bearing assembly; 6 cylinder standard transmission models; 10" clutch
CB-1312 C	release bearing assembly; 6 cylinder fluid drive models; 9¼" clutch
CD-728	clutch disc; 6 cylinder standard transmission models; 10" clutch
CD-729	clutch disc; heavy duty; fleet and taxi 11" clutch; 11" O.D., 10 spline, 1" hub
CD-756	clutch disc; 6 cylinder fluid drive models; 9¼" clutch
MU-938	matched unit of cover and clutch; 6 cylinder standard transmission models; 10" clutch

MU-952 matched unit of cover and clutch; 6 cylinder fluid drive models; 9¼" clutch

Durkee-Atwood—Fan/Generator Belts and Hoses

Durkee-Atwood was advertised as "The V-Belt People." Belts were formed with a center body of tough, pre-stretched cord, impregnated with liquid rubber and then locked into a layer of highly elastic, heat resistant "Tie-Gum" rubber. A molded covering completed the belt. The Durkee-Atwood Company was located in Minneapolis, Minnesota.

8-703 single molded and curved lower radiator hose; substitution for all models
140-A fan/generator V belt; all models
140-B heavy duty fan/generator V belt; all models
280-A fan/generator V belt; all models
280-B heavy duty fan/generator V belt; all models
V-446 fan/generator V belt; all models

Echlin—Ignition and Electrical Replacement Parts

Echlin Manufacturing Company advertised itself as "The Largest Independent Ignition Parts Manufacturer in the World." Replacement parts for Auto-Lite, Delco-Remy, Ford and Foreign Car Systems were equal to or better than the products they replaced. Echlin was located in Branford, Connecticut, and parts were distributed through NAPA and independent jobbers.

4258 starter bushing; drive end; MAW and MZ starters
4259 starter bushing; commutator end; MAW starters
4270 distributor housing bushing
4278 generator bushing
A-410 generator brush set
A-502 starter brush set; MZ starter
A-505 starter brush set; MAW starter
AL-60 distributor contact arm (used in contact set CS-12)
AL-62 distributor rotor
AL-63 distributor cap
AL-64 distributor condenser; standard
AL-81 distributor contact bracket (bar used in contact set CS-12)
AL-220 upper distributor breaker plate
AL-864 distributor condenser; universal
CS-12 distributor contact set; standard
CS-24 contact set; standard
CS-24A contact set assembled; standard
CS-712 contact set; heavy duty
CS-724A contact assembled; heavy duty
DS-103 dimmer switch

HR-104	horn relay
IC-7	service ignition coil
ICB-7	ignition coil bracket
LW-1	distributor ground lead wire
LW-6	distributor primary lead wire
SL-133	stoplight switch
ST-62	starter switch
VC-105	distributor vacuum control
VR-23	voltage regulator

Eclipse—Brake Shoes

Eclipse advertised "Duo Friction" brakes for passenger cars consisting of segments that were rigid, full-molded and engineered to form the correct friction for the particular car and type of brake to be serviced. Eclipse was a division of Bendix Aviation Corporation of Troy, New York.

192-A	front axle brake set (4 pieces); 5 passenger models with 11" drums
192½ BE	front axle brake shoe set (4 segments) for 5 passenger models; drilled
1105-A	front axle brake set (4 pieces); 7 passenger models with 12" drums
1105½ BE	front brake shoe set (4 segments) for 7 passenger models; drilled
1161-A	rear axle brake set (4 pieces); 5 passenger models with 11" drums
1161½ BE	rear axle brake shoe set (4 segments) for 5 passenger models; drilled
1179	rear axle brake set (4 pieces); 7 passenger models with 12" drums
1179½ BE	rear brake shoe set (4 segments) for 7 passenger models; drilled

EIS—Hydraulic Brake Parts

EIS supplied a complete line of wheel cylinders and master cylinders for passenger cars and trucks. Cylinders were accurately made and finished with the highest grade of wear resistant rubber. Each had engineered expanders and springs for a longer lasting seal and pistons were vacuum impregnated with lubricant to reduce corrosion and wear. EIS supplied a special rib-molded wheel cylinder cup for Chrysler Product Cars (including Dodge—854 038) that provided better wall tension and sealing. A complete line of tools and fluids were also available. EIS Automotive Corp. was located in Middletown, Connecticut.

BZ	kit for servicing wheel cylinders with two piece piston
BZ-P	complete kit for standard cup wheel cylinders
C-574	front and/or rear wheel cylinder repair kit; replacement number for CA-P
C-615	front and/or rear wheel cylinder repair kit; replacement number for DR
CA-P	front and or rear wheel cylinder repair kit
DR	front and/or rear wheel cylinder repair kit; two piece piston kit

EW-3241	brake master cylinder
EW-10580	upper left front wheel cylinder
EW-10581	upper right front wheel cylinder
EW-10582	lower left front wheel cylinder
EW-10583	lower right front wheel cylinder
EW-10588	right and/or left rear wheel cylinder
HHH	master cylinder repair kit; replacement number for UU
K-80	stop light switch
M-46	master cylinder repair kit; replacement number for UU and HHH
P-783	anodized, surface hardened wheel cylinder piston; replaces 865 953
P-934	wheel cylinder kit contains (R-933 cup and P-783 piston assembly
R-911	front and/or rear wheel cylinder with plain type rubber cup; replaces 854 038
R-933	front and/or rear wheel cylinder with ribbed rubber cup; replaces 854 038
SP-790	flexible rear hydraulic brake hose; 16⅞" long
SP-890	flexible front hydraulic brake hose
SP-967	flexible right and/or left front wheel hydraulic hose; newer number; 10⅞" long
UU	master cylinder repair kit

Ennis Manufacturing—Water Pumps

Ennis Manufacturing was a member of the Automotive Parts Rebuilders Association and advertised their factory rebuilt water pumps as "the standard for quality in the rebuilding industry." Warehouses were located in eleven cities for rapid distribution to jobbers across the country. Ennis Manufacturing was located in Clio, Michigan.

WP-53	factory rebuilt water pump; replaces bushing type pump with "half moon" in back plate with original casting No. 637437; also replaces bearing type pump with original casting No. 642398

Ertel Products (EP)—Engine Rebuild Parts, Bushings, Chassis and Suspension Replacement Parts

Ertel Manufacturing Corporation was founded in 1917. They soon became a major supplier of replacement chassis, suspension and engine parts for automobiles, trucks, buses and tractors. Ertel Products was located in Indianapolis, Indiana.

37-P	piston; U-slot 3¼" diameter; 3¹¹⁄₁₆" length
98-P	piston; 3¼" diameter; all models
1075	rear spring, front bushing; all models
1415-M	main bearing set
11011-M	cam bearing set
19185-SB	connecting rod bearing
19186-SB	main bearing; position #1
19187-SB	main bearing; position #2, #3

19188-SA	main bearing; position #4
C-21	lower; inner shaft bushing kit; excludes 7 passenger models
C-40	lower, outer pivot pin kit; 7 passenger sedan and limousine models
C-42	lower, outer pivot pin kit; models with 16" wheels; excludes 7 passenger models
C-44	coil spring spacers; excludes 7 passenger models
C-47	lower, inner shaft and bushing kit; 7 passenger sedan and limousine models
C-67	upper, outer pin and bushing kit; models with 16" wheels; excludes 7 passenger models
C-68	upper, inner shaft and bushing kit; excludes 7 passenger models
C-83	upper, outer pin and bushing kit; 7 passenger sedan and limousine models
C-84	upper, inner shaft and bushing kit; 7 passenger sedan and limousine models
C-88	upper shock absorber stud; all models
C-94	upper, outer pin and bushing kit; models with 15" wheels; excludes 7 passenger models
C-95	lower, outer pivot pin kit; models with 15" wheels; excludes 7 passenger models
C-124	lower, inner shaft and bushing kit; excludes 7 passenger models
C-240	lower shock absorber stud; all models
C-722	steering knuckle support; right or left; excludes 7 passenger models
C-764	upper control arm; left or right; excludes 7 passenger models
C-1538	lower control arm bumper; all models
ES-60	tie rod ends; right hand assembly; all models
ES-131	tie rod ends; left hand assembly; all models
G-337	exhaust valve guide
G-338	intake valve guide
HB-735	rear spring, rear bushing; early type; all models
HB-779	front and rear shock absorber bushing; upper and lower; all models
HB-850	rear spring, rear bushing; all models
K-540	water pump repair kit for P-540 water pump; replaces factory number 1064 752
K-554	optional replacement water pump kit for water pump P-554; replaces factory number 1325 977
KB-541	king bolt set; 5 passenger models to Detroit serial number 31006517 and to Los Angeles serial number 45022935; excludes 7 passenger sedan and limousine
KB-542	king bolt set; 5 passenger models from Detroit serial number 31006517 to 31057047 and after 31084245; from Los Angeles 45022935 to 45029117; excludes 7 passenger sedan and limousine
KB-542 A	king bolt set; 5 passenger models from Detroit serial number 31057047 to 31084245 and after Los Angeles serial number 45029117; excludes 7 passenger sedan and limousine

KB-543	king bolt set; 7 passenger sedan and limousine
P-32	piston pin
P-540	water pump; replaces factory number 1064 750
P-554	optional replacement water pump; replaces factory number 1325 973
PB-35	piston pin bushing; standard
PB-35 X	piston pin bushing; .008" oversize
RS-504 N	rear spring, rear shackle; all models
S-1689	exhaust valve
SL-317FS	cylinder sleeve; ³⁄₃₂" wall
V-1690	intake valve
VR-31	valve retainer
VS-31	valve spring; exhaust or intake

Eveready—Electric Lamps and Electric Bulbs

Eveready automobile lamps were advertised as "Always Dependable." Bulbs were made with exacting care from selected quality materials and carefully inspected, tested and packaged before shipment. Eveready was a trademark of the Union Carbide Corporation, New York, New York.

51	instrument lamp
55	instrument lamp
63	parking
87	dome
1129	directional
1158	stop, tail, directional
4030	headlight

EZ Ride—Shock Absorbers

EZ Ride was advertised as "The All Star Performance Team" for shock absorbers. The "Standard" shock absorbers were designed to meet or exceed original equipment specifications and the bore of heavy duty series was 50 percent larger than factory installed originals. Their heavy duty shocks were calibrated and valved for maximum stability and comfort. Special engineered features provided more rapid heat dissipation and protection from road hazards for the most demanding driving requirements.

A-10	standard rear axle shock absorber
J-610	heavy duty rear axle shock absorber
J-619	heavy duty front wheel shock absorber

Federal—Clutch Release Bearings

Federal Ball Bearing Company, Inc., produced clutch release bearings and clutch release assemblies for passenger cars and trucks. Federal was located in Poughkeepsie, New York.

2-P1054 clutch release bearing and carrier assembly; replaces 658 998; all models without fluid drive

1054 clutch release bearing; replaces factory number 658 998; all models without fluid drive

1055 clutch release bearing; replaces factory number 658 948; all models with fluid drive

1116 clutch release bearing; replaces factory number 658 998; all models without fluid drive

1148 clutch release bearing; replaces factory number 658 998; all models without fluid drive

BA 3 clutch release bearing and sleeve assembly; replaces factory number 862 859; all models without fluid drive

BA 6 clutch release bearing and sleeve assembly; replaces factory number 867 735; all models with fluid drive

C-1055 clutch release bearing and carrier assembly; replaces 658 948; all models with fluid drive

Federal-Mogul—Engine Replacement Parts, Pistons, Bearings, Rods and Bushings

Federal-Mogul advertised that their research, engineering and production provided the best bearings that could be made. They supplied more part numbers, undersizes and lining alloy bearings than any other company. Company owned service branches provided immediate service and technical support to customers nationwide. Federal-Mogul was located in Detroit, Michigan.

37-P	3.250" diameter piston with .8593 pin diameter
415M-SB	main camshaft bearing set; all models
855M-CB	main camshaft bearing set; all models
1010-M	cam bearing set; all models
1631-P	3.250" diameter piston with .8593" pin diameter
8649-V	connecting rod pin bushing set; split bushing; all models
8649-XA	connecting rod pin bushing set; solid bronze
8649-XAS	connecting rod pin bushing set; solid bronze
9076	cam shaft bearing #1; all models
9185-SB/CA	connecting rod bearing; all rods; all models
9186-SB/CA	main crankshaft #1 bearing; all models
9187-SB/CA	main crankshaft #2 and/or #3 bearing; all models
9188-SB/CA	main crankshaft #4 bearing; flanged; all models
9207	cam shaft bearing #2; all models
9208	cam shaft bearing #3; all models
L-2101CF	3.250" diameter piston with .8593" pin diameter
R-22N	connecting rods; number 1,3,5, rods; all models
R-22P	connecting rods; number 2,4,6, rods; all models
R-22U	connecting rods; number 1,3,5, rods; all models
R-22V	connecting rods; number 2,4,6, rods; all models

Federated—Thermostats, Fuel, Radiator and Oil Caps

Federated supplied a line of low and high temperature thermostats and specialized caps for vintage automobiles and trucks. Federated was located in Staunton, Virginia.

30026	low temperature (160°F) thermostat; 1946–1948
30028	low temperature (180°F) thermostat; 1946–1948
30963	thermostat paper gasket for the 6 cylinder models
46002	radiator cap; 1946–1948; all models
46105	fuel cap; 1946–1948; all models
46312	locking fuel cap; 1946–1948; all models
46501	oil filler cap; 1946–1948; all models

Fel-Pro—Gaskets

Fel-Pro supplied single and individual gaskets as well as gasket sets for a complete engine rebuild. Gaskets were equal to or surpassed the original equipment specifications and many were available in more than one type of material. Gaskets were available for most cars and trucks from the water pump to the rear axle and generally packaged in sealed envelopes with an identifying Fel-Pro number. Fel-Pro was a division of Felt Products Mfg. Co. and was located in Skokie, Illinois.

5955-C	spark plug gasket
7075-C	head gasket
7564-C	head gasket
8531	carburetor mounting gasket; models without governor
11920-C	oil pan drain plug gasket
14110	timing cover seal
35063	water outlet gasket
A-9533	carburetor mounting gasket; models with governor
BS-6300	rear main bearing gasket set; used up to engine number 272298
BS-10085-3	rear main bearing gasket set; used after engine number 272298
C-773	fuel pump bowl gasket; models without glass bowl
C-5019	fuel pump bowl gasket
FS-7075 C	full gasket set
FS-7564 C	full gasket set
HS-7075 C	head gasket set
HS-7564 C	head gasket set
K-675	water outlet gasket
K-3122	oil pressure relief valve gasket
K-4267	water pump to block gasket
K-4271	water pump by-pass gasket
K-4275	oil pump body gasket
K-4279	fuel pump mounting gasket; single action fuel pumps
LB-8011	intake to exhaust manifold gasket set
LB-8247	exhaust pipe flange gasket

MS-8009 B	intake and exhaust manifold gasket set
OS-4250 D	oil pan gasket set
R-3115	thermostat gasket
R-4253	valve cover pan gasket
R-4281	valve cover stud seal gasket
R-6311	oil pump cover gasket
R-6312	oil pan front end oil seal plate gasket
RDS-4290	differential carrier gasket
T-4155	timing cover set and gasket; 1947–1948 after engine number 38058
T-4258	timing cover set and gasket; 1946–1947 up to engine number 38058
TCS-4155-1	timing cover set and gasket; 1947–1948 after engine number 38058
TCS-4258-2	timing cover set and gasket; 1946–1947 up to engine number 38058
TS-3120-A-1	standard and fluid drive trans. gasket set
VS-4253 R	valve cover pan gasket

Filko—Ignition and Electrical Replacement Parts

Filko was advertised as "The Crown Jewels of Ignition" and used a royal crown as a logo on a green and yellow or green and white packaging. Filko had a complete line of stock parts conveniently located throughout the world and were able to supply replacement parts immediately worldwide. Filko was advertised as "More Than a Replacement Part … A True Improvement in Ignition." Filko was the product name for F & B Manufacturing Co., located in Chicago, Illinois.

66-91	contact points set
66-91A	contact points set; assembled
66-91AHD	contact points set; assembled; heavy duty
74-91A	contact set; for IGS distributor; later number; includes arm and bar
74-91S	contact set; for IGS distributor; early number; includes arm and bar
258	starter bushing; drive end
270	distributor bushing
278	generator bushing; commutator end
3259	heater switch; 6 volt; 4-position; two screw terminals
3260	fog light switch
3261	door jamb switch; circuit is closed when door is opened
3262	back up light switch
3263	pillar switch; the circuit is closed when the door is opened
3273	headlight switch
AC-32	ignition coil
AC-32HS	ignition coil; high speed

AL-97	distributor rotor
AL-97HD	distributor rotor; heavy duty
AL-104	distributor cap
AL-104HD	distributor cap; heavy duty
AL-214	distributor condenser
AL-242	condenser; strap type; copper strap can be shortened to fit most installations
AL-243	condenser that may be substituted for AL-242; flexible wire type
DL-2	distributor lead; 1⅞"
DL-5	distributor lead; 1¹⁵⁄₁₆"
DL-21	primary distributor lead; 2½" long
DL-23	ground distributor lead; 2" long.
DS-4	dimmer switch
DS-4HD	dimmer switch; heavy duty
E16-18	Canadian Dodge brush set; starter MZ-4133
E37-38	starter brush set
E-45X	generator brush set; standard
E-57X	generator brush set; consists of (2) E-57 brushes
E-59X	generator brush set; for special high output generator GEG-4823B; police, taxi
FF-6	fuel filter
FP-588	fuel pump; all models
HR-13	horn relay
RF-60	voltage regulator fuse; 45-60 amp rating
SLS-22	stoplight switch
SS-9R	starter Bendix spring
SSB-82	starter button
SW-83	starter switch solenoid
UC-102	ignition coil; 6-volt; early number
VRA-340HD	voltage regulator; for special high output generator GEG-4823B; police, taxi; 6-volt, 40-51 Amps, positive ground
VRA-345HD	voltage regulator; standard; 6 volt, 35-45 Amps, positive ground
VRA-349HD	voltage regulator; 6-volt, 40-51 amp; uses RF regulator fuse 60

Firestone—Fan/Generator Belts

Firestone fan and generator belts were advertised as "Scientifically Balanced for High Speed Engines." Belts were constructed of special rayon cords that provided strength, flexibility and heat resistance to assure longer life. All fan belts were built to original equipment specifications. Firestone was located in Akron, Ohio.

3-J-27	fan and generator belt; all models
20	heavy duty fan/generator V belt; all models
36	fan/generator V belt; all models
64	heavy duty fan/generator V belt; all models

Fitzgerald—Gaskets

Fitzgerald was one of the largest gasket manufacturers in the U.S. and offered complete gasket replacement for most passenger cars and trucks. Gaskets were cut and formed using patented technology and materials exclusive to Fitzgerald. Specialty gaskets were also available from the factory. Fitzgerald was located in Torrington, Connecticut.

0550 C	cylinder head gasket; with internal by-pass; copper and asbestos; replaces 1326 318
0550 L	cylinder head gasket; with internal by-pass; steel and asbestos; replaces S1401 345
1392 C	cylinder head gasket; with external by-pass; copper and asbestos; replaces 1117 542
1392 L	cylinder head gasket; with external by-pass; steel and asbestos; replaces 859 224
1555 B	exhaust pipe flange gasket; $2^{11}/_{32}$" center holes; replaces 623 361, 1636 571
4407 MK	manifold—intake gaskets and exhaust end gaskets; replaces 318 042
5128 MK	intake to exhaust manifold gasket; replaces 601 420
5129 MK	manifold center gasket; replaces 601 275
5156	manifold many-in-one gasket; replaces 854 395
5510 MK	carburetor to manifold gasket; replaces 637 191
8012 A	timing chain case cover plate screw gasket; replaces 114 622
8050 S	spark plug gasket; replaces 321 918
8097 AH	oil pan drain plug gasket; replaces 105 456
9891	oil pressure relief valve cap gasket; replaces 618 622
10311	thermostat gasket; replaces 863 220
10312	oil pump cover gasket; 1946–1947; replaces 863 724
10394	oil pump cover gasket; 1948; replaces 1124 984
10395	oil pan front end oil seal; 1948; replaces 1066 873
10407	differential carrier; replaces 1318 011
20152	timing chain case cover oil seal gasket; replaces 1088 603
20533	carburetor to air cleaner gasket; replaces 952 062
24517	transmission case extension; replaces 1635 273
26165	timing chain case cover; 1947–1948 after engine No. 79100
44036	transmission remote control selection retainer gasket; replaces 857 309
61607	water outlet gasket; replaces 50 082
62309	timing chain case cover; 1946–1947 up to engine No. 79100; replaces 600 752
63444	oil pump body gasket; replaces 695 442
63465	differential carrier gasket; 7 passenger sedan; replaces 1121 940
63770	water pump body cover plate gasket; replaces 637 439
63773	water pump body to cylinder block; replaces 637 440
63775	water pump by-pass elbow; replaces 622 772

63776	oil pan front end oil seal; 1947–1947; replaces 600 764
63840	crankshaft rear bearing oil seal retainer gasket; replaces 633 298
63843	universal joint housing gasket; 2 or 4 needed; replaces 602 819
64218	transmission rear bearing retainer gasket; replaces 601 130
64327	fuel pump flange gasket; replaces 688 481
64396	transmission case to clutch housing; replaces 852 623
64411	transmission case extension; standard transmission; replaces 853 895
64503	transmission case cover; replaces 854 801
64585	valve spring cover nut gasket; replaces 693 959 or 53 170
64601	transmission case to clutch housing; replaces 865 170
68762	transmission drive pin bearing retainer gasket; .009" thick; replaces 865 180
68798	transmission drive pin bearing retainer gasket; .0165" thick; replaces 865 180
70978	valve spring cover gasket; 2 or 4 required; replaces 600 882
71652	fuel pump strainer bowl; replaces 689 504
84505	crankshaft rear bearing oil seal; replaces 863 214
84505 S	crankshaft rear bearing oil seal; replaces 863 214
84513	timing chain case cover oil seal; replaces 1064 730
AS-10407	differential carrier set
AS-63465	differential carrier set; 7 passenger
CBS-17	crankshaft rear main bearing oil seal set; replaces 891 458
CS-0550L	complete engine gasket set; with internal by-pass; steel and asbestos head gasket
ES-26165	timing chain case cover set; 1947–1948 after engine No. 79100
ES-62309	timing chain case cover set; 1946–1947 to engine No. 79100
GS-0550C	engine gasket set; with internal by-pass; with copper and asbestos head gasket
GS-1392C	engine gasket set; with external by-pass; with copper and asbestos head gasket
GS-1392L	engine gasket set; with external by-pass; with steel and asbestos head gasket
KS-80157	oil pan set; replaces 780 477 or 9933 438
MS-5128MK	manifold set
MS-5129MK	manifold set; replaces 780 460
RS-1392C-2	rebuilding set; with external by-pass; with copper and asbestos head gasket
RS-1392L-1	rebuilding set; with external by-pass; with steel and asbestos head gasket
RS-1392L-2	rebuilding set; with external by-pass; with steel and asbestos head gasket
TS-64601-1	transmission set; standard transmission; replaces 1450 232
TS-64601-2	transmission set; without fluid drive; replaces 1450 231
VK-125	valve cover set; replaces 780 469 or 980 583

Gabriel—Shock Absorbers and Thermostats

Gabriel advertised a complete line of shock absorbers with several grades of quality. The 1" bore "Hydroshox" was their number one replacement line for standard equipment passenger cars. The "Adjustable" heavy duty came in several bore sizes and offered three way adjustments of regular, firm, or extra firm ride for cars and light trucks. They also supplied a line of thermostats with gaskets. Gabriel Co. was located in Cleveland, Ohio.

50-4503	front axle direct-action airplane type hydraulic shock absorber
50-8002	rear axle direct-action airplane type hydraulic shock absorber
3001	thermostat gasket; all models
18234	front shock absorber; standard 1" bore replacement; all models
18253	rear shock absorber; standard 1" bore replacement; all models
45003	front shock absorber; heavy duty; all models
45010	rear shock absorber; heavy duty; all models
63176	front shock absorber; extra heavy duty; all models
63177	rear shock absorber; extra heavy duty; all models
ERB-375	front axle heavy-duty shock absorber
ERB-725	rear axle heavy-duty shock absorber
G-92	bellows type thermostat; standard temperature; 160 degrees F; all models
G-92H	bellows type thermostat; high temperature; 180 degrees F; all models
G-108	pellet type thermostat; standard temperature; 160 degrees F; all models
G-108H	pellet type thermostat; high temperature; 180 degrees F; all models

Gates—Fan/Generator Belts, Hoses, Thermostats and Fuel, Radiator, Oil Caps

Gates was best known for its fan/generator belts and hoses. Gates engineers designed and developed fan belts with a special rubber-impregnated fabric covering. This tightly wrapped V-belt cover protected the inner core from water, antifreeze, oil and gasoline, yet left the belt flexible for running over pulleys. The Gates Rubber Company was located in Denver, Colorado.

3	radiator cap
4X	oil cap
20	exterior gas cap
20X	exterior gas cap
30	exterior gas cap
44-TS	fan/generator belt; all models
50X	locking gas cap
58X	locking gas cap
61	oil cap
61X	oil cap
79	locking gas cap

79X	locking gas cap
604-TG	fan/generator belt; all models
660	fan/generator V belt; all models
660-T	heavy duty fan/generator V belt; all models
734	fan/generator V belt; all models
734-T	heavy duty fan/generator V belt; all models
5139	universal rear car mat; all models
5142	universal front car mat; all models
5164	universal trunk mat; all models
5526	160 degree F. thermostat
5528	180 degree F. thermostat
8098-T	fan/generator belt; all models
8506-TR	heavy duty fan/generator V belt; all models
33026	low temperature (160 degree F) thermostat; all models
33028	high temperature (180 degree F) thermostat; all models
33625	thermostat gasket; all models
CH-121	single molded and curved lower radiator hose; substitution for all models
CH-122	single molded and curved lower radiator hose; substitution for all models
CH-142	single molded and curved lower radiator hose; substitution for all models
CH-177	single molded and curved lower radiator hose; substitution for all models
VF-5	upper radiator hose; "Vulcoflex"; all models
VF-13	lower radiator hose; "Vulcoflex"; all models

General Armature Manufacturing Co. (GAMCO)—
Armatures, Generators and Starters

This company started in Lock Haven, Pennsylvania, about 1930 for the fabrication of automotive replacement parts. The company expanded to nearby Mill Hall, Pennsylvania, and by 1950 was one of the largest independent replacement manufacturers of replacement starters and generators. They developed the patented B-V (balanced-ventilated) process for wiring starters and generators.

1164	generator armature; replaces Auto-Lite generator armature GDZ-2006 in the GDZ-4801 generator
1180	generator armature; heavy duty police armature; replaces armature GEB-2006F
1269	generator armature; heavy duty police armature; replaces armature GEG-2006F
1899	starter armature; replaces armature MZ-2108
1970	starter armature; replaces armature MAW-2030
2033	starting motor armature; replaces Auto-Lite starting motor armature MAW-2128 in the MAW-4041 starter

7432	generator field coil; replaces Auto-Lite field coil for generator GDZ-4801
9329	generator; replaces Auto-Lite generator GDZ-4801
9769	starting motor; replaces Auto-Lite starting motor MAW-4041

General Automotive Products—Ignition and Electrical Replacement Parts

"The General Line" supplied ignition and general merchandise repair parts for most popular passenger cars before and after World War II. The Chicago General Accessories Co. was located in Chicago, Illinois.

M-101	ignition coil
M-1260	voltage regulator for the GDZ generators
MA-5	ignition rotor
MA-2105	ignition contact set
MC-55	ignition condenser
MEX-16-18S	starter brush set
MEX-45-2	generator brush set for the GDZ generator
MEX-46-2	generator brush set for the GEG and GGJ generators
MH-70	distributor cap

G-H (Geary-Hershey)—Chassis and Suspension Replacement Parts

Hershey Metal Products (later Geary-Hershey) was founded in 1925 and produced one of the highest quality lines of suspension and chassis parts available in the U.S.A. It was one of the largest metal machining plants in the country devoted to producing replacement parts that were equal to or better than original equipment. Hershey Metal Products, Inc. was located in Derby, Connecticut.

G-240	lower support outer pin and bushing kit; right or left; all 7 passenger and limousine
G-244	coil spring spacers; right or left; excludes 7 passenger and limousine
G-247	lower control arm inner shaft; right or left; all 7 passenger and limousine
G-268	upper control arm inner shaft kit; right or left; excludes 7 passenger and limousine
G-2124	lower control arm inner shaft kit; straight type; right or left; excludes 7 passenger and limousine
G-2124S	lower control arm inner shaft kit; offset type; right or left; excludes 7 passenger and limousine
G-2701	upper support outer pin and bushing kit; right or left; excludes 7 passenger and limousine
G-2702	lower support outer pin and bushing kit; right or left; excludes 7 passenger and limousine
G-2706	upper control arm; right or left; excludes 7 passenger and limousine

G-2707	upper shock absorber stud; right or left; excludes 7 passenger and limousine
G-2711	upper support outer pin and bushing kit; right or left; all 7 passenger and limousine
G-2713	upper control arm inner shaft; right or left; all 7 passenger and limousine
G-2722	steering knuckle support; right or left; excludes 7 passenger and limousine
G-A 94	king bolt set; excludes 7 passenger and limousine
G-A 146	king bolt set; includes 7 passenger and limousine
G-ES60	tie rod end set; right hand assembly; all models
G-ES60 L	left tie rod end; right hand assembly; all models
G-ES60 R	right tie rod end; right hand assembly; all models
G-ES131	tie rod end set; left hand assembly; all models
G-ES131L	left tie rod end; left hand assembly; all models
G-ES131R	right tie rod end; left hand assembly; all models

Gibson—Brake Shoe Hold Down Parts

Gibson was best known for brake shoe hold down kits that hold the brake shoe against the backing plate under constant tension at all times whether the car is parked or rolling or brakes are in release or being operated. They also supplied replacement brake lines, brake shoe pull back springs and adjusting screw springs for most cars and light trucks. Gibson was located in Cleveland, Ohio.

ASK-700	anti-squeak kit; services two wheels; all models
BK-120	two wheel kit
C-10	bottom cup
C-20	top (locking) cup
GW-15	anchor pin " C" washer
KK-20	four wheel kit
P-20	pin; 2³⁄₁₆" long
PS-23	brake shoe pull back spring; front wheel
S-10	brake hold down spring

Gilmer—Fan/Generator Belts

Gilmer started in Philadelphia, Pennsylvania, in the very early days of motoring and developed a process to vulcanize woven belting with rubber that resisted oil, moisture and heat. They were advertised as "Makers of the World's Best Known Fan Belts" and by 1920, 8 out of 10 cars in the automotive industry were factory equipped with Gilmer fan belts. Their "V Belts" were engineered and built to close tolerances with accurate fit that reduced stretch and maintenance. Gilmer became a member of Johns-Manville, New York, New York.

V-87	fan/generator V belt; all models
V-115	fan/generator V belt; all models
V-132	fan/generator V belt; all models

Globe—Fan/Generator Belts, Hoses and Rubber Replacement Parts

Globe Rubber Products Corp., was a manufacturer of original equipment and replacement parts for the automotive industry. They produced engine/transmission mounts, grommets, bushings, belts, hoses and rubber brake parts for passenger cars and trucks. In addition they produced many miscellaneous rubber items such as fender flaps, splash guards and floor mats. Globe was located in Philadelphia, Pennsylvania.

1660	fan/generator belt; all models
C-1121	custom lower radiator hose; all models
GB-1220	flat type spring and shackle bushing; early 1946
GB-1230	shock absorber grommets for standard shock absorbers; all models
GB-1231	shock absorber grommets for oversize shock absorbers; front upper; all models
GB-3678	tail pipe support spacer grommet; all models
GB-6586	gear shift control rod bushing; all models
GB-7704	grooved type spring and shackle bushing; late 1946–1948
MO-1290	front motor mount; 1 required
MO-1292	rear lower motor mount; 2 required
MO-1294	rear upper motor mount; 2 required
P-120	brake and/or clutch pedal; all models
S-1235	brake and clutch weather pad; all models
S-3268	drive shaft insulator; all models
S-4470	control arm bumper plug; lower; all models
S-4499	steering gear arm insulator; all models
U-100	curved lower radiator hose; cut to length; all models

Goerlich—Exhaust Mufflers and Pipes

Goerlich Muffler stressed first and foremost the "Inner Construction" of mufflers and followed the original equipment design specifications. These mufflers provided peak performance of gas flow in back pressure elimination and sound wave diffusion. Goerlich was founded by (AP-Auto Parts founder) John Goerlich and was located in Toledo, Ohio.

BR-6	tail pipe bracket; all models except the 7 passenger sedan, limousine and convertible coupe
BR-11	rear exhaust bracket; all models
BR-15	rear exhaust bracket; all models
BR-21	inlet muffler clamp; all models
BR-22	outlet muffler clamp; all models
BR-30	front exhaust bracket; all models
EP-188	exhaust pipe; all models except the 7 passenger, limousine and convertible
M-511	muffler; all models including the 7 passenger sedan, limousine and convertible

TP-225 tail pipe; all models except the convertible, 7 passenger sedan and limousine

TP-312 tail pipe; convertible

Gold Seal—Oil Filters

Gold Seal produced the insert refill type of oil filters that were used in the D24 Dodge. They advertised oil filters that were made from the finest materials available, lasted 5000 miles (under normal service life) and were equal in quality and performance to the original filter used by the car manufacturer. All filters conformed to the United States Army and the Society of Automotive Engineers (S.A.E.) specifications. The Gold Seal Filter Company was located in Edison, New Jersey.

G-70FF full flow oil filter; replacement filter for D24 Dodge; all models

Gould—Armatures, Generators and Starters

Gould was advertised as "The Complete Line" of precision rebuilt starters and generators for passenger cars and trucks. Gould Precision-Built Parts was located in Grand Rapids, Michigan.

4 rebuilt GDZ-2006 generator armature for the GDZ-4801 generator; all models

1745 rebuilt MAW-2128 starter armature for the MAW-4041 starter; all models

3246 rebuilt MAW-4041 starter; all models

9413 rebuilt GDZ-4801 generator; all models

Grand—Mufflers

Grand engineered, developed and produced a muffler that set exhaust gases into a spiraling motion that eliminated the pulsations of the engine exhaust. Longer perforated and louvered chambers gave a smoother flow of gases that eliminated muffler vibration. The overall result was a "Quiet-Tone" muffler with efficient circulation of gases that reduced internal corrosion and rusting out. Grand was located in Melrose Park, Illinois.

6300 Grand "quiet-tone" muffler; all models

MC-458X inlet muffler clamp; all models

MC-459X outlet muffler clamp; all models

TH-199X rear tailpipe hanger; all models

TH-392X front tail pipe hanger; all models

Green—Clutch Bearings

Green produced some of the highest quality clutch release bearings and sleeve assemblies for cars and trucks available in the U.S. Bearings were usually marked with a "Green" imprint and wrapped in a green colored box. The Green Ball Bearing Co. was located in Cleveland, Ohio.

CB-1054	clutch release bearing; models without fluid drive; replaces 658 998
CB-1055	clutch release bearing; models with fluid drive; replaces 658 948
CB-1310-C	clutch release bearing and carrier assembly; models without fluid drive; replaces 862 859
CB-1312-C	clutch release bearing and carrier assembly; models with fluid drive; 867 735

Grey-Rock—Brake Shoes and Clutch Plates

Grey-Rock produced "Balanced Brake sets" from materials that provided safe, sure and fast stops with long lasting "Balanced" brake action. Bonded, drilled, countersunk, and chamfered brake sets were available. A line of fan and generator V-belts was also available. Grey-Rock was located in Manheim, Pennsylvania.

993A	clutch facing; Custom, DeLuxe; 5 and 7 passenger; fluid drive models; 9¼" outside diameter and 6" inside diameter
1008A	clutch facing; Custom, DeLuxe; 5 and 7 passenger; standard drive models; 10" outside diameter and 7" inside diameter
BB192A-1161AD	heavy duty brake set; 192A—front axle; 1161—rear axle; Custom, DeLuxe; 5 passenger; 11" brake drum
BB1105A-1179D	heavy duty brake set; 1105—front axle; 1179—rear axle; Custom, DeLuxe; 7 passenger; 12" brake drum
BBS192AP	heavy duty bonded brake set; front axle; Custom, DeLuxe; 5 passenger; 11" brake drum
BBS1105AP	heavy duty bonded brake set; front axle; Custom, DeLuxe; 7 passenger; 12" brake drum
BBS1161AP	heavy duty bonded brake set; rear axle; Custom, DeLuxe; 5 passenger; 11" brake drum
BBS1179P	heavy duty bonded brake set; rear axle; Custom, DeLuxe; 7 passenger; 12" brake drum
CH-67	single molded and curved lower radiator hose
DMS192AP	economy duty bonded brake set; front axle; Custom, DeLuxe; 5 passenger; 11" brake drum
DMS1105AP	economy duty bonded brake set; front axle; Custom, DeLuxe; 7 passenger; 12" brake drum
DMS1161AP	economy duty bonded brake set; rear axle; D24 Custom, DeLuxe; 5 passenger; 11" brake drum
DMS1179P	economy duty bonded brake set; rear axle; Custom, DeLuxe; 7 passenger; 12" brake drum
V-560	fan and generator V-belt
V-560HD	heavy duty fan and generator V-belt
WB192A-1161AD	economy duty brake set; 192A—front axle; 1161—rear axle; Custom, DeLuxe; 5 passenger; 11" brake drum
WB1105A-1179D	economy brake set; 1105—front axle, 1179—rear axle; Custom, DeLuxe; 7 passenger; brake drum

Grizzly—Brake Shoes

Every brake shoe was inspected for distortion, shot blasted to remove any burrs and cleaned to assure proper adhesion of premium brake lining that won't glaze under high speed driving conditions. Grizzly brakes meet or exceed all original equipment specifications. Grizzly was located in Chicago, Illinois.

192A	front axle brake shoe set; 5 passenger models
1105A	front and/or rear brake shoe set; 7 passenger models
1161A	rear axle brake shoe set; 5 passenger models

Guaranteed Parts (GP)—Ignition and Electrical Replacement Parts

GP started manufacturing replacement parts for automobiles around 1910 and quickly became a leader in the ignition replacement parts industry by adapting the best materials available for each part. Parts fit accurately and met or surpassed the original factory specifications for domestic and foreign ignitions. They were a leader in the use and development of Bakelite for distributor caps and rotors and tungsten for contact points. GP parts were readily available since cabinets filled with GP parts were located in almost every garage across the country. Guaranteed Parts Co. was located in Seneca Falls, New York.

4258	starter bushing; drive end
4278	generator bushing; commutator end
AL-83	distributor cap
AL-99	distributor rotor
AL-8190	distributor contact points
AL-8190S	distributor contact points; heavy duty
AL-8890	regular points set
AL-8890AS	pre-assembled heavy duty ventilated points set
AL-8890S	heavy duty ventilated points set
ALC-54	distributor condenser
ALC-54S	distributor condenser; heavy duty
ALC-72	distributor condenser
ALC-72U	this condenser can substitute for ALC-72
BK-5	coil bracket
BX-9R	starter Bendix spring
DS-3	dimmer switch
DS-3S	dimmer switch; heavy duty
EX-37-38	starter brush set
EX-57	generator brush set
GC-20S	universal ignition coil; heavy duty
GC-102	coil
GL-13	distributor primary lead and/or ground lead
HR-19	horn relay
SLS-24	stop light switch

SS-46   starter switch
VCA-2   distributor vacuum chamber
VR-222   voltage regulator; 6 volt; 35-45 amp; positive ground
VR-222S   voltage regulator; 6 volt; 35-45 amp; positive ground; heavy duty

HaDees—Thermostats

HaDees started in the early 1920s to manufacture and supply heaters, fluids and thermostats for automobiles and trucks. The thermostats listed below were advertised to provide dependable temperature control for top engine and heater performance. The company logo was a devil blowing warm air. HaDees was located in Rockford, Illinois, and Detroit, Michigan.

H-96   bellows type thermostat; standard temperature; 160 degrees F; all models
H-96HT   bellows type thermostat; high temperature; 180 degrees F; all models
H-108   pellet type thermostat; standard temperature; 160 degrees F; all models
H-108HT   pellet type thermostat; high temperature;180 degrees F; all models

Hampden—Brake Shoes and Water Pumps

Hampden supplied a quality line of rebuilt bonded brake shoes. Brakes were available in single front or rear axle boxed sets or dual front and rear axle boxed sets. They also supplied rebuilt water pumps for most U.S. cars, trucks and tractors that featured 100 percent new bearings and new seal assemblies. Hampden stressed only the highest quality replacement parts and was a member of the Automotive Parts Rebuilders Association. Hampden was located in Newark, New Jersey.

192-44   front bonded brake shoe set for 5 passenger models
1105-45 front and rear bonded brake shoe set for 7 passenger models
1161-44 rear bonded brake shoe set for 5 passenger models
1179-45 rear bonded brake shoe set for 7 passenger models
BB-2   bonded emergency brake shoe for all models with fluid drive transmission
BB-7   bonded emergency brake shoe for all models with standard transmission
WP-53   replaces bushing type water pump for all models—including those with a half-moon outlet in the back plate and all with the original casting number 637437; also replaces bearing type water pump for all models—including those with a half-moon outlet in the back plate and all with the original casting number 642398

Harrison—Thermostats

Harrison was a recognized leader in the efficient control of water and engine temperature using in-line thermostats. Their 150 degree bellows type thermostats were designed for either alcohol base or permanent type antifreeze, while the 160, 170 and 180 degree thermostats were to be used with permanent type antifreeze only. Harrison was located in Flint, Michigan.

155	150 degrees; bellows type thermostat; fits all models
156 P	160 degrees; bellows type thermostat; fits all models
157	170 degrees; bellows type thermostat; fits all models
158	180 degrees; bellows type thermostat; fits all models
158 P	180 degrees; bellows type thermostat; fits all models
3121244	150 degrees; bellows type thermostat; fits all models
3121245	170 degrees; bellows type thermostat; fits all models
3126285	180 degrees; bellows type thermostat; fits all models

Hastings—Piston Rings, Fuel Pumps and Oil Filters

Hastings supplied a line of replacement piston rings, fuel pumps, spark plugs and filters for passenger cars and trucks. All parts were engineered for "exact-fit" to give extra miles of satisfactory service. Hastings was located in Hastings, Michigan.

2C-144	high quality ring set with chrome where needed
9-144	ring set that includes cast iron oil ring with an inner spring—suggested for use with factory replacement engines
14-106	hotter spark plug used to prevent fouling in 1946 engine
14-126	spark plug recommended for normal conditions for 1946 engines; used to prevent fouling in 1947–1948 engines
14-141	spark plug recommended for normal conditions for 1947–1948 engines;
14-141R	spark plug with built-in resistor recommended for normal conditions for 1947–1948 engines
144	standard ring set with chrome rails on oil ring only
215-3¼"	GL spacers for use on top groove if top groove is widened to get a true surface
316	replacement oil filter; all models; replaces 1121 694
M 847	fuel pump; all models
VA-300-6	valve spring insert .060" thick (suggested for use with old springs and valve grind)
VB-300-6	valve spring insert .030" thick (suggested for use with new springs or old springs with no valve grind)

Hastings Company (The)—Brakes, Clutch Assemblies and Water Pumps

The Hastings Company supplied rebuilt clutch assemblies, bonded brake shoes, brake cylinders and water pumps for passenger cars and light trucks. They were a member of both the Parts Rebuilders Automotive Association and the National Standard Parts Association (NSPA). Rebuilt Hastings products were only distributed to wholesale jobbers and the company was located in King, North Carolina.

192-A	bonded brake shoes; front; 5 passenger models
1105	bonded brake shoes; front; 7 passenger
1161-A	bonded brake shoes; rear; 5 passenger models
1179	bonded brake shoes; rear; 7 passenger
CA-929	clutch cover assembly; models with 11" clutch
CA-952	clutch cover assembly; models with fluid drive
CA-957	clutch cover assembly; models with standard transmission
CP-723	clutch plate standard transmission
CP-756	clutch plate fluid drive models
CP-1850	clutch plate; models with 11" clutch
M-3241	master cylinder all models
MS-716	matched set of clutch plate and cover assembly; models with 11" clutch
MS-813	matched set of clutch plate and cover assembly; models with fluid drive
MS-814	matched set of clutch plate and cover assembly; models with standard transmission
W-10580	front wheel; left cylinder
W-10581	front wheel; right cylinder
W-10582	front wheel; left cylinder
W-10583	front wheel; right cylinder
W-10588	rear wheel cylinder; left or right
WCR-11R	water pump; all models

HE Ignition—*See* Hoosick Engineering

Hoosick Engineering (HE)—Ignition

Hoosick Engineering was advertised as "The Best in Ignition Replacement Parts." They specialized in replacement distributor caps, rotors, contact sets and condensers for Auto-Lite, Delco-Remy and Ford ignition systems. HE used only molded Bakelite for replacement caps and rotors. Standard and heavy duty contact parts were available. Hoosick Engineering was located in Hoosick Falls, New York.

201	distributor cap; D24 models with IGS distributor; replaces factory no. IGC-1107 or IGC 1107S
204	distributor rotor; D24 models with IGS distributor; replaces factory no. IGS-1016 or 1016B
AL-15	distributor condenser; regular; D24 models with IGS distributor; replaces factory no. IG-3927-A
HE-30	point set; regular; D24 models with IGS distributor; replaces factory no. IGP-3028-ES
HE-30 HD	point set; heavy duty; D24 models with IGS distributor; replaces factory no. IGP-3028-ES

Hoover—Bearings and Tie Rod Ends

Hoover bearings offered perfectly balanced and honed raceways that were an exclusive Hoover construction. Micro-lapped chrome steel balls were accurate to

0.000025" and were held within balanced retainers that offered silent operation and supreme performance. High carbon chrome steel outer supports provided more load and longer life. Hoover was located in Ann Arbor, Michigan.

5-C	bearing cone; steering gear upper and lower bearings; 5 passenger models only
6-A	bearing cup; steering gear upper bearing; 5 passenger models only
6-C	bearing cup; steering gear lower bearing; 5 passenger models only
11-C	bearing cone; steering gear upper and lower bearings; 7 passenger models only
13	bearing cup; steering gear upper bearing; 7 passenger models only
14-C	bearing cup; steering gear lower bearing; 7 passenger models only
203	generator bearing
206	transmission main shaft extension bearing
206-N	fluid coupling bearing
207	transmission main shaft rear bearing
1729	bearing cup; outer front wheel; 7 passenger models only
1755	bearing cone; outer front wheel; 7 passenger models only
2523	bearing cup; inner front wheel; 7 passenger models only
2585	bearing cone; inner front wheel; 7 passenger models only
2736	bearing cup; rear wheel; 7 passenger models only
2780	bearing cone; rear wheel; 7 passenger models only
3041	king pin thrust bearing; all models
3069	throwout bearing; standard transmission models without fluid drive
3420	bearing cup; rear axle front pinion; 7 passenger models only
3476	bearing cone; rear axle front pinion; 7 passenger models only
3820	bearing cup; rear axle rear pinion; 7 passenger models only
3875	bearing cone; rear axle rear pinion; 7 passenger models only
7207	propeller shaft bearing; 7 passenger model only; transmission main extension—fluid drive
7207-G	transmission rear drive shaft bearing
09074	bearing cone; outer front wheel; 5 passenger models only
09194	bearing cup; outer front wheel; 5 passenger models only
14125-A	bearing cone; inner front wheel; 5 passenger model only
14276	bearing cup; inner front wheel; 5 passenger models only
25520	bearing cup; right and left differential
25580	bearing cone; right and left differential
25821	bearing cup; rear wheel; 5 passenger models only
25877	bearing cone; rear wheel; 5 passenger models only
31520	bearing cup; rear axle front and rear pinion; 5 passenger models only
31590	bearing cone; rear axle front pinion; 5 passenger models only
31593	bearing cone; rear axle rear pinion bearing; 5 passenger models only

CT-1054	clutch release bearing; conventional drive models without fluid drive
CT-1055	clutch release bearing; fluid drive models
CT-1312	clutch release bearing and carrier assembly; fluid drive models
ES-60	tie rod end; used for right hand assembly; 5 passenger models; 2 required
ES-131	tie rod end; used for left hand assembly; 5 passenger models, 2 required
N-1055	throwout bearing; fluid drive models
NE-7	transmission main shaft front needles
NE-8	transmission countershaft; front and rear needles; reverse idler needles

Houdaille—Shock Absorbers

Houdaille (HOO-DYE) shock absorbers were brand new and not rebuilt. They were one of the pioneer builders, with the longest experience of producing hydraulic shock absorbers in the automobile industry. Houdaille shocks were engineered from hardened, heavy duty parts for stability, control and performance at all temperatures. The Houdaille-Hershey Corporation was located in Detroit, Michigan.

D-137	direct action shock absorbers; rear; standard size "Hercules" matched pair with bushings; all models
D-137-1	new number for D-137
D-138	direct action shock absorbers; front; standard size "Hercules" matched pair with bushings; all models
D-138-1	new number for D-138
G-1	single bushing for shock absorbers
G-1-8	box of 8 shock absorber rubber bushings
G-7	single bushing for shock absorbers; new number
G-7-4	box of 4 shock absorber rubber bushings
H-10	direct action shock absorber; rear; standard size "Hercules" single shock absorber without bushings; all models
H-11	new number for H-10
H-20	direct action shock absorber; front; standard size "Hercules" single shock absorber without bushings; all models
H-21	new number for H-20
HH-10	direct action shock absorber; rear; heavy duty "Husky" single shock absorber without bushings; all models
HH-11	new number for HH-10
HH-20	direct action shock absorber; front; heavy duty "Husky" single shock absorber without bushings; all models
HH-21	new number for HH-20
HHD-137	direct action shock absorbers; rear; heavy duty "Husky" matched pair with bushings; all models
HHD-137-1	new number for HHD-137

HHD-138   direct action shock absorbers; front; heavy duty "Husky" matched pair with bushings; all models

HHD-138-1   new number for HHD-138

Hygrade—Fuel Pumps

Hygrade supplied only new fuel pumps. Each pump was accurately assembled, completely tested and sealing surfaces were polished mirror-smooth to prevent abrasion of the diaphragm. The diaphragm was specially constructed to resist alcohol, gasoline and high temperatures, and the rocker arm was heat treated for strength and specially processed to prevent corrosion. Hygrade Products was located in Long Island City, New York.

577   fuel pump; replaces original pump number 1539042 (577); 1947–1948 models

588   fuel pump; replaces original pump number 1523647 (588); 1946 models

40588   fuel pump; all models with single diaphragm pumps

FP-411A   fuel pump diaphragm kit; 588 and 577 fuel pumps

FP-411C   diaphragm kit for pump number H-588AT (588) and/or pump H-577BQ (577)

FP-714   "contain all" fuel pump repair kit for H-588AT (588) pump

FP-755   "contain all" fuel pump repair kit for H-577BQ (577) pump

H-505AT   pump that may be substituted for pump H-588AT

H-577BQ   fuel pump; replaces original pump number 1539042 (577); 1947–1948 models

H-588AT   fuel pump; replaces original pump number 1523647 (588); 1946 models

Imparco—Exhaust Mufflers and Pipes

Imparco mufflers had a double heavy steel gauge steel jacket with a rust resistant finish for protection against rust and corrosion. Inlet and outlet pipes were firmly anchored into the muffler body to assure permanent and rigid muffler mounting and unusual strength. The Imparco Brand was supplied by International Parts Corporation, Chicago, Illinois.

3E-185   exhaust pipe, excludes convertible and 7 passenger models

7-T196   tail pipe; excludes convertible and 7 passenger models

468   muffler; all models

F-839   rear hanger

F-840   front hanger

MP-126   inlet clamp

MP-127   outlet clamp

Imperial—Rebuilt Armatures, Generators and Starters

Imperial supplied rebuilt starters, generators and voltage regulators for passenger cars and trucks. Imperial Armatures, Inc., was located in Boston, Massachusetts.

4	rebuilt generator armature; replaces Auto- Lite GDZ-2006 armature
129	generator armature for police and taxi D24 models; replaces generator armature GDZ 2600
1745	rebuilt starter armature; replaces Auto-Lite MAW-2128 armature
3246	starting motor; replaces Auto-Lite starting motor MAX 4041
9413	generator; replaces Auto-Lite generator GDZ 4801
9444	generator for police and taxi models; replaces Auto-Lite generator GEG 4818 or GEG 4823
A-413	rebuilt generator; replaces Auto-Lite GDZ-4801-A, GDZ-4801-B or GDZ-4801-R generators
A-2991	rebuilt starter drive
P	rebuilt voltage regulator; replaces Auto-Lite VRP-4503-A regulator
S-246	rebuilt starter; replaces Auto-Lite MAW-4041 starter

Inlite—Brake Linings

Inlite passenger car brakes came in matched sets and were engineered "to give equalized brakes on all four wheels and to stop the car in a smooth quiet way without dangerous wheel slide." Sets were compounded from material selected and blended to give dependable service and long life under the severest kind of heavy duty operation. Inlite brakes were a product of the United Motors Line of General Motors of Flint, Michigan.

192-A	front brakes; drilled brake set that requires 40 rivets size 4-5; set contains: 4 pieces for 11" diameter drum size
192-BA	front brakes; bonded and undrilled; set contains: 4 pieces for 11" diameter drum size
1161-A	rear brakes; drilled brake set that requires 36 rivets size 4-5; set contains: 4 pieces for 11" diameter drum size
1161-BS	rear brakes; bonded and undrilled; set contains: 4 pieces for 11" diameter drum size

International Parts—General Line of Replacement Parts

International Parts supplied dozens of parts for the aftermarket passenger car and truck market. Their extensive inventory was too large for one catalog and therefore their available parts were covered in several counter and aftermarket catalogs found in garages and repair shops nationwide. The Field Guide reflects this hugeness by dividing their inventory into several categories. International Parts Corporation was located in Chicago, Illinois.

Engine

588	fuel pump; all models
C-542	water pump; all models
E-381	ignition cable set; 6 cylinder; all models
E-488	voltage regulator; positive ground

E-498   solenoid starter switch
E-501   regular ignition coil
E-519   heavy duty ignition coil
E-609   ignition points set
E-657   distributor cap
E-675   distributor rotor
E-682   distributor condenser
EN-1278 valve tappet; intake or exhaust valve; all models
EX-16   starter brush set
EX-45   generator brush set
F-469   front motor mount; all models
F-895   rear upper motor mount; all models
F-1347   rear lower motor mount; all models
G-306P   oil filter; all models
G-423   gasoline filter; all models
G-665   Stromberg carburetor tune-up kit; models with fluid drive
G-833   Stromberg carburetor tune-up kit; models without fluid drive
G-15208 Stromberg carburetor tune-up kit; models with fluid drive
G-15384 Stromberg carburetor tune-up kit; models without fluid drive
M-5   spark plug
R-258   thermostat; 160 degrees F; all models
R-259   thermostat; 180 degrees F; all models
S-108   starter drive
TC-401   timing chain; all models
V-98   fan/generator belt; all models

Exhaust

360   muffler; excludes 7 passenger models
EX-147   exhaust pipe; 5 passenger models; excludes 7 passenger and
         convertible
F-838   rear tail pipe hanger; factory type; all models
F-840   front tail pipe hanger; factory type; all models
MP-126   muffler inlet clamp; factory type; all models
MP-127   muffler outlet clamp; factory type; all models
TA-196   tail pipe; 5 passenger models; excludes 7 passenger and convertible

Brakes

10268   front wheel brake hose; left and/or right wheel; all models
10304   rear wheel brake hose; all models
10595   front wheel brake hose; all models
B-218   emergency brake cable; models without fluid drive
B-230   emergency brake cable; models with fluid drive
B-523   front and/or rear wheel cylinder repair kit; all models
B-562   master cylinder repair kit; all models

B-588   master cylinder; all models
B-728   brake set; replaces 192A front and/or 1161A rear; all 5 passenger models
B-730   brake set; replaces 1105A front and/or 1179 rear; all 7 passenger models
B-10580 left front upper wheel cylinder; all models
B-10581 right front upper wheel cylinder; all models
B-10582 left front lower wheel cylinder; all models
B-10583 right front lower wheel cylinder; all models
B-10588 rear wheel cylinder; right and/or left wheel; all models
E-448   hydraulic stop light switch; all models
BR-105   front wheel brake return spring; all models
BR-106   rear wheel brake return spring; all models

Suspension, Chassis

09067   front wheel outer bearing cone; 5 passenger models
09195   front wheel outer bearing cup; 5 passenger models
14125A   front wheel inner bearing cone; 5 passenger models
14276   front wheel inner bearing cup; 5 passenger models
25821   rear wheel bearing cup; 5 passenger
25877   rear wheel bearing cone; 5 passenger models
AX-411   front wheel grease retainer; 5 passenger models
AX-412   rear wheel inner grease retainer; excludes 7 passenger
AX-500   rear wheel outer grease seal; leather; 5 passenger models
AX-671   rear wheel outer grease seal; 5 passenger models
AX-755   rear wheel outer grease seal; 7 passenger models
ES-60L   right hand rod; left tie rod end; all models
ES-60R   right hand rod; right tie rod end; all models
ES-131L left hand rod; left tie rod end; all models
ES-131R left hand rod; right tie rod end; all models
F-382   eye spring bushing; all models
F-548   rear spring and shackle bushing; flat type; all models
F-549   rear shackle set; all models
F-761   front or rear shock absorber replacement grommets; all models
F-878   spring/shackle dome top bushing; standard; all models
F-879   rear spring and shackle bushing; grooved type; all models
F-1000   shock absorber helper spring; all models
F-1100   overload helper spring; all models
F-1101   extra overload helper spring; all models
J-302   universal joint; front and rear; 7 passenger models
J-311   universal joint front and rear; all models; excludes early 1946 front
J-315   universal joint repair kit; 5 passenger Detroit type
K-25B   king bolt set; up to serial number 31006517; replaces 933 435; 5 passenger models

K-59B　　king bolt set; after serial number 31006517 to 31057047; replaces 947 557; 5 passenger models

SH-137-1　rear shock absorber; standard; all models

SH-138-1　front shock absorber; standard; all models

SHH-137-1 rear shock absorber; heavy duty; all models

SHH-138-1 front shock absorber; heavy duty; all models

TG-243-50 transmission small parts kit

Clutch

CP-243　　clutch plate; 9¼" clutch; models with fluid drive

CP-246　　clutch plate; 10" clutch; models without fluid drive

CP-371　　clutch fork assembly; models without fluid drive

CP-372　　clutch fork assembly; models with fluid drive

CP-470　　clutch throwout bearing; models without fluid drive

CP-471　　clutch throwout bearing; models with fluid drive

CP-487　　clutch fork ball; all models

ST-993A　clutch facing; 9¼" clutch; models with fluid drive

1008A　　clutch facing; 10" clutch; models without fluid drive

ST-993A　clutch facing; 9¼"; models with fluid drive

ST-1008A clutch facing; 10" models without fluid drive

Miscellaneous

6968　　speedometer cable; 67"; models with fluid drive

6971　　speedometer cable; 64"; models without fluid drive

7007　　speedometer cable and casing set; 67"; models with fluid drive

7008　　speedometer cable and casing set; 64"; models without fluid drive

D-142　inside door handle; all models

D-143　inside window handle; all models

D-150　glove compartment lock

D-154　trunk lock

D-156　ignition lock switch

D-177　left front and/or right rear door striker repair kit

D-178　right front and/or left rear door striker repair kit

D-179　left front and/or right rear door rotary lock repair kit

D-180　right front and/or left rear door rotary lock repair kit

D-423　trunk handle; all models

E-427　headlamp switch

E-436　dimmer switch

E-493　door jamb switch

E-497　back-up light switch

E-733　battery cable; positive

E-747　battery cable; negative

F-335　battery hold-down; 15 plate battery

F-336   battery hold-down; 17 plate battery
X-480   front floor mat

Jiffy-Kit—Carburetors

The Jiffy repair kit contains everything that is needed for a quick and reliable carburetor rebuild in one compact package. Each tune-up part is engineered to fit perfectly and outlast the original. Jiffy-Kit was a trademark of Hygrade Products located in Long Island City, New York.

1386   original number for C-1212 carburetor repair kit
C-1212   repair kit for Carter BB-D6J1 carburetor; all models
RK-130   original number for repair kit for Stromberg BXV-3 carburetor; models without fluid drive
RK-131   original number for repair kit for Stromberg BXVD-3 carburetor; models with fluid drive
S-1215   repair kit for Stromberg BXV-3 carburetor; models without fluid drive
S-1216   repair kit for Stromberg BXVD-3 carburetor; models with fluid drive.

Johns-Manville—Clutch Facings and Brake Shoes

The Johns-Manville (JM) company was formed in 1901 and started producing brake lining and clutch facings soon afterwards. Catalogs printed following World War II advertised JM as the oldest name in brake lining and featured the new "Wire-clad Brakes" and "Spiral Wound Clutch Facings." The General Headquarters was located in New York, New York.

192A   front axle brake set; 4 pieces; 5 passenger models
192A-1161AD   brake set; 192A front axle and 1161AD rear axle; 5 passenger models
993   clutch facing; fluid drive transmission; $9\frac{1}{4}$" × 6" × $\frac{1}{8}$" with 18 pre-drilled holes; 5 passenger and 7 passenger models
1008A   clutch facing standard drive transmission; 10" × 7" × $\frac{1}{8}$"; 18 pre-drilled holes; 5 passenger and 7 passenger models
1105A   front axle brake set; 4 pieces; 7 passenger models
1105A-1179D   brake set; 1105A front axle and 1179D rear axle; 7 passenger models
1161A   rear axle brake set; 4 pieces; 5 passenger models
1179   rear axle brake set; 4 pieces; 7 passenger models
RX-192AD   lined brake shoe exchange; front axle; 4 brake shoes; 5 passenger models
RX-1161AD   lined brake shoe exchange; rear axle; 4 brake shoes; 5 passenger models
US-192A   unlined brake shoe; front axle; 5 passenger models
US-1161AD   unlined brake shoe; rear axle; 5 passenger models
WK-192A-1161AD   brake set; WK-192A front axle; 8 pieces; 5 passenger models

Johnson—Piston Rings

Johnson supplied piston ring sets for cars, trucks, and tractors that were designed to give greater efficiency, longer wear and unmatched durability. They produced "Perfect Seal" chrome treated and "Super Seal" perma-black treated replacement piston rings designed for heavy duty operation under severe conditions. Rings were engineered to reduce oil consumption, increase gas mileage, eliminate "blow-by" and adapt to irregularities of the cylinder wall. The Johnson Piston Ring Company was located in Detroit, Michigan.

51	piston rings; all models with 3¼" pistons

K.O. Lee—Valve Inserts

In 1926 K.O. Lee developed a machine and process for repairing automobile engine valve seats with inserts. Soon thereafter, they produced a wide range of machines used in engine repair and rebuilding. Valve inserts were sold across the U.S. through local NAPA stores. K.O. Lee was located in Aberdeen, South Dakota.

9	intake valve seat insert ring; 6 cylinder
9BR	exhaust valve seat insert ring; 6 cylinder

Kem—Ignition and Fuel Pumps

The Kem Field Guide information is divided into two sections: (1) ignition and (2) fuel pump. Kem started producing ignition and fuel pump aftermarket replacement parts in 1920. Kem parts are "Pre-fitted" to each specified installation so as to function satisfactorily under the most adverse service conditions. Pre-fitted parts assure easy installation and long service life. Kem Manufacturing Co. Inc., was located in Fair Lawn, New Jersey.

Ignition

340 L	Kem "high ratio" coil
1650	rotor
1651	distributor cap
1658	condenser
1700	universal type condenser
BB 258	starter bushing—drive end
BB 259	starter bushing—commutator end
BB 278	generator bushing—commutator end (excludes GEG generators)
DS 104	dimmer switch
EG 1039	stop light switch
ES 16-18S	starter brush set for MZ starters
ES 37-38	starter brush set for MAW starters
ES 57	generator brush set
HR 6	horn relay
KL 18	distributor primary lead

KL 19	distributor ground lead
KVR 109	voltage regulator (excludes GGW generators) positive ground, 6 volt, 35–45 amp.
KVR 126	voltage regulator (for GGW generators) positive ground, 6 volt, 40–51 amp.
SW 16	starter switch (solenoid)
TC 13	contact set (regular) contains (1) T1656 arm and (1) 11661 bar
TV 13	contact set—one-piece heavy duty "vent-o-lated"
U 11A	regular coil
VC 101	vacuum chamber for IGS distributor

Fuel Pump

4-P	glass filter bowl for the 588 AT fuel pump
52-P	gasket for glass filter bowl for the 588 AT fuel pump
588	fuel pump; all models
588-AT	fuel pump with a glass filter bowl; replaces manufacturers number 152 3647
706	fuel pump number replaced by 9926-BQ
9926	fuel pump without a glass bowl and filter
9926-BQ	fuel pump without a glass bowl and filter; replaces manufacturers number 153 9042
FPA 48	fuel pump repair kit for the 588-AT fuel pump; a rocker arm is not included with this kit
FPA 94	fuel pump repair kit for the 588-AT fuel pump; a rocker arm is included with this kit
FPA 170	fuel pump repair kit for the 9926-BQ fuel pump; a rocker arm is included with the kit
KF 111	fuel filter

King Products—Engine and Suspension Replacement Parts

King supplied a large variety of aftermarket replacement engine and suspension parts for passenger cars and trucks. The product line is so long that the Field Guide conveniently divides the parts list into engine and suspension groups for easier use by the D24 owner. King Products was located in St. Louis, Missouri.

Engine

1639	service special piston ring set; all models
2568	connecting rod bearing; all models
2568S	connecting rod bearing set; all models
2569	front #1 position main bearing; all models
2570	#2 and/or #3 position main bearing; all models
2571	rear #4 position main bearing; all models
3640	special flange semi-finished rear #4 bearing; all models

4339	rebore-rebuild piston ring set; all models
C-4339	chrome rebore-rebuild piston ring set; all models
CBS	complete camshaft bearing set; split precision type; all models
CBS-34	complete camshaft bearing set; solid precision type; all models
G-254R	intake and/or exhaust valve guide; all models
L-339	leak-proof piston ring set; all models
L-339C	leak-proof chrome control piston rings set; all models
LR-4	piston pin lock; all models
M-201	water pump pulley hub; all models
MA-10R	water pump seal kit; all models
MB-17F	camshaft #1 bearing; split precision type; all models
MB-17SF	camshaft #1 bearing; split ream type; all models
MB-18F	camshaft #2 bearing; split precision type; all models
MB-18SF	camshaft #2 bearing; split ream type; all models
MB-19F	camshaft #3 bearing; split precision type; all models
MB-19SF	camshaft #3 bearing; split ream type; all models
MB-136F	camshaft #1 bearing; solid precision type; all models
MB-137F	camshaft #2 bearing; solid precision type; all models
MB-138F	camshaft #3 bearing; solid precision type; all models
MBS-51	main bearing complete set; all models
P-337AX	cam ground U-slot piston; 3¼" diameter; original type piston interchangeable in complete sets; all models
PA-117R	water pump repair kit; all models
PC-11R	complete water pump; all models
PX-23	piston expander for U-slot pistons; all models
PY-17	water pump pulley; all models
SD-59	dry cylinder piston sleeve; cut to length; all models
TU-1	water distribution tube; steel; all models
TU-2	water distribution tube; brass; all models
V-1334	exhaust valve; all models
V-1335N	intake valve; all models
V-1581N	"silichrome" intake valve; all models
VK-84	intake and/or exhaust valve keepers; all models
VS-348	intake and/or exhaust valve springs; all models
W-9226	piston pin; all models
WB-1824	piston pin bushing; all models

Suspension

ES-60L	right tie rod; left tie rod end
ES-60R	right tie rod; right tie rod end
ES-131L	left tie rod; left tie rod end
ES-131R	left tie rod; right tie rod end
FA-024	control arm lower shaft assembly; all 5 passenger models
FA-029	knuckle support lower pin assembly; all 7 passenger models

FA-030	control arm lower shaft assembly; all 7 passenger models
FA-039	knuckle support upper pin assembly; 5 passenger models up to Detroit 30993973 and Los Angeles 450021591
FA-040S	control arm upper shaft assembly; all 5 passenger models
FA-042	knuckle support upper pin assembly; all 7 passenger models
FA-043	control arm upper shaft assembly; all 7 passenger models
FA-045	knuckle support lower pin assembly; 5 passenger models up to Detroit 30993973 and Los Angeles 450021591
FA-119	knuckle support upper pin assembly; 5 passenger models after Detroit 30993973 and Los Angeles 450021591
FA-134	knuckle support lower pin assembly; 5 passenger models after Detroit 30993973 and Los Angeles 450021591
FCS-250	regular duty front coil spring; all 5 passenger models
FCS-258	regular duty front coil spring; all 7 passenger models and heavy duty all 5 passenger models
FSC-260	heavy duty front coil spring; all 7 passenger models
FN-8	right and/or left steering knuckle support; all 5 passenger models
KA-16	king bolt set; 5 passenger models
KA-135	king bolt set; 7 passenger models
M-634	front coil spring upper spacer; 5 passenger models
M-683	front coil spring upper silencer—5 passenger models; upper and/or lower silencer—7 passenger models
M-684	front coil spring lower silencer; all 5 passenger models
SK-34	rear spring front bolt kit; all models
SK-44	rear spring shackle kit; all models

KM (Ken Mar)—Water Pumps

Ken Mar supplied rebuilt water pumps for passenger cars, truck and tractors. Core pumps were inspected to meet all factory specifications before being rebuilt with the highest quality materials. Ken Mar Automotive Products was located in Cincinnati, Ohio.

| WP-53 | water pump; half-moon outlet in back; all models |

Lasco—Brake Shoes

Old brake shoes were thoroughly cleaned, inspected and tested for trueness to insure maximum surface adhesion of "Super Bond" bonding cement. Shoes were tested for bonding strength. All brake shoes were precision surface ground to insure maximum drum to lining contact. Lasco Brake Products was a member of Laher Industries, St. Louis, Missouri.

| BLS 260 | "Blue Label" Lasco brake shoes; front brakes; 5 passenger Custom and DeLuxe FMSI number on the box is 192 A |
| BLS 261 | "Blue Label" Lasco brake shoes; rear brakes; 5 passenger Custom and DeLuxe FMSI number on the box is 1161 A |

BLS 263	"Blue Label" Lasco brake shoes; front brakes; 7 passenger; FMSI number on the box is 1105 A
BLS 264	"Blue Label" Lasco brake shoes; rear brakes; 7 passenger; FMSI number on the box is 1179
LS 260	Lasco shoe exchange; front brakes; 5 Passenger Custom and DeLuxe; FMSI number on the box is 192 A
LS 261	Lasco shoe exchange; rear brakes; 5 Passenger Custom and Deluxe; FMSI number on the box is 1161 A
LS 263	Lasco shoe exchange; front brakes; 7 Passenger; FMSI number on the box is 1105 A
LS 264	Lasco shoe exchange; rear brakes;7 Passenger; FMSI number on the box is 1179

Lempco—Clutch Bearings, Timing Chains and Axle Shafts

Lempco was founded in 1917 as a manufacturer of die sets for the production of small metal parts for World War I. Following the war the product line was expanded to include clutch bearings and assemblies, precision matched timing chains, gears and sprockets and replacement axles, for automobiles and trucks. Lempco always included the original factory part number in their catalogs to provide the exact replacement information for all original parts. Lempco Automotive, Inc., was located in Cleveland, Ohio.

1054	clutch release bearing; replaces factory number 658 998; conventional drive models without fluid drive
1055	clutch release bearing; replaces factory number 658 948; fluid drive models
BA-3	clutch release bearing and carrier assembly; replaces factory number 862 859 models without fluid drive
BA-6	clutch release bearing and carrier assembly; replaces factory number 867 735 fluid drive models
C-200	rear axle; model D24; all 7 passenger models; length 32¼"; 10 splines; replaces factory number 1118 137
P-85	rear axle; model D24; excludes 7 passenger models; length 32¼"; 10 splines; replaces factory number 1118 136
PT-771	clutch release bearing; models without fluid drive (old number)
PT-777	clutch release bearing; models without fluid drive (old number)
PT-800	clutch release bearing and carrier assembly; models without fluid drive (old number)
PT-903	clutch release bearing; fluid drive models (old number)
S-126	cam gear; 38 teeth; replaces factory number 601 757; all models
S-127	crank gear; 19 teeth; replaces factory number 601 760; all models
TC-401	timing chain; 48 links; replaces factory number 1075 001; all models

Limpco—Clutch Assemblies and Clutch Plates

Limpco clutches were remanufactured to give as good or better than new service.

Adherence to very close tolerances guaranteed long and trouble free driving. Limpco Manufacturing Co. was located in Jeannette, Pennsylvania.

CA-938   pressure plate assembly; all standard drive transmission models
CA-1329   pressure plate assembly; all fluid drive models
CD-728   clutch disc; all standard drive transmission models; 10" diameter
CD-756   clutch disc; all fluid drive models; 9¼" diameter
MU-938   matched clutch disc and pressure plate; all standard drive transmission models
MU-1329   matched clutch disc and pressure plate; all fluid drive models

Link-Belt—Timing Chains and Gears

Link-Belt produced timing chains, camshaft and crankshaft gears that provided smooth, quiet and efficient performance for trouble free service. Timing chains and gears were designed to equalize load pressure across the face of the teeth to reduce wear and assure longer life. Link-Belt was located in Philadelphia, Pennsylvania, with warehouses in major cities across the country.

401   timing chain; 230 engine; 48 links; replaces 1075 001
S-126   camshaft gear; 230 engine; 38 teeth
S-127   crankshaft gear; 230 engine; 19 teeth

Lion—Fuel Pumps and Suspension Replacement Parts

Lion front end suspension parts were manufactured from the highest grade steel, heat treated to ensure maximum strength and safety and precisely machined to manufacturers' specifications for perfect interchangeability with original equipment. Lion also supplied single action and combination fuel/vacuum pumps for most passenger cars, light and heavy-duty trucks. Pumps were new—not rebuilt. Repair kits contained all the essential parts necessary to service and overhaul single or dual action pumps. The Lion Auto Parts and Manufacturing Co. was located in Chicago, Illinois.

FP-14DK   fuel pump repair kit; for models 577 and 588 without glass bowl and 505 and 588 with glass bowl
FP-505(AT)   fuel pump; type AT pump with glass bowl; replaces original pump number 1523647; 1946 models with glass bowl
FP-577(BQ)   fuel pump; type BQ pump without glass bowl; replaces original pump number 1539042; 1947–1948 models without glass bowl
FP-588(AT)   fuel pump; type AT pump with glass bowl; replaces original pump number 1523647; 1946 models with glass bowl
FP-588(BQ)   fuel pump; type BQ pump without glass bowl; replaces original pump number 1539042; 1947–1948 models without glass bowl
FPK-6   diaphragm repair kit; for models 577 and 588 without glass bowl and 505 and 588 with glass bowl
K-140   lower support—outer (pivot pin); 7 passenger sedan and limousine; 2 required

K-142	lower support—outer; excludes 7 passenger sedan and limousine; 2 required
K-147	lower control arm—inner shaft; 7 passenger sedan and limousine; 2 required
K-167	upper support—outer; excludes 7 passenger sedan and limousine; 2 required
K-168	upper control arm—inner shaft; excludes 7 passenger sedan and limousine; 2 required
K-224	lower control arm—inner shaft; excludes 7 passenger sedan and limousine; 2 required

Maremont—Exhaust Mufflers and Pipes

Maremont mufflers and pipes were advertised as "The Right Design for Every Engine." Maremont exhaust systems were easily installed and heavy duty with low back pressure and quiet performance. Maremont Automotive Products, Inc., was located in Chicago, Illinois.

CR-46	muffler; 5 passenger models; excludes conv. coupe and 7 passenger models; replaces Mopar 676 955
EP-336	exhaust pipe; 5 passenger models; excludes conv. coupe and 7 passenger models; replaces Mopar 958 122
ST-44	muffler; 5 passenger models; excludes conv. coupe and 7 passenger models; replaces 676 955
T7-325	tail pipe; 5 passenger models; excludes conv. coupe and 7 passenger models; replaces 1122 759
TH-54	rear tail pipe hanger; replaces 681 934
TH-71	front tail pipe hanger; replaces 861 392
TP-325	tail pipe; 5 passenger models; excludes conv. coupe and 7 passenger models; replaces Mopar 1122 759
X-120	factory duplicate muffler outlet clamp; all models
X-180	factory duplicate muffler inlet clamp; all models

Martin—Oil Filters

Martin produced the insert refill type oil filters that were used on the D24 Dodge. They advertised oil filters that "Removed Sludge and Acid" from motor oil. All filters conformed to the Society of Automotive Engineers (S.A.E.) specifications. The Martin Filter Corporation was located in Edison, New Jersey.

M-70FF full flow oil filter; replacement filter for D24 Dodge; all models

Master—*See* Chefford/Chefford-Master—Clutch Bearings, Fuel Pumps and Universal Joints

McCord Motor Gaskets—Gaskets

McCord started producing gaskets as early as 1895 and was the originator of the cylinder head gasket. They developed many of the gaskets associated with the early automobile industry. They originated the idea of packing all the necessary gaskets for engine overhaul and valve grinding into an individual envelope. Gaskets made by McCord for repair and replacement are the same high quality as those supplied to automobile manufacturers. McCord Corporation was located in Detroit, Michigan.

2952	one piece manifold gasket
3337 L	rear main bearing cap; left
3337 R	rear main bearing cap; right
3338	rear main bearing oil seal; crankshaft
3408	thermostat gasket
3410	oil pump cover gasket; 1 required
6213	cylinder head gasket; asbestos and copper
6213 S	cylinder head gasket; asbestos and steel
9016	engine valve grind set; asbestos and copper; set contains (1) 6213, (1) SMS 2031, (1) CV 441, (1) S 859 J, (1) S3050, (1) V 8423, (1) 3408, (1) 30057
9016 S	engine valve grind set; asbestos and steel; set contains (1) 6213 S, (1) SMS 2031, (1) CV 441, (1) S 859 J, (1) 3050, (1) 8423, (1) 3408, (1) 30057
9274	engine overhaul set; asbestos and copper; contains timing gear cover oil seal—does not contain rear main bearing seal
9274 S	engine overhaul set; asbestos and steel; contains timing gear cover oil seal—does not contain rear main bearing seal
16172	oil pump to cylinder block
30057	cylinder head water outlet
38243	timing gear cover oil seal
BS-14	rear main bearing oil seal set
C-3309	valve cover gasket
C-3381	oil pan; right gasket
C-3382	oil pan; left gasket
C-3635	oil pan end gaskets; 2 required
C-4492	fuel pump strainer
CS-2255	oil pan gasket set
CV-441	valve cover set
ES-1137	timing gear cover gasket set; used up to engine number 79100
ES-1138	timing gear cover plate set
ES-1195	timing gear cover gasket set; used after engine number 79100
ES-4033	differential carrier gasket set; excludes 7 passenger sedan and limousine
ES-4146	differential carrier gasket set; 7 passenger sedan and limousine
MS-2505	manifold set one piece
S-821A	exhaust and intake end gaskets
S-859 J	exhaust pipe flange gasket
S-2553	intake to exhaust
S-2554	exhaust center gasket

S-2829	carburetor gasket; without governor
S-2864	automatic choke gasket
SMS-2031	manifold set
V-1137	timing gear cover gasket; 1946–1947; up to engine number 79100
V-1138	timing chain cove plate gasket
V-1195	timing gear cover gasket; 1947–1948; used after engine number 79100
V-4033	differential carrier gasket; excludes 7 passenger sedan and limousine
V-8202	fuel pump flange gasket; used on pump without booster
V-8253	universal joint body gasket; 2–4 required
V-8423	water pump by-pass elbow gasket
V-8978	water pump body cover plate gasket
V-8979	water pump body to cylinder block gasket
VTS-166	transmission gasket set

McQuay-Norris—General Line of Popular Engine and Suspension Replacement Parts

McQuay-Norris produced dozens of major aftermarket parts for passenger cars and automobiles. So many parts in fact for the D24 Dodge that the aftermarket information has been divided into three sections: (1) engine rebuild, (2) suspension and (3) additional. McQuay-Norris Manufacturing was located in St. Louis, Missouri.

Engine Rebuild

1639	service special piston ring set
2568	connecting rod bearing
2568S	complete connecting rod bearing set
2569	front main bearing
2570	center and intermediate main bearing
2571	rear main bearing
3640	rear main bearing; semi-finished
4339	rebore-rebuild piston ring set
C-4339	chrome rebore-rebuild piston ring set
CBS-2	complete camshaft bearing set
CBS-34	complete camshaft bearing set; standard
G-254R	valve guide
L-339	leak-proof piston ring set
L-339C	leak-proof chrome control piston ring set
LR-4	piston pin lock pin
MB-17F	front camshaft bearing
MB-17SF	split ream front camshaft bearing
MB-18F	center camshaft bearing
MB-18SF	split ream center camshaft bearing
MB-19F	rear camshaft bearing

MB-19SF	split ream rear camshaft bearing
MB-136F	front camshaft bearing; standard
MB-137F	center camshaft bearing; standard
MB-138F	rear camshaft bearing; standard
MBS-51	complete main bearing set
P-171NTX	piston; 3¼" diameter; 3¹¹⁄₁₆" length; all models
P-215ARX	piston; 3¼" diameter; 3¹¹⁄₁₆" length; all models
P-337AX	piston; 3¼" diameter; 3¹¹⁄₁₆" length; all models
PX-23	piston expander; U-slot pistons
SD-59	dry cylinder sleeve; cut-to-length
TU-1	water distribution tube; steel
TU-2B	water distribution tube; brass
V-1334	exhaust valve
V-1335N	intake valve
V-1581N	silichrome intake valve
VK-84	valve keeper
VS-348	valve spring
W-9226	piston pin
WB-1824	piston pin bushing

Suspension

ES-60	tie rod end; right rod; all models
ES-131	tie rod end; left rod; all models
FA-024	lower control arm; inner shaft assembly; 5 passenger
FA-029	lower knuckle support pin assembly; 7 passenger
FA-030	lower control arm shaft assembly; 7 passenger
FA-039	upper knuckle support pin assembly; 5 passenger models
FA-040S	upper control arm shaft assembly; 5 passenger
FA-042	upper knuckle support pin assembly; 7 passenger
FA-043	upper control arm shaft assembly; 7 passenger
FA-044	upper control arm inner shaft assembly; 5 passenger models
FA-045	lower knuckle support pin assembly; 5 passenger
FA-117	upper knuckle support pin; after No, 30993973 Detroit and 45021591 Los Angeles
FA-134	lower knuckle support pin; after No. 30993973 Detroit and 45021591 Los Angeles
FCS-250	front coil spring; regular; 5 passenger
FCS-258	front coil spring; heavy duty-5 passenger; regular duty-7 passenger
FCS-260	front coil spring; heavy duty; 7 passenger
FN-8	left and/or right steering knuckle support; 5 passenger
HB-779	shock absorber bushing; standard-all models; lower oversize bushing-all models
HB-947	upper shock absorber bushing; oversize; all models
KA-16	king bolt set; 5 passenger models

KA-135	king bolt set; 7 passenger models
M-634	upper front coil spacer; 5 passenger models
M-683	upper front coil silencer; 5 passenger models; upper and lower-7 passenger models
M-684	lower front coil silencer; 5 passenger
SK-34	rear spring shackle kit; all models

Additional

DV-3H	high temperature (180 F) thermostat; all models
DV-5	low temperature (160 F) thermostat; all models
MA-10R	water pump seal kit
PA-117R	water pump repair kit
PC-11	factory duplicate type water pump
PC-11R	water pump; complete
PY-17	water pump pulley

Merit—Exhaust Clamps, Pipes and Mufflers

Merit Mufflers provided anti-rust protection with hot gases going to every inner chamber. Every chamber was at a temperature above 212 degrees F and there were no corrosive moisture collecting areas. Heavier and thicker outer shells were crimped with a double-locked seam to provide low back pressure with maximum silencing. Merit was located in Toledo, Ohio.

742	muffler; 6 cylinder
80225	tail pipe; 6 cylinder; excludes convertible, 7 passenger sedan and limousine
BR-21	front muffler clamp; all models
BR-22	rear muffler clamp; all models
BR-30	front tail pipe bracket; all models
BR-31	rear tail pipe bracket; all models
C 134	muffler rear clamp
C 200	muffler front clamp

Metro Auto Electric—Generators

Metro Auto Electric Inc. supplied rebuilt original Auto-Lite, Ford, Delco-Remy and North-East generators for passenger cars and trucks from the 1920s through the 1950s. Metro was located in Detroit, Michigan.

GA-32	rebuilt generator to replace Auto-Lite GDZ-4801 generator

Michigan Engine Bearings—Engine and Camshaft Bearings

Michigan Engine Bearings produced by the Detroit Aluminum and Brass Corporation (DAB) advertised their replacement service bearings as having original equipment quality. DAB was a supplier of original equipment bearings to the automotive industry starting in 1925 and produced replacement bearings with the exact same standards and precise tolerances as the bearings produced for original equipment. The company was located in Detroit, Michigan.

14-CS	camshaft bearing No. 1; all models; replaces MoPar 632 465
15-CS	camshaft bearing No. 2; all models: replaces MoPar 632 466
16-CS	camshaft bearing No. 3; all models; replaces MoPar 632 467
86-CS	camshaft bearing set; all models
315	engine main bearing set; all models
15098	connecting rod bearing; 6 required
15099	main engine bearing No. 1
15100	main engine bearing No. 2 and/or No. 3
15101	main engine bearing No. 4
SB-86 CS	camshaft bearing set; all models
SB-315	main bearing set; all models
SB-5098T	connecting rod bearing; 6 pair required; all models
SB-5099	front main bearing; 1 pair required; all models
SB-5100	intermediate main bearings; 2 pair required; all models
SB-5101	rear main bearing; 1 pair required; all models

MicroTest—Axles and Gears

MicroTest produced many heavy duty foundry type parts such as gears and axles for passenger cars and trucks. They later became well known for their automatic transmission parts and repair kits. The MicroTest Gear Co. was located in Indianapolis, Indiana, and parts were sold through NAPA stores.

5-126	camshaft gear; 230engine; 38 teeth; replaces 601 757
6	axle nut; 5 passenger models
7	axle nut; 7 passenger models
8-127	crankshaft gear; 230 engine; 19 teeth; replaces 601 760
9-401	timing chain; 230 engine; 48 teeth; replaces 1075 001
78-8802	ring and pinion set (41-10); 5 passenger modes
78-8808	ring and pinion set (39-19); 5 passenger models
78-8809	ring and pinion set (43-10); 5 passenger models
78-8812	ring and pinion set (41-10); 7 passenger models
78-8813	ring and pinion set (39-9); 7 passenger models
1262	axle shaft; 5 passenger models
1286	axle shaft; 7 passenger models

Mo-Car—Starter Drives

Mo-Car starter drives were assembly-inspected and torque-tested to assure proper fit and dependable service. Each starter drive was required to meet three times the maximum original equipment specification torque or be rejected. Motor Car Parts Company (Mo-Car) was located in Kokomo, Indiana.

3-521	replacement starter drive; all models

Modac—Fan/Generator Belts and Hoses

Modac supplied quality fan/generator belts and hoses for passenger cars, trucks and tractors. Modac advertised quality, durability and accuracy of size and fit for longer belt and hose life. Radiator and heater hoses were made to duplicate originals or universal hoses could be cut to size. Modac was a member of Haywood Industries of Waynesville, North Carolina, and their belts and hoses were sold through local NAPA stores.

109	fan and generator V-belt; all models
109-H	heavy duty fan and generator V-belt; all models
706	upper radiator hose; all models
762	lower radiator hose; all models
7011	lower curved radiator hose; all models
MH-704	"cut to fit" lower curved radiator hose; all models

Molec—Armatures, Generators and Starters

Molec was advertised as the "Sign of Quality—Serving the Jobber Trade" for rebuilt starters and generators for passenger cars and trucks. Molec was located in Elkhart, Indiana.

4	rebuilt GDZ-2006, F generator armature for the GDZ-4801A, B, R generator; all models
1745	rebuilt MAW-2128 starter armature for the MAW-4041 starter; all models
5019	rebuilt MAW-4041 starter; all models
9069	rebuilt GDZ-4801A, B, R generator; all models

Monmouth—Engine, Clutch and Suspension/Chassis Replacement Parts

Monmouth advertised that "The World's Finest Replacement Parts Bear the Name of Monmouth." Monmouth produced dozens of quality parts and so the Monmouth aftermarket information has been divided into three sections: (1) engine rebuild, (2) clutch, and (3) suspension/chassis.

Engine Rebuild

CB-60	connecting rod bearing; 6 required; replaces MoPar 958-944
CB-60 M	connecting rod bearing set; 6 in the set; steel back and babbitt lined; standard and several undersized sizes; replaces factory numbers 958 944 and 1238 553
MB-0120	main engine bearing No. 1; replaces MoPar 959-966-71
MB-0121	main engine bearing No. 2 and/or No. 3; replaces 959-976
MB-0122	main engine bearing No. 4; replaces 959-981-86
MB-120 M	main bearings for position 1; not flanged; steel back and babbitt lined; standard and several undersized sizes; replaces factory numbers 959 966 to 959 971 and 1238432

MB-121 M	main bearings for position 2-3; flanged; steel back and babbitt lined; standard and several undersized sizes; replaces factory numbers 959 976 and 1238 433
MB-122 M	main bearing for position 4; not flanged; steel back and babbitt lined; standard and several undersized sizes; replaces factory numbers 959 981 to 959 986 and 1238 434
MS-101 M	main bearing set; steel back and babbitt lined; standard and several undersized sizes
SH-23	camshaft bearing; position 1; precision fit
SH-23 R	camshaft bearing; position 1; ream to fit
SH-23 R–S	camshaft bearing set; positions 1-2-3; ream to fit
SH-23 S	camshaft bearing set; positions 1-2-3; precision fit
SH-24	camshaft bearing; position 2; precision fit
SH-24 R	camshaft bearing; position 2; ream to fit
SH-25	camshaft bearing; position 3; precision fit
SH-25 R	camshaft bearing; position 3; ream to fit

Any bearing with the suffix "R" or "Semi" is resizable to standard. Any bearing without this suffix is not resizable.

Clutch

07114	flexible clutch plate; all models with 10" plate, 10 spline, 1" diameter; standard transmission
07150	flexible clutch plate; all models with 9¼" plate, 10 spline, 1¼" diameter; fluid drive
9157	rigid clutch plate; all models with 9¼" plate, 10 spline, 1¼" diameter; fluid drive
CA-952	clutch cover assembly; all models with 9¼" plate, 10 spline, 1¼" diameter; fluid drive
CA-957	clutch cover assembly; all models with 10" plate, 10 spline, 1" diameter; standard transmission
PT-771	clutch release bearing; conventional drive models without fluid drive
PT-777	clutch release bearing; conventional drive models without fluid drive
PT-800	clutch release bearing and carrier assembly; conventional drive models without fluid drive
PT-903	clutch release bearing; fluid drive models

Suspension/Chassis

1228	spring bolt bushing; rear spring fixed eye end; all models
1591	spring bolt; rear spring fixed eye end; all models
5060 L	left tie rod end for the right hand rod; all models; replaces factory number 951 303
5060 R	right tie rod end for the right hand rod; all models; replaces factory number 951 302

5131 L   left tie rod end for the left hand rod; all models; replaces factory number 951 305

5131 R   right tie rod end for the left hand rod; all models; replaces factory number 951 302

A-283   replaces king pin assembly on D24 Detroit built models after serial number 31006517 and up to serial number 31057047 and after serial number 31084245; excludes 7 passenger sedan; replaces manufacturer's king pin 626 975 within manufacturer's king pin assembly service package 947 557; also replaces king pin assembly on D24 Los Angeles built models after serial number 45022935 and up to serial number 45029117; excludes 7 passenger sedan; replaces manufacturer's king pin 626 975 within manufacturer's king pin assembly service package 947 557.

A-290   replaces king pin assembly on D24 Detroit built models up to serial number 31006517; excludes 7 passenger sedan; replaces manufacturer's king pin 626 975 within manufacturer's king pin assembly service package 933 435; also replaces king pin assembly on D24 Los Angeles built models up to serial number 45022935 excludes 7 passenger sedan; replaces manufacturer's king pin 626 975 within manufacturer's king pin assembly service package 933 435.

A-322   replaces king pin assembly on D24 7 passenger sedan; replaces manufacturer's king pin 634 036 within the manufacturer's king pin assembly service package 1311 059.

A-356   replaces king pin assembly on D24 Detroit models from serial number 3105740 to serial number 31084245; excludes 7 passenger sedan; replaces manufacturer's king pin 626 975 within the manufacturer's king pin assembly service package 1243 731; also replaces king pin assembly on D24 Los Angeles built models after serial number 45029117; excludes 7 passenger sedan; replaces manufacturer's king pin 626 975 within the manufacturer's king pin assembly service package 1243 731.

CS-14   lower control arm set; front suspension; excludes 7 passenger

CS-18   upper control arm set; front suspension; excludes 7 passenger

HB-735   shackle bushings; rear spring—shackle end

HB-779   front shock absorber pivot bushing; upper—standard size; lower—standard or oversize; all models; rear axle transverse strut bushing—7 passenger and conv. coupe

HB-850   shackle bushings; rear spring—shackle end

HB-947   front shock absorber pivot bushing; lower—oversize; all models

HB-978   rear axle transverse strut bushing; excludes 7 passenger and convertible

HS-105   complete shackle; rear spring—shackle end

K-22   upper and lower steering knuckle support pin; front suspension; excludes 7 passenger

KA-24   lower control arm—inner shaft; excludes 7 passenger sedan and limousine; 2 required

KA-29   lower support—outer (pivot pin); 7 passenger sedan and limousine; 2 required

KA-39   upper support—outer; excludes 7 passenger sedan and limousine; 2 required

KA-40   upper control arm—inner shaft; excludes 7 passenger sedan and limousine; 2 required

KA-45   lower support—outer (pivot pin); excludes 7 passenger sedan and limousine; 2 required

KB-26   lower steering knuckle support bushing; front suspension; excludes 7 passenger

KB-46   upper steering knuckle support bushing; front suspension; excludes 7 passenger

KB-47   upper control arm bushing; front suspension; excludes 7 passenger

NS-6   steering knuckle support; right or left; 2 required; 5 passenger models

SK-107 bolt and bushing kit; rear spring fixed eye end; all models

Monroe—Shock Absorbers

Monroe direct-action airplane type shock absorbers were used as standard equipment on more makes of cars after the war than any other shock absorber. Monroe shock absorbers were also standard equipment on many makes of cars for export. Replacement conversion kits were available to upgrade prewar models to the newer type shock absorbers. Monroe Equipment Co., was located in Monroe, Michigan.

1   bushing set containing 16- 10687-A bushings

10687-A   bushing; 4 required per each shock absorber

K-11148   front axle direct-action airplane type hydraulic shock absorber

K-11149   rear axle direct-action airplane type hydraulic shock absorber

KB-18167   front wheel shock absorber; all models

KB-18168   rear wheel shock absorber; all models

L-12024   rear axle super duty shock absorber

L-12066   front axle super duty shock absorber

Moog—Chassis and Suspension Replacement Parts

Moog advertised they had solved the "Excessive Looseness" problem in suspension with their new "Gusher Bearings." Gusher bearings fight friction and constantly lubricate surfaces to prevent dry metal to metal contact. Chassis parts were made to the closest tolerances in the industry. Moog Industries, Inc., was located in St. Louis, Missouri.

722   steering knuckle support; 5 passenger models

728   front coil spring; heavy duty; 5 passenger models

742   front coil spring; regular duty; 5 passenger models

1538   lower arm bumper; 5 and 7 passenger models

8302B   king bolt kit; 5 passenger models

8328B   king bolt kit; 5 and 7 passenger models

8398B   king bolt kit; factory duplicate; 7 passenger models

ES-60L	right tie rod; left tie rod end; all models
ES-60R	right tie rod; right tie rod end; all models
ES-131L	left tie rod; left tie rod end; all models
ES-131R	left tie rod; right tie rod end; all models
K-40	lower control arm; outer shaft; 7 passenger models
K-68	upper control arm; inner shaft; 5 passenger models
K-83	upper control arm; outer shaft; 7 passenger models
K-84	upper control arm; inner shaft; 7 passenger
K-90	upper arm bumper; 5 and 7 passenger models
K-91	shock absorber grommets; front and/or rear shock absorbers
K-94	upper control arm; outer shaft; 5 passenger models
K-95	lower control arm; outer shaft; 5 passenger models
K-124	lower control arm; inner shaft; 5 passenger
MS-304A	rear spring rear eye shackle
N-603	rear spring front eye bolt kit

Morse—Timing Chains

Morse specialized in the production of front-end-drive timing chains. They maintained a leadership position in the field by supplying manufacturers with chains that provided dependable operation and smooth performance. Morse engineers always searched for improvements in design and construction. Morse was located in Ithaca, New York, and Detroit, Michigan.

TC 401   6 cylinder timing chain; 48 links; all models

Monteith—Armatures, Generators and Starters

Monteith Brothers Inc. offered dependable delivery of remanufactured generators, armatures and starters for passenger cars and trucks to auto supply stores and garages across the country. The Monteith main office was located in Elkhart, Indiana, with factories in Auburn, Indiana, and Paola, Kansas.

4	generator armature; replaces GDZ-2006F armature used in the GDZ-4801A, B generator
1745	starter armature; replaces MAW-2128 armature used in the MAW-4041 starter
5019	starter; replaces MAW-4041 starter
9069	generator; replaces GDZ-4801A, B generator

Motor Master—Universal Joints

Motor Master supplied new, high quality universal joints and kits for passenger cars and light trucks. Motor Master Products Corp., was located in Defiance, Ohio.

2318-A	universal joint; front; early 1946 only; all 5 passenger models; replaces 1134 579
2387-A	universal joint; front and rear; all 7 passenger models; replaces 947 550

| MR-52 | universal joint; front, late 1946–1948; rear 1946–1948; all 5 passenger models; replaces 939-700 |
| MR-52A | universal joint kit for model MR-52; without body |

MRC—Clutch Bearings

MRC (Marlin Rockwell Corporation) produced quality ball, roller, and thrust bearings for passenger cars, trucks and industry. They were the oldest maker of ball bearings in the United States. MRC was located in Jamestown, New York.

208-CTC-1	clutch release bearing; conventional drive models without fluid drive
306-TN-334	clutch release bearing; conventional drive models without fluid drive
306-TN-342	clutch release bearing; conventional drive models without fluid drive
316-TN-332	clutch release bearing; fluid drive models

Muskegon—Piston Rings

Muskegon first started producing piston rings in 1922. Piston ring sets are specifically designed for each engine application and each ring set contains the combination of compression and oil rings that best satisfy the requirements of the engine. The Muskegon Piston Ring Company manufactured ring sets for passenger cars, trucks, buses and industrial engines and was located in Muskegon, Michigan.

BC-1304	chrome piston ring set; 230 engine; 3¼" cylinder diameter
C-1304	chrome piston ring set; 230 engine; 3¼" cylinder diameter
PS-1304	premium piston ring set; 230 engine; 3¼" cylinder diameter

National—Grease and Oil Seals

The National Motor Bearing Company provided the first complete line of replacement oil and grease seals for automobiles and light trucks. All seals were designed and manufactured to meet or exceed factory specifications. National offices were located in Redwood City, California, with manufacturing plants in California and Ohio.

5400	crankshaft rear bearing oil seal set; bolt on type; all models
5415	crankshaft rear bearing oil seal set; rope type; all models
5745	front pinion bearing oil seal; 7 passenger models
5792	front wheel inner bearing dust seal; 7 passenger models
5836	front wheel inner bearing dust seal; 5 passenger models
5851	front pinion bearing oil seal; 5 passenger models
5983	rear axle inner seal; 1946–47 models; 5 passenger models
6186	timing chain case cover oil seal and gasket; all models
6241S	rear wheel outer seal; 5 passenger models
6338	rear wheel inner seal; early 1948; 7 passenger models
6339	rear wheel inner seal; 1948; 5 passenger models

6405   crankshaft rear bearing oil seal retainer only; all models
6966S   rear wheel outer seal; 7 passenger models
10684S   transmission main shaft extension seal; all models
50061   rear wheel inner seal with spring; 1946–1947; 5 passenger models
50062   rear wheel inner seal with spring; 1946–47; 7 passenger models
50356   steering gear pitman shaft seal; all models
50746   rear wheel inner seal; late 1948; 7 passenger models
50776   rear wheel inner seal with spring; 1948; 5 passenger models

Nice—Clutch Assemblies and Bearings

Nice produced a line of clutch release bearings and clutch release assemblies for passenger cars and trucks. Nice Bearings was a Division of SKF Industries, Inc., of Philadelphia, Pennsylvania.

N-494   clutch release bearing; models with fluid drive
N-591   clutch release bearing; models with fluid drive
N-681   clutch release bearing; models with fluid drive
N-845   clutch release bearing; models without fluid drive
N-956   clutch release bearing; models without fluid drive
N-988   clutch release bearing; models with fluid drive
N-1054   clutch release bearing; models without fluid drive
N-1055   clutch release bearing; models with fluid drive
N-1070   clutch release bearing; models without fluid drive
N-1097   clutch release bearing; models without fluid drive
N-1116   clutch release bearing; models without fluid drive
N-1148   clutch release bearing; models without fluid drive
N-1150   clutch release bearing; models with fluid drive
N-1310   clutch release bearing and carrier assembly; models without fluid drive
N-1312   clutch release bearing and carrier assembly; models with fluid drive

Norwalk—Fan/Generator Belts

Norwalk was best known as an early supplier of tires and tubes for passenger cars and trucks. They also supplied a line of fan/generator belts and radiator hoses. Norwalk Tire and Rubber Co., was located in Norwalk, Connecticut.

V-31   heavy duty fan/generator V belt; all models
V-98   fan/generator V belt; all models
V-128   fan/generator V belt; all models

Nylen—Pistons

Nylen produced and supplied both aluminum and iron pistons in boxed sets with available matched piston pins for passenger cars and trucks. Nylen Products Company was located in St. Joseph, Michigan.

AD-41   piston; 3¼" diameter; 6 cylinder models

Ohio Pistons—Pistons

Ohio Piston started in 1913 and produced high grade pistons, piston pins and cylinder sleeves. Ohio was known nationwide for quality, reliability and products that were made in accordance with original equipment specifications. Ohio Piston and Pin Co., Inc., was located in Indianapolis, Indiana.

L-133 piston; 3¼" diameter and 3¹¹⁄₁₆" length; all models; aluminum alloy

L-369 piston; special ³⁄₆₄" destroked piston to compensate for head and block surface reductions; eliminates gasket problems; 3¼" diameter and 3⁴¹⁄₆₄" length; all models; aluminum alloy

L-17733 piston; 3¼" diameter and 3¹¹⁄₁₆" length; all models; aluminum alloy

P-613 piston pin; all models; .859"diameter and 2⁴⁷⁄₆₄" length; full floating type

P & D—Ignition

P&D advertised "Precision in Manufacturing … Dependability in Quality" in the production of replacement ignition parts. Every part was guaranteed to perfectly fit the ignition system for which it was intended. Only the very best grade of raw materials were used in the manufacture of P&D parts. P&D Manufacturing Co., Inc., was located in Long Island City, New York.

258	starter bushing; drive end; all models
278	generator bushing, commutator end
AU-18-21	regular contact set; all models
AU-93	distributor rotor; all models
AU-102	distributor cap; all models
AUC-114	distributor condenser; all models
DS-5	dimmer switch; all models
HR-2	horn relay; all models
SE-37X	starter brush set; all models
SE-57	generator brush set
SW-58	stoplight switch; all models
SW-60	starter switch; all models
SW-61	stoplight switch; all 1946 models
UC-1	heavy duty ignition coil; all models
UC-1S	regular duty coil; all models
VC-205	distributor vacuum chamber; all models
VR-112H	voltage regulator; all models
XAU-18-21	pre-assembled contact set; all models

Pacco—Carburetors

Pacco offered a line of tune-up kits that contained the necessary gaskets, needles and seats to rebuild passenger car and truck carburetors. Pacco engineers developed a non-magnetic seat and needle with a precision tapered tip that prevented carburetor flooding due to an accumulation of iron oxides—a common reason for needle leakage. The precision tapered tip assured accurate fuel flow that maintained proper float setting. Precision Automotive Components Company (Pacco), was located in Baldwin, Missouri.

10-04	resilient needle carburetor tune-up kit; models with BXV-3 Stromberg 1 barrel carburetor
10-106	resilient needle carburetor tune-up kit; models with BXVD-3 Stromberg 1 barrel carburetor
25-299A	Paccon resilient-tip needle and seat assembly carburetor tune-up kit; models with BXVD-3 Stromberg 1 barrel carburetor
25-330A	Paccon resilient-tip needle and seat assembly carburetor tune-up kit; models with BXV-3 Stromberg 1 barrel carburetor
501	steel needle carburetor tune-up kit; models with BXV-3 Stromberg 1 barrel carburetor
505X	steel needle carburetor tune-up kit; models with BXVD-3 Stromberg 1 barrel carburetor

Packard—Wires and Cables

Packard automotive wire and cable was known as "The Standard Wiring Equipment of the Automotive Industry" for starting, lighting and ignition. Packard Electric was a Division of General Motors and was located in Warren, Ohio.

1L-16	battery to switch cable; lead-alloy terminal; all models
1L-23	battery to switch cable; lead-alloy terminal; all models
1U-16	battery to switch cable; leaded brass terminal; all models
1U-23	battery to ground cable; leaded brass terminal; all models
440-E	ignition cable (spark plug) set without protectors; all models
440-EB	ignition cable (spark plug) set with protectors; all models
SS-19	starter switch to starter cable

Partex—Fuel Pumps

Partex produced a variety of premium remanufactured car parts for passenger cars and trucks. Partex was a member of Safeguard Automotive located in San Francisco, California.

20-120R	remanufactured starter drive; all models
588	remanufactured fuel pump; all models
9926-S	remanufactured fuel pump that may substitute for number 588

Parts Specialties (PS)—Water Pumps

Part Specialties (PS) produced remanufactured water pumps with precision care to the exact specifications and tolerances as prescribed by the original car manufacturer. They were known for quality, service, and dependability and were advertised as "The Complete Line" of water pumps. Parts Specialties was located in Detroit, Michigan.

PS-40	water pump; all models; replaces manufacturers No. 1064 705 and casting No. 865 490.

Pedrick—Piston Rings

Pedrick piston rings were advertised as superior to the competition in quality, service and performance because they featured a solid chrome coating and a patented "Heat-Shaping" manufacturing process. They also developed an "Equalizer Oil Ring" for uniform and continuous ring pressure to control oil at the cylinder wall/piston interface. Pedrick was owned by Wilkening Manufacturing Co. of Philadelphia, Pennsylvania.

A-34	"formflex" type "A" piston ring set with "equalizer" expander; chrome
E-34	"E" engineered type piston ring set
Ec-34	chrome engineered piston ring set
F-34	factory-type piston ring set
SX-34	rebore piston ring set
SXc-34	rebore chrome piston ring set

Perfect Circle—Piston Rings and Chassis/Suspension Replacement Parts

Perfect Circle started in 1921 to supply piston rings for engine repair of passenger cars and trucks. They soon became a world leader in piston ring engineering, innovation and manufacturing technology. Perfect Circle also included a variety of aftermarket parts for suspension and chassis. Perfect Circle was located in Hagerstown, Maryland, and parts were sold through NAPA Stores nationwide.

439	piston ring set; re-ring and/or re-bore; 3¼" piston diameter
539	piston ring set; steel expansion type; 3¼" piston diameter
647	piston expander set
739	piston ring set; plain type 3¼" piston diameter
8089	piston ring set; cast expansion type; 3¼" piston diameter
FS-2701	upper knuckle support pin assembly; front suspension; excludes 7 passenger
FS-2702	lower knuckle support pin assembly; front suspension; excludes 7 passenger
HB-735	rear spring shackle bushing; flat head type; all models
HB-850	rear spring shackle bushing; dome head type; all models
KA-789B	king bolt set; Detroit serial numbers through 31006517; Los Angeles numbers through 45022935
KA-879B	king bolt set; bearing type; Detroit serial numbers 31006518 through 31057047 and after 31084245; Los Angeles numbers 45022936 through 45029117; excludes 7 passenger models
KA-1480B	king bolt set; bushing type; Detroit serial numbers 31006518 through 31057047 and after 31084245; Los Angeles numbers 45022936 through 45029117; excludes 7 passenger models
SC-60	connecting rod bearing adjuster set
SM-0120	main bearing adjuster set
ST-160L	tie rod end; right outer; all models

| ST-160R | tie rod end; inner; all models |
| ST-1131 | tie rod end; left outer; all models |

Perfect Parts—Clutch Bearings, Wheel Bearings and Engine Rebuild Parts

Perfect Parts supplied quality aftermarket parts for passenger cars and trucks. They specialized in fasteners, clamps, springs and gaskets that were found in display cabinets on shelves, counters, and walls of garages and repair shops across the country. Perfect Parts, Inc., was located in New York, New York.

09074	front wheel bearing outer cone; 5 passenger models
09194	front wheel bearing outer cup; 5 passenger models
1729	front wheel bearing outer cup; 7 passenger models
1755	front wheel bearing outer cone; 7 passenger models
2523	front wheel bearing inner cup; 7 passenger models
2585	front wheel bearing inner cone; 7 passenger models
2736	rear wheel bearing inner cup; 7 passenger models
2780	rear wheel bearing inner cone; 7 passenger models
14123	front wheel bearing inner cone; 5 passenger models
14276	front wheel bearing inner cup; 5 passenger models
25821	rear wheel bearing inner cup; 5 passenger models
25877	rear wheel bearing inner cone; 5 passenger models
A-873C	clutch throwout bearing assembly; 5 passenger with fluid drive
A-874C	clutch throwout bearing assembly; 5 passenger without fluid drive
B-778	piston pin bushing; all models
CB-103	cam shaft bearing No. 1; all models
CB-104	cam shaft bearing No. 2; all models
CB-105	cam shaft bearing No. 3; all models
CB-1103	cam bearing set; all models
CS-8BR	exhaust valve seat; all models
CS-10	intake valve seat; all models
FL-1001	oil line; all models
FL-1057	flexible gas line; 1946–1947 models
FL-1083	flexible gas line; 1948 models
G-22348	water outlet gasket; all models
GR-373	oil/grease retainer; 5 passenger models
MB-1348	main bearing packing seal; all models
P-753K	clutch fork repair kit; all models
P-823	clutch fork assembly; all models
PB-5	clutch pilot bushing; all models
PP-731	piston pin; all models
PR-62	piston pin retainer; all models
R-101	valve keeper; all models
RB-118	rear spring bushing; flat type; all models
RB-241	rear spring bushing; dome type; all models

RG-103	shock absorber grommet; all models
VG-337	exhaust valve guide; all models
VG-338	intake valve guide; all models
VS-495	engine valve spring; all models

Perfection—Clutch Assemblies, Bearings and Plates

Perfection produced a line of clutch sets, plates, bearings and assemblies for the D24 fluid drive, standard transmission 10" clutch and standard transmission heavy duty 11" clutch models. They produced silent timing chains and matching sprockets for most cars and trucks that had the timing chain located in the front of the engine. The Perfection Gear Company was located in Harvey, Illinois.

161	complete fluid drive assembly
CA-929	clutch cover assembly; models without fluid drive and 11" clutch; police and taxi
CA-938	clutch cover assembly; models without fluid drive and 10" clutch
CA-952	clutch cover assembly; models with fluid drive
CA-957	clutch cover assembly; models without fluid drive and 10" clutch
CF-354	dual flex clutch plate; models without fluid drive and 10" clutch
CF-355	dual flex clutch plate; models without fluid drive and 11" clutch; police and taxi
CF-381	dual flex clutch plate; models with fluid drive
P-507	clutch set; models with fluid drive
P-509	clutch set; models without fluid drive and 10" clutch
ST-286	pilot bushing; models without fluid drive and 10" or 11" clutch
ST-653	torque shaft pivot bearing; models with fluid drive
ST-771	clutch release bearing; models without fluid drive and 10" or 11" clutch
ST-782	clutch release bearing pull-back spring; models without fluid drive and 10" clutch
ST-821A	clutch fork assembly; models with fluid drive and models without fluid drive
ST-831	clutch release bearing; models with fluid drive
ST-831S	clutch release bearing and carrier assembly; models with fluid drive
ST-873	clutch release bearing, carrier assembly and spring; models without fluid drive and 10" clutch
ST-882	front pilot bushing; models with fluid drive
ST-883	rear pilot bushing; models with fluid drive
ST-1310C	clutch release bearing and assembly; models without fluid drive and 10" or 11" clutch
ST-1312C	clutch release bearing and assembly; models with fluid drive

Permite—Engine Bearings and Pistons

Permite advertised and produced a complete line of engine, chassis and exhaust replacement parts. They also produced a long-lasting line of ready mixed aluminum paints that used pure aluminum as the paint pigment. Permite was the brand name for Aluminum Industries, Inc., located in Cincinnati, Ohio.

801-P	piston; 3¼" diameter; all models
1009	piston; 3¼" diameter; all models
1009-P	piston; 3¼" diameter; all models
1012	piston; 3¼" diameter; all models
1012-P	piston; 3¼" diameter; all models
PP-8010	factory duplicate type water pump; all models
S-5097	connecting rod bearing; 6 required
S-5100	main engine bearing No. 1
S-5102	main engine bearing No. 2 and/or No. 3
S-5104	main engine bearing No. 4

Pick—Brake Shoes

Pick re-manufactured brake shoes provide long life and effective stopping power under all driving conditions. Exchange shoes are tested with the same dies used in making new shoes and every bonded lining is checked under hydraulic pressure before grinding to perfect fit specifications. The Pick Manufacturing Co. was located in West Bend, Wisconsin

817-E	front or rear brake set; bonded "green dot" (heavy duty service brakes); front BLMA or FMS number 192-44 or rear BLMA or FMS number 1161-44; all 5 passenger models
817F-B	front brake set; bonded "red dot" (regular service brakes); BLMA or FMS number 192-44; all 5 passenger models
817F-PE	front brake set; bonded "blue dot" (multi-stop service brakes); BLMA or FMS number192-44; all 5 passenger models
817R-B	rear brake set; bonded "red dot" (regular service brakes); BLMA or FMS number 1161-44; all 5 passenger models
817R-PE	rear brake set; bonded "blue dot" (multi-stop service brakes); BLMA or FMS number 1161-44; all 5 passenger models
818-B	front or rear brake set; bonded "red dot" (regular service brakes); BLMA or FMS number 1105-45; all 7 passenger models
818-E	front or rear brake set; bonded "green dot" (heavy duty service brakes); BLMA or FMS number 1105-45; all 7 passenger models
818-PE	front or rear brake set; bonded "blue dot" (multi-stop service brakes); BLMA or FMS number 1105-45; all 7 passenger models

Pierce—Fuel Pumps

The Pierce Company started producing quality automotive products in 1913. New, leak tested and flow tested mechanical fuel pumps were a company specialty. Pierce was located in Upland, Indiana.

588	fuel pump; all models with single diaphragm pumps

Pilot—Master Cylinders, Wheel Cylinders, Universal Joints and Universal Joint Repair Kits

Pilot produced complete wheel cylinder and master cylinder assemblies for quick dependable and secure replacement for most passenger cars and trucks. Individual repair parts were also available in bulk on shelf and counter displays for garage or customer rebuild of cylinders. Brake hose and stop light switches were also available as well as universal joint assemblies and repair kits. Pilot was the trade name for the Motive Equipment Manufacturers, Inc. of Chicago.

18 P	master cylinder repair kit
91	wheel cylinder repair kit; front or rear; right or left
91 S	wheel cylinder repair kit; front or rear; right or left
3241	master cylinder assembly
5550	stoplight switch
10304	rear wheel brake hose
10580	wheel cylinder assembly; front; upper; left side
10581	wheel cylinder assembly; front; upper; right side
10582	wheel cylinder assembly; front; lower; left side
10583	wheel cylinder assembly; front; lower; right side
10588	wheel cylinder assembly; rear; right or left side
11110	front wheel brake hose
11352R	universal joint repair kit without body; substitutes for 11360 R or 11355 R; includes early 1946-front; late 1946–1948 front and rear; excludes 7 passenger sedan and limousine
11355R	universal joint repair kit; front; Detroit ball and roller bearing type; body included; early 1946; excludes 7 passenger sedan and limousine
11360R	universal joint repair kit; front and rear; Detroit ball and roller bearing type; body included; late 1946–1948; excludes 7 passenger sedan and limousine
17220	universal joint repair kit; rear; Detroit cross and bearing type; bearing straps included; excludes 7 passenger sedan and limousine
17227	replacement number for 17220
17228	universal joint repair kit; front and rear; Detroit cross and bearing type; bearing straps included; 7 passenger sedan and limousine

Powell—Exhaust Mufflers and Pipes

Powell advertised as "Built Stronger to Last Longer" and "The Most Complete Line in the Exhaust System Parts Field." They produced mufflers, exhaust pipes and tail pipes for most cars and trucks. Powell was located in Chicago, Illinois.

30-A	muffler; 5 passenger models; excludes conv. coupe and 7 passenger models; replaces MoPar 676-955
EE-192	exhaust pipe; 5 passenger models; excludes conv. coupe and 7 passenger models; replaces MoPar 958-122
TT-226	tail pipe; 5 passenger models; excludes conv. coupe and 7 passenger models; replaces MoPar 1122-759

Pratt—Exhaust Mufflers and Pipes

Pratt produced an aftermarket line of "Spiral" mufflers that were advertised as "Built Like a Cannon, Not Like a Stovepipe." They produced quality mufflers, tail pipes, exhaust pipes, and clamps. Pratt industries, Inc., was located in Frankfort, New York.

30-RR   muffler; 5 passenger models; excludes conv. coupe and 7 passenger models; replaces MoPar 676-955

E30-8   exhaust pipe; 5 passenger models; excludes conv. coupe and 7 passenger models; replaces MoPar 958-122

T30-11   tail pipe; 5 passenger models; excludes conv. coupe and 7 passenger models; replaces MoPar 1122-759

Purolator—Oil Filters

Purolator developed the "Micronic" filter that removed particles that were measured in microns and was advertised as the "World's Finest Filter." Filters were waterproof, warp-proof and unaffected by engine temperature. Purolator Products, Inc., was located in Rahway, New Jersey.

P-70   replacement oil filter; all models; replaces 1121 694

P-70FF   replacement oil filter; all models; replaces 1121 694

Quality Service Parts—Ignition and Electrical Replacement Parts

4258	starter bushing—drive end
4259	starter bushing—commutator end
4278	generator bushing—commutator end
5550	stop light switch (Wagner original number)
AL 30	regular quality point set
AL 522	regular quality distributor condenser
AL 923	distributor rotor
AL 930	distributor cap
AL 1030	heavy duty point set
AL 1030MV	heavy duty matched and ventilated point set
AL 1030VT	heavy duty ventilated point set
AL 1522	heavy duty distributor condenser
C 807	coil
C 809	universal application coil
EX 18	starter brush set
EX 37	starter brush set for MAW starter
EX 45	generator brush set
EX 46	generator brush set for use on GEG-4823A and GEG-4823B generators
EX 46M	generator brush set for use with GGJ generators
EX 57	generator brush set for use with GGU generators

F 4804	stop light switch
HR 604	4 terminal horn relay
TK 109	tune-up kit
UDS 400	universal dimmer switch
UDS 408	dimmer switch
VR 662	voltage regulator for use on GEG-4823A and GEG-4823B generators
VR 665	voltage regulator (excludes GEG-4823A and GEG-4823B generators)

Ramco—Piston Rings

Ramco engineered and developed chrome and molybdenum piston rings that seated fast, reduced blow-by, delivered more horsepower, reduced cylinder-wall drag, lasted longer and provided greater reliability. Ramco advertised the "Harmonized" piston ring sets that were designed, engineered and tested to work together in perfect harmony. Ring sets were available for passenger cars, trucks, agriculture, industry and marine engines. Ramsey Corporation was located in St. Louis, Missouri.

1195	non-chrome piston rings; re-ring and re-bore set; all models with 3¼" pistons
1195-H	chrome piston rings; re-ring and re-bore set; all models with 3¼" pistons
1195-M	molybdenum filled compression rings; re-ring and re-bore set; all models with 3¼" pistons
SDR-331	groove spacer used for standard to .060"; for sets 1195, 1195-H, 1195-M; all models
SRD-325	groove spacer used for standard to .040"; for sets 1195, 1195-H, 1195-M; all models

Raybestos—Brake Shoes, Brake Cylinders and Cylinder Repair Kits

Raybestos was best known for aftermarket replacement clutch and brake sets. Brakes were made from quality ingredients and molded under tremendous heat and pressure on exclusive Raybestos equipment. Raybestos brakes were engineered with the exclusive "Drop Center Warp" that assured a uniform flat surface for long wear, non-fade and safe performance. Brake boxes were often marked with the letters "PG" (Proving Ground Tested) or "WM" (Wire Molded). Raybestos was located in Bridgeport, Connecticut.

112	front and/or rear wheel brake cylinder repair kit; all models
143	master cylinder repair kit; all models
192-44PGP	front axle relined brake shoe set; 5 passenger models
201	front wheel brake cylinder overhaul repair kit; all models
202	rear wheel brake cylinder overhaul repair kit; all models
1105-45PGP	front and/or rear axle relined brake shoe set; 7 passenger models

1161-44PGP	rear axle relined brake shoe set; 5 passenger models
3241	master cylinder; all models
5550	stop light switch; all models
10304	rear wheel brake hose; all models
10580	left front wheel upper brake cylinder; all models
10581	right front wheel upper brake cylinder; all models
10582	left front wheel lower brake cylinder; all models
10583	right front wheel lower brake cylinder; all models
10588	rear wheel brake cylinder; right and/or left; all models
10595	front wheel hydraulic brake hose; right and/or left; all models
PG-192A	front axle brake shoe set; 5 passenger models
PG-1105AD	front axle brake shoe set; 7 passenger models
PG-1161AD	rear axle brake shoe set; 5 passenger models
PG-1179D	rear axle brake shoe set; 7 passenger models
RL-993A	clutch facing; all models
V-560	fan/generator belt; replaces 1117 603; all models
WM-192AD	front axle brake shoe set; 5 passenger
WM-1161AD	rear axle brake shoe set; 5 passenger

Rayloc—Brake Shoes, Clutch Assemblies, Fuel, Oil and Water Pumps

Rayloc started rebuilding automobile parts in 1931 and soon expanded into a company that rebuilt dozens of different parts for passenger cars and trucks. Rayloc was located in Hancock, Maryland, and rebuilt products were sold through NAPA stores nationwide.

0922	connecting rod; cylinders 2,4,6
41-9100	rebuilt oil pump; all models
588	fuel pump; single; rebuilt; all models
922	connecting rod; cylinders 1,3,5
4588	fuel pump; single; new; all models
B-44	brake shoe set (4 pieces); front and/or rear axle 11" drum; F.M.S.I. No. 192-44 or 1161-44; 5 passenger models
B-45	brake shoe set (4 pieces); front and/or rear axle 12" drum; F.M.S.I. No. 1105-45; 7 passenger models
B-314	emergency brake; all models; 6" × 2" × ³⁄₁₆".
CA-938	clutch cover assembly; all with 10" clutch standard drive;
CA-952	clutch cover assembly; all with fluid drive transmission
FP-38	fuel pump repair kit; diaphragm service kit
FP-99	fuel pump repair kit; kit contains rocker arm
W-53	water pump; all models

ReNu—Fuel Pumps

ReNu supplied a line of remanufactured fuel pumps for passenger cars and trucks. ReNu was a division of Maremont Products, Chicago, Illinois.

| 77-0588 | remanufactured, glass bowl, fuel pump; all models |
| 77-9926 | remanufactured, metal bowl, fuel pump; all models |

Republic Automotive—Timing Chains, Universal Joints and Universal Joint Repair Kits

Republic automotive timing chains were known to be long lasting, silent and easily installed. Simple design and construction allows the chain to operate in either direction on the sprockets, and there is no front or reverse side. Republic also produced a complete line of high quality Detroit, Spicer and Cleveland type universal joints for passenger cars and trucks. Republic was located in Detroit, Michigan.

AD-5200	universal joint with body; early 1946
AD-5200	universal joint without body; early 1946
AD-5200 AR	front and/or rear universal joint repair kit (body not included); 1947–1948
AD-5200 R	front and/or rear universal joint with body included; 1947–1948
AD-5500 AR	front universal joint repair kit (body not included) 1946
AD-5500 R	front universal joint with body included;1946
CB-7225	front and/or rear universal joint for 1946–1948; 7 passenger sedan and limousine; a discontinued number—replaced by CB-72625-2
CB-72525-3	front and/or rear universal joint for 1946–1948; 7 passenger sedan and limousine; a discontinued number—replaced by CB-72625-2
CB-72625-2	front and/or rear universal joint for 1946–1948; 7 passenger sedan and limousine
CB-83254	rear universal joint; 1946
CB-83254-A	rear universal joint; 1946 (includes bearing caps, screws, and lock washers)
R-401	timing chain; 230 engine; 48 links; replaces 1075 001 or 601 765
RS-126	camshaft gear; 230 engine; 38 teeth; replaces 601 757
T-127	crankshaft gear; 230 engine; 19 teeth; replaces 601 760

Robertshaw—Thermostats

Frederick W. Robertshaw invented the thermostat in 1899 and soon after founded a manufacturing company that produced specialty application thermostats for temperature control for auto, home and industry. Robertshaw automobile and truck thermostat boxes may also have the names Autostat, Fulton or Fulton-Sylphon printed on the box (see Autostat introduction). Robertshaw was located in Knoxville, Tennessee.

| 97-160 | low temperature (160°F) thermostat; all models |
| 97-180 | low temperature (180°F) thermostat; all models |

Rusco—Brakes Shoes and Fan/Generator Belts

The Russell Manufacturing Company (Rusco) produced brake linings treated with a special compound that was unaffected by water. Brake advertisements boasted

"It holds in wet weather just as well as in dry." Brakes also resisted heat, oil, dirt and wear. Clutch facings and fan/generator belts were also major products of the company. Rusco was located in Middletown, Connecticut.

139	heavy duty fan/generator V belt; all models
148	heavy duty fan/generator V belt; all models
158	fan/generator V belt; all models
192A	front wheel brake set; 5 passenger models
536	fan/generator V belt; all models
585	fan/generator V belt; all models
1105	front wheel brake set; 7 passenger models
1161A	rear wheel brake set; 5 passenger models; can be substituted by 192A
1179	rear wheel brake set; 7 passenger models; can be substituted by 1105

Sachs—Clutch, Water Pumps

Every Sachs clutch cover assembly was carefully rebuilt and balanced to exacting factory standards using the same balancing machine employed in this process by Chrysler and many other well-known manufacturers. Perfect static and dynamic balance was obtained that removed vibration, bearing wear and poor clutch performance. Sachs supplied rebuilt water pumps for passenger cars, trucks, tractors and industries. All water pumps were vacuum tested to locate the smallest of cracks in the housing. Sachs used the highest quality bearings, gaskets and washers in the rebuilding process and finished all pumps in their "Natural Casting Color." Sachs Automotive Products Company was located in Chicago, Illinois.

BU-2501	balanced CF 354 IW clutch plate and CA 957 pressure plate; 10" clutch models without fluid drive
BU-2502	balanced CF 381 IW clutch plate and CA 952 pressure plate; models with fluid drive
BU-2504	balanced CF 361 IW clutch plate and CA 926 pressure plate; 9¼" clutch models without fluid drive
CA-926	clutch cover assembly; models without fluid drive; 9¼" clutch
CA-952	clutch cover assembly; models with fluid drive
CA-957	clutch cover assembly; models without fluid drive; 10" clutch
CF-354	clutch plate; 10" clutch models without fluid drive
CF-361	clutch plate; 9¼" clutch models without fluid drive
CF-381	clutch plate; models with fluid drive
W1601	rebuilt water pump; all models

Safeguard—Fuel Pumps

Safeguard produced fuel pumps having strength, dependability, ruggedness and the highest standards of workmanship. Fuel pumps were new, not rebuilt, of the best quality, thoroughly tested and fully warranted. Safeguard Automotive Corp., was located in San Francisco, California.

9926	fuel pump; all models; replaces manufacturers number 1523 647

Scandinavia—Brake, Clutch Lining

Scandinavia produced riveted and bonded brake lining sets for passenger cars and trucks. They advertised their brakes as "For Better and Safer Braking." Clutch facings were also produced for most popular cars and trucks. The Scandinavian Belting Company was located in Newark, New Jersey.

192	bonded brake set; 11" brake drum; front axle; 4 pieces; 5 passenger models
192AD	brake set; 11" brake drum; front axle; 4 pieces; 5 passenger models
192AD-1161AD	brake set; 11" brake drum; 192AD front axle—4 pieces; 1161AD rear axle—4 pieces; 5 passenger models
993A	clutch facing; fluid drive models; 5 and 7 passenger; 9¼" outside diameter and 6" inside diameter
1008A	clutch facing; standard drive; 10"outside diameter and 7" inside diameter
1105	bonded brake shoe set; 12" brake drum; 4 pieces; 7 passenger models
1105AD	brake set; front axle; 12" brake drum; 4 pieces; 7 passenger models
1105AD-1179D	brake set; 12" brake drum; 1105AD front axle—4 pieces; 1179D rear axle—4 pieces; 7 passenger models
1161	bonded brake shoe set; 11" brake drum; 4 pieces; 5 passenger models
1161AD	brake set; 11" brake drum; rear axle—4 pieces; 5 passenger models
1179	bonded brake set; 12" brake drum; 4 pieces; 7 passenger models
1179D	brake set; 12" brake drum; rear axle—4 pieces ; 7 passenger models

Sealed Power—Piston Rings

Sealed Power supplied standard conventional oil rings in their piston ring sets and their newly developed steel "Full-Flow" oil ring. Boxes with an "X" added to the part number featured oil rings of constant spring tension, longer life and greater oil flow. Sealed Power operated one of the finest facilities in the piston ring industry and they were located in Muskegon, Michigan.

453	factory type piston ring set with cast iron oil rings for Canadian models with 3⅜" cylinder diameter
589	expander type piston ring set with cast iron oil rings; recommended as a re-bore set or re-sleeve set; 3¼" cylinder diameter
589X	expander type piston ring set with steel oil rings; recommended as a re-ring set; 3¼" cylinder diameter
709	conventional type piston ring set; 3¼" cylinder diameter

771   conventional type piston ring set for Canadian models with; 3⅜" cylinder diameter

932   expander type piston ring set with cast iron oil rings; recommended as a re-bore or re-sleeve for Canadian models with; 3⅜" cylinder diameter

Shurhit—Ignition and Electrical Replacement Parts

Shurhit advertised itself as the "Manufacturer of the World's Finest Automotive Ignition." Careful attention to detail was followed in every step of the production process for repair and replacement parts. Parts were guaranteed to give satisfactory service and dependability. Shurhit Products, Inc., was located in Waukegan, Illinois.

81	regular point set
82	contact point set that may substitute for regular point set
191	starter brush set
260	generator brush set
A-81	assembled point set
A-82	assembled point set that may substitute for A-81 assembled point set
BB-1	generator bushing; drive end
C-123	distributor cap
D-103	distributor rotor
DB-70	distributor bushing
DL-10	distributor lead; 2"
DL-13	distributor lead; 1¹⁵⁄₁₆"
DL-30	distributor primary lead; 1⅞"
DS-38	dimmer switch
E-5	ignition coil
E-5H	heavy duty ignition coil
G-87	distributor condenser
G-122	distributor condenser
GB-78	generator bushing; commutator end
MB-13	coil bracket
NE-16R	starter Bendix spring
PB-4	push button start switch
R-118	voltage regulator; 6 volt; 35-45 Amps; positive ground
R-118TT	voltage regulator
R-160	horn relay
S-57	starter switch solenoid
S-130	headlight switch
S-193	stoplight switch
SB-58	starter bushing; drive end
SB-59	starter bushing; commutator end
SB-64	starter bushing; drive end
V-101	vacuum control
X-191	starter brush set
X-260	generator brush set

Silv-O-Lite—Pistons

United Engine and Machine Company has been manufacturing aftermarket pistons for cars and trucks under the Silv-O-Lite trademark since 1922. Pistons were produced to exact tolerances using alloy aluminum to assure tighter piston to cylinder wall clearances and longer piston life. Silv-O-Lite was located in San Leandro, California.

1203	piston; 3¼" diameter; all models
1204	piston; 3¼" diameter; all models
1213	piston; 3¼" diameter; all models
1225	piston; 3¼" diameter; all models
1280	piston; 3¼" diameter; all models

Sorensen—Ignition and Electrical Replacement Parts

The P. Sorensen Manufacturing Company was founded in 1900 and nearly a half-century later they supplied D24 Dodge owners with replacement parts that were designed to be the highest quality duplication of original equipment design and specifications.

Sorensen products represented the best of research, development and manufacturing experience available in the aftermarket industry. Parts were designed to be heat, moisture and vibration proof. Sorensen was located in Glasgow, Kentucky.

588	fuel pump; all models
652-M	weatherproof type spark plug cable set
652-R	glass core weatherproof type spark plug cable set
653	regular type spark plug cable set
A-43	distributor condenser
A-55	distributor condenser
A-56	distributor condenser
AL-15	contact set arm
AL-15-17	contact set
AL-15-17H	contact set; heavy duty
AL-16-22M	assembled and matched contact set
AL-16-22MX	"cross-cut" heavy duty contact set
AL-17	contact set bar
AL-64	distributor rotor
AL-99	distributor cap
AL-225	upper brake plate assembly
AL-503	dimmer switch
DJ-1	door jamb switch
DR-502N	dimmer switch used to replace AL-503
FL-15	distributor ground lead; 1¹⁵⁄₁₆" length
FL-181	distributor primary lead; 1⅞" length
HR-3	horn relay; 4-terminal relay
HR-4	horn relay used to replace HR-3
LL-18-1	starter switch to starter cable

PB-5	starter push button switch
PL-1	pillar switch
SC-4	coil
SC-5X	heavy duty coil
SS-4	starter switch
SS-9R	starter drive spring
SW-9	stoplight switch
VR-66	voltage regulator
W-16-1	battery to switch cable
W-23-1	battery to ground cable
X-4258	starter bushing; drive end
X-4259	starter bushing; commutator end
X-4270	distributor bushing; upper and/or lower
X-4278	generator bushing; commutator end
XE-37S	starter brush set
XE-45	generator brush set

Soundmaster—Exhaust Clamps, Pipes and Mufflers

Soundmaster advertised mufflers that "Have What It Takes" for power, silence and endurance. Mufflers had extra large internal gas flow tubes covered with a specialized welded shell construction. Non-corrosive materials were used throughout. Soundmaster was located in Racine, Wisconsin, and mufflers were sold through NAPA stores nationwide.

156	muffler; excludes 7 passenger
2034	outlet clamp; original type; excludes 7 passenger
2035	inlet clamp; original type; excludes 7 passenger
4073	outlet clamp; U-type; excludes 7 passenger
4075	inlet clamp; U-type; excludes 7 passenger
4414	tail pipe; excludes 7 passenger and convertible
4549	tail pipe; convertible
5334	exhaust pipe; excludes 7 passenger and convertible

Springfield Electrical Specialties—Ignition

Springfield Electrical Specialties, Inc. (SES) manufactured limited, but superior quality ignition replacement parts for cars and light trucks. They supplied a line of "Superseal" condensers that resisted moisture accumulation, and a line of "Superpoint" tungsten contact points that provided perfect alignment. Points and condensers were inspected and tested at every stage of manufacture. SES was located in New York, New York.

30	regular duty ignition contact set
AL-15	ignition condenser
HD-30	heavy duty ignition contact set

Standard—Thermostats

Standard thermostats were of all metal construction and were not affected by antifreeze solutions. Thermostats were of simple, accurate and dependable design that gave better performance and longer life. Standard thermostats were ideal for pressurized cooling systems. Standard Motor Products, Inc., was located in Long Island City, New York.

16	standard temperature thermostat
16-HT	high temperature thermostat

Standard/Blue Streak—Ignition and Electrical Replacement Parts

Standard was advertised in aftermarket catalogs as "The World's Leading Manufacturer of Tune-Up Engineered Automobile Parts." They specialized in heavy-duty ignition parts, automobile wire and cable and "Jiffy-Kits" for carburetor tune-ups. Standard Motor Products, Inc., was located in Long Island City, New York.

4264	starter bushing—drive end
4278	generator bushing—commutator end
AL-3J	standard ignition coil
AL-50	breaker point arm
AL-50X	breaker point arm
AL-57	stationary contact point
AL-57X	stationary contact point
AL-96	distributor cap
AL-98	rotor
AL-101	condenser
AL-101X	condenser
AL-5057	breaker point set
AL-5057X	breaker point set
BX-9R	starter drive spring
DS-47	dimmer switch
DS-47X	dimmer switch
E-37	starter brush (needs 2)
E-37X	starter brush (needs 2)
E-38	starter brush (needs 2)
E-38X	starter brush (needs 2)
E-45	generator main brush (needs 2) excludes generators GCB-4802A,B or GEB-4801A
E-46	generator main brush if generator GCB-4802A,B or GEB-4801A is used (needs 2)
EX-37	starter brush set
EX-38	starter brush (needs 2)
EX-45	generator brush set, excludes generators GCB-4802A,B or GEB-4801A

EX-46	generator brush set if generator GCB-4802A,B or GEB-4801A is used
HR-114	horn relay
SLS-27	stop light switch
SS-549	starter switch
UC-500R	ignition coil (heavy duty)
VR-313	voltage regulator; positive ground; for GEB-4801A generator
VR-313X	voltage regulator; positive ground; for GEB-4801A generator
VR-322	voltage regulator; positive ground; excludes generator GEB-4801A
VR-322X	voltage regulator; positive ground; excludes GEB-4801A generator
X-4264	starter bushing—drive end
X-4278	generator bushing—commutator end

Stant—Thermostats, Gas, Oil and Radiator Caps

Stant was advertised as the "Recognized Standard of the Industry" in the production of radiator, gas and oil filler/breather caps. Stant developed the "Lev-R-Vent" safety pressure cap that eliminates burn hazard by releasing steam pressure through the overflow tube. Stant Manufacturing Company was located in Connersville, Indiana.

G-20	stainless steel gas cap; all models
G-70	stainless steel locking gas cap; all models
GW-50	locking gas cap; all models
R-3	standard under hood radiator cap; all models
S-97	low temperature (160°F) thermostat; 1946–1948; all models
S-97H	low temperature (180°F) thermostat; 1946–1948; all models
SO-69	oil filler/breather cap; all models

Sterling—Thermostats

Sterling produced thermostats, gaskets, hose clamps and pressure caps. Thermostats were suitable for winter driving with permanent antifreeze. Sterling was made by Carol Cable Company of Pawtucket, Rhode Island.

35-S	low temperature (160 degree F) thermostat; all models
35-H	low temperature (180 degree F) thermostat; all models

Sterling Products—Pistons

Sterling provided replacement pistons in single piston boxes or boxed sets of matched pistons for a complete engine overhaul. Sterling Aluminum Products, Inc., was located in St. Charles and St. Louis, Missouri.

37-P	piston; 3¼" diameter; 6 cylinder models
134-P	piston; 3¼" diameter; 6 cylinder models
1000-P	piston; 3¼" diameter; 6 cylinder models

Stromberg—Carburetor and Carburetor Repair Kit

Stromberg produced carburetors for passenger cars, light trucks and industrial engines. The single barrel, downdraft, float-type BXV-3 and BXVD-3 carburetors provided the exact amount of atomized fuel air mixture for the Dodge 230 engine. Stromberg was a member of the Bendix Corporation that was located in South Bend, Indiana.

384956	float and needle seat for BXV-3 carburetor
385100	piston pump for BXV-3 and/or BXVD-3 carburetor
BXV-3	Stromberg carburetor; all models without fluid drive
BXVD-3	Stromberg carburetor; all models with fluid drive
J-5968	gasket set for BXV-3 and/or BXVD-3 carburetor
P-21918	float and needle seat for BXVD-3 carburetor
RK-131	repair kit for BXVD-3 carburetor with 3-77 code number
RK-139	repair kit for BXV-3 carburetor
RK-143	repair kit for BXVD-3 carburetor with 3-82 code number

Superior—Armatures, Generators and Starters

The Superior Manufacturing Co. used the "VMC" (ventilated, matched coils) process to produce armatures that duplicated original factory methods. VMC armatures assured better balance, greater dependability, longer life and greater output. The company was located in Scranton, Pennsylvania.

4	generator armature; replaces Auto-Lite armature GDZ 2006 in the GDZ 4801 generator
1745	starter armature; replaces Auto-Lite armature MAW 2128 in the MAX 4041 starter
3246	starter; replaces Auto-Lite MAW 4041 starter
9413	generator; replaces Auto-Lite GDZ 4801 generator
RP-4503	voltage regulator

Superior—Piston Rings

The Superior piston ring company pioneered the design and manufacture of piston rings with emphasis on engine compression and oil control. Ring sets were engineered, starting in 1920, to cover engine replacements from slightly worn to rebore and total rebuild. Superior advertised that their ring sets for re-ring purposes "cannot be excelled." Superior was located in Detroit, Michigan.

330	"steel-master" piston ring set fits 3¼" diameter pistons; designed as a re-ring set; steel compression ring in the set is designed to seal in worn grooves on the intake stroke to provide even gasoline distribution and a smoother running engine; steel oil ring is designed to scrape excess oil from worn cylinders
722	"super-flo" piston ring set; designed as a re-ring set; very effective in worn cylinders
1330	"sealzit" conventional (plain) piston ring set; suggested for rebored engines
3330	"sealzit" flexible scraper piston ring set
SF-330	"sealzit" flexible piston ring set

Thermoid—Brake Lining, Clutch Facing, Belts and Hoses

Thermoid was a diversified company that produced quality brake linings, clutch facings, hoses and belts for passenger cars and trucks. Thermoid products were used as original equipment for many of the automotive manufacturers and all replacement products were custom built and certified to match original equipment specifications. Thermoid Company was located in Trenton, New Jersey.

192 A	brake lining; front axle 11" drum (4 pieces); 5 passenger models
993 A	clutch facing (2 required); 5 and 7 passenger fluid drive models
1008 A	clutch facing (2 required); 5 and 7 passenger standard drive models
1105 A	brake lining; front axle 12" drum (4 pieces; 7 passenger models
1161 A	brake lining; rear axle 11" drum (4 pieces); 5 passenger models
1179	brake lining; rear axle 12" drum (4 pieces); 7 passenger models
CB-192A	brake lining; front axle 11" drum (4 pieces); 5 passenger models
CB-192A/1161AD	brake lining; front and rear axle 11" drum (8 pieces); 5 passenger models
CB-1105A	brake lining; front axle 12" drum (4 pieces); 7 passenger models
CB-1105A/1179D	brake lining; front and rear axle 12" drum (8 pieces); 7 passenger models
CB-1161A	brake lining; rear axle; 11" drum (4 pieces); 5 passenger models
CB-1179	brake lining; rear axle 12" drum (4 pieces); 7 passenger models
CH-1502	single molded and curved lower radiator hose substitution; all models
CH-1607	single molded and curved lower radiator hose substitution; all models
R6017	lower radiator hose; by-pass; new number; all models
R7006	upper radiator hose; new number; all models
RC-505	lower radiator hose; by-pass; old number; all models
RC-507	upper radiator hose; old number; all models
V-11	fan/generator V belt; all models
V-15	heavy duty fan/generator V belt; all models
V-122	fan/generator V belt; all models
VH-122	fan and generator belt

Thompson Products—Engine Rebuild and Suspension Replacement Parts

Thompson Products engineers worked hand-in-hand with factory engineers and made major improvements in factory original parts and replacement parts for passenger cars, trucks and the aviation industry. Thompson replacement engine and chassis parts available as aftermarket were the same precision and quality as original factory equipment. Thompson Products Inc., was located in Cleveland, Ohio.

Engine

13C	bellows type thermostat; standard 160 degrees F; all models
55	pellet type thermostat; standard 160 degrees F; all models
113C	bellows type thermostat; high temperature 180 degrees F; all models
155	bellows type thermostat; high temperature 180 degrees F; all models
AS-1689	exhaust valve; all models
CB-60G	connecting rod bearing; all models
CB-60M	connecting rod bearing; all models
CR-01205	connecting rod; numbers 2,4,6; all models
CR-1205	connecting rod; numbers 1,3,5; all models
FH-11	fan hub
G-337	exhaust valve guide; all models
G-338	intake valve guide; all models
IS-101	valve seat; all models
IS-207	valve seat; all models
L-100F	piston; 3¼" diameter; all models
L-843	piston; 3¼" diameter; all models
L-843F	piston; 3¼" diameter; all models
L-1001F	piston; 3¼" diameter; all models
L-2101F	piston; 3¼" diameter; all models
L-10001	piston; 3¼" diameter; all models
LK-83	valve spring keeper; all models
MB-120M	main engine bearing #1; all models
MB-121M	main engine bearing #2 and #3; all models
MB-122M	main engine bearing #4; all models
MS-120M	main engine bearing set; all models
P-731	piston pin; all models
PB-671	piston pin bushings; all models
S-1689	exhaust valve; all models
SH-23RS	cam bearing set; all models
SH-23S	cam bearing set; all models
SL-318F	dry cylinder sleeve
V-1690	intake valve; all models
V-1690X	intake valve; all models

VS-495	valve spring; all models
WP-953N	water pump; all models
WS-15	water pump repair kit; all models

Suspension

0345	rear spring attaching bolt; all models
10029	lower support outer pivot pin kit; 7 passenger models
10039	upper support outer pivot pin kit; 5 passenger models
10045	lower support outer pivot pin kit; 5 passenger models
10045N	lower knuckle support pin kit; 5 passenger models
10071	upper knuckle support pin kit; 7 passenger models
10072	upper knuckle support pin kit; 5 passenger models
13014A	lower control arm shaft kit; 5 passenger models
13018A	upper control arm shaft kit; 5 passenger models
13020A	lower control arm shaft kit; 7 passenger models
18253	coil spring shim spacer; 5 passenger models
18300	upper coil spring silencer—5 passenger models; upper and lower silencer—7 passenger models
18301	lower coil spring silencer—5 passenger models
DA-142	rear shock absorber; regular duty; all models
DA-143	front shock absorber; regular duty; all models
DA-342	rear shock absorber; heavy duty; all models
DA-343	front shock absorber; heavy duty; all models
ES-60L	right hand tie rod; left tie rod end; all models
ES-60R	right hand tie rod; right tie rod end; all models
ES-131L	left hand tie rod; left tie rod end; all models
ES-131R	left hand tie rod; right tie rod end; all models
HB-735	rear spring grommet; flat head; all models
HB-827	shock absorber bushing; front and/or rear; all models
HB-850	rear spring grommet; dome head; all models
HB-947	shock absorber bushing; upper; all models
HS-104N	rear spring shackle; all models
K-64	king bolt set; 5 passenger; up to Detroit 31006517 and Los Angeles up to 45022935
K-342	king bolt set; factory duplicate; 5 passenger; from Detroit 31006517 to 31057047 and after 31084245; and from Los Angeles 45022935 to 45029117
K-342E	king bolt set; optional bronze bushing; 5 passenger; from Detroit 31006517 to 31057047 and after 31084245; and from Los Angeles 45022935 to 45029117
K-361	king bolt set; factory duplicate; 7 passenger models
K-362	king bolt set; optional bronze bushings; 7 passenger models
TC-250	front coil spring; 5 passenger models
TC-258	front coil spring; 7 passenger models

Timken—Bearings

Timken, in 1899, was the first company to produce tapered roller bearings for carriages and the newly developing automobile industry. They soon became a world leader in bearings for passenger cars, trucks and railroads. All bearings were made of case-hardened shock resistant steel and stamped with the "Timken" trademark on both the cone and the cup. The Timken Roller Bearing Company was located in Canton, Ohio.

09074	front wheel bearing outer cone; 5 passenger models
09194	front wheel bearing outer cup; 5 passenger models
5BC	steering gear bearing cone; upper and lower; 5 passenger models
6A	steering gear bearing cup; upper; 5 passenger models
6C	steering gear bearing cup; lower; 5 passenger models
11BC	steering gear bearing cone; upper and lower; 7 passenger models
13	steering gear bearing cup; upper; 7 passenger models
14C	steering gear bearing cup; lower; 7 passenger models
1729	front wheel bearing outer cup; 7 passenger models
1755	front wheel bearing outer cone; 7 passenger models
2523	front wheel bearing inner cup; 7 passenger models
2585	front wheel bearing inner cone; 7 passenger models
2736	rear axle wheel bearing cup; 7 passenger models
2780	rear axle wheel bearing cone; 7 passenger models
3420	rear axle drive pinion front bearing cup; 7 passenger models
3476	rear axle drive pinion front bearing cone; 7 passenger models
3820	rear axle drive pinion rear bearing cup; 7 passenger models
3875	rear axle drive pinion rear bearing cone; 7 passenger models
14125A	front wheel bearing inner cone; 5 passenger models
14276	front wheel bearing inner cup; 5 passenger models
25520	rear axle differential side bearing cup; all models
25580	rear axle differential side bearing cone; all models
25821	rear axle wheel bearing cup; 5 passenger
25877	rear axle wheel bearing cone; 5 passenger
31520	rear axle drive pinion front and rear bearing cup; 5 passenger models
31590	rear axle drive pinion front bearing cone; 5 passenger models
31593	rear axle drive pinion rear bearing cone; 5 passenger models

Toledo Steel—Engine Rebuild and Suspension Replacement Parts

Toledo Steel advertised their parts "Make Good Engines Better." Toledo engineers kept pace with the new demands of higher speed and higher powered engines through continued research and improved manufacturing methods. The Toledo Steel Products Company was located in Cleveland, Ohio.

Engine

AS-1689	exhaust valve; all models
CB-60M	connecting rod bearing; all models
CR-01205	connecting rod; numbers 2,4,6; all models
CR-1205	connecting rod; numbers 1,3,5; all models
CS-1003	cam shaft bearing set; ream type; all models
CS-1103	cam shaft bearing set; precision type; all models
FH-11	fan hub
G-337	exhaust valve guide; all models
G-338	intake valve guide; all models
L-100F	piston; 3¼" diameter; all models
L-843	piston; 3¼" diameter; all models
L-843F	piston; 3¼" diameter; all models
L-2101F	piston; 3¼" diameter; all models
L-1001F	piston; 3¼" diameter; all models
L-10001	piston; 3¼" diameter; all models
LK-83	valve spring keeper; all models
MB-120M	main engine bearing #1; all models
MB-121M	main engine bearing #2 and #3; all models
MB-122M	main engine bearing #4; all models
MS-120M	main engine bearing set; all models
P-731	piston pin; all models
PB-671	piston pin bushings; all models
S-1689	exhaust valve; all models
V-1690	intake valve; all models
V-1690X	intake valve; all models
VS-495	valve spring; all models
WP-953N	water pump; all models
WS-15	water pump repair kit; all models

Suspension

0345	rear spring attaching bolt; all models
10029	lower knuckle support pin kit; 7 passenger models
10045N	lower knuckle support pin kit; 5 passenger models
10071	upper knuckle support pin kit; 7 passenger models
10072	upper knuckle support pin kit; 5 passenger models
13014A	lower control arm shaft kit; 5 passenger models
13018A	upper control arm shaft kit; 5 passenger models
13020A	lower control arm shaft kit; 7 passenger models
13026A	upper control arm shaft kit; 7 passenger models
15024	knuckle support; right and/or left side`
16500	lower control arm; right hand side
16501	lower control arm; left hand side

18253	coil spring shim spacer; 5 passenger models
18300	upper coil spring silencer—5 passenger models; upper and lower silencer—7 passenger models
18301	lower coil spring silencer—5 passenger models
ES-60L	right hand tie rod; left tie rod end; all models
ES-60R	right hand tie rod; right tie rod end; all models
ES-131L	left hand tie rod; left tie rod end; all models
ES-131R	left hand tie rod; right tie rod end; all models
HB-735	rear spring grommet; flat head; all models
HB-779	shock absorber bushing; lower; all models
HB-850	rear spring grommet; dome head; all models
HB-947	shock absorber bushing; upper; all models
HS-104N	rear spring shackle; all models
K-64	king bolt set; 5 passenger; up to Detroit 31006517 and Los Angeles up to 45022935
K-342	king bolt set; factory duplicate; 5 passenger; from Detroit 31006517 to 31057047 and after 31084245; and from Los Angeles 45022935 to 45029117
K-342D	king bolt set; 5 passenger; from Detroit 31057047 to 31084245; and after Los Angeles 45029117
K-342E	king bolt set; optional bronze bushing; 5 passenger; from Detroit 31006517 to 31057047 and after 31084245; and from Los Angeles 45022935 to 45029117
K-361	king bolt set; factory duplicate; 7 passenger models
K-362	king bolt set; optional bronze bushings; 7 passenger models
TC-250	front coil spring; 5 passenger models
TC-258	front coil spring; 7 passenger models

Triangle—Springs

Triangle produced and advertised "Matched Pairs" of front coil replacement springs for most passenger cars and station wagons. Triangle Auto Spring Corporation was located in DuBois, Pennsylvania.

| 250 | front coil spring; 5 passenger models; regular duty |

Triplex—Pistons

Triplex Corporation of America was known for its boxed sets of matched pistons for passenger cars and trucks. Triplex was located in Pueblo, Colorado.

TC-9	piston; 3¼" diameter; 6 cylinder models
TC-27-N	piston; 3¼" diameter; 6 cylinder models
TC-113	piston; 3¼" diameter; 6 cylinder models

Tru-Power—Carburetor Repair Kits

Tru-Power produced carburetor kits for cars, trucks, marine and small air cooled engines. Kits included the "Tru-Power Needle and Seat Assembly" that included a flexible needle that makes a tight seal at all times and prevents carburetor flooding and regulates fuel flow even when the fuel may be contaminated with iron oxides. The company was located in Ballwin, Missouri.

For the following carburetors: BXV-3 or BXVD-3 with numbers 3-82, 3-83 or 3-93

100-2	carburetor gasket set
K-501	carburetor tune-up kit
K-503	carburetor tune-up kit
K-505X	replaces K—503 tune-up kit
S25-48A	carburetor needle and seat assembly
S25-58A	carburetor needle and seat assembly
S64-84A	carburetor pump plunger

Tru-Torque—Brake Part Kits

Tru-Torque developed a special wheel cylinder spring and expander assembly that eliminated leaks and assured smooth and easy brake action. Heat resistant rubber reduced spongy pedal and fade-out. Tru-Torque was located in St. Louis, Missouri.

10590	front or rear wheel cylinder cup (1⅛")
T-077	front or rear wheel cylinder cup (1⅛")
T-093	front or rear wheel cylinder piston
TM-13504	master cylinder repair kit
TT-010 B	front or rear wheel cylinder repair kit
TT-095	wheel cylinder repair kit for four wheels
TT-095 B	wheel cylinder repair kit for four wheels including boots
TT-098	wheel cylinder repair kit for front wheels only

TRW—Engine Rebuild and Suspension Replacement Parts

TRW was advertised as the "World's Largest Independent Manufacturer of Chassis Parts." All parts were engineered and designed to improve customer safety and to meet or exceed original equipment standards. TRW also produced new aftermarket replacement engine parts for passenger cars and trucks. TRW was located in Cleveland, Ohio.

Engine

50013	oil pump; all models
55006	fuel pump all models
CB-608	connecting rod bearing; all models
G-337	exhaust valve guide; all models
G-338	intake valve guide; all models
IS-104	intake valve seat; all models
KD-8	exhaust valve seat; all models

KD-10	intake valve seat; all models
L-3056F	aluminum piston; all models
LK-83	valve spring lock; all models
MS-2523	main bearing set; all models
PB-719	piston pin bushing; .008" oversize; all models
PB-778	piston pin bushing; standard size; all models
S-2251	exhaust valve; all models
SH-23S	camshaft bearing set; all models
SL-318F	dry piston sleeve; cut to length; all models
SS-126	timing cam sprocket; all models
SS-127	timing crank sprocket; all models
T-1195	piston ring set; all models
T-1195M	piston ring set; moly; all models
TC-401	timing chain; all models
VS-495	valve springs; all models

Suspension

0345	rear spring front attaching bolt; all models
10029N	knuckle support pin kit; lower; 7 passenger models
10045N	knuckle support pin kit; lower; 5 passenger models
10071	knuckle support pin kit; upper; 7 passenger models
10072	knuckle support pin kit; upper; 5 passenger models
13014A	front control arm shaft kit; lower; 5 passenger models
13018A	front control arm shaft kit; upper; 5 passenger models
B-176	rear spring front attaching bushing; all models
DA-141	front shock absorbers; regular duty; all models
DA-142	rear shock absorber; regular duty; 5 passenger models
DA-765	rear shock absorber; regular duty—7 passenger models; heavy duty—5 passenger models
DA-964	rear shock absorber; heavy duty; 7 passenger models
ES-60L	right hand tie rod; left tie rod end; all models
ES-60R	right hand tie rod; right tie rod end; all models
ES-131L	left hand tie rod; left tie rod end; all models
ES-131R	left hand tie rod; right tie rod end; all models
HB-735	shackle bushing; early type flat head bushing; all models
HB-779	front shock absorber bushings; all models
HB-827	rear shock absorber regular bushing; regular and/or heavy duty shock absorbers; all models
HB-850	shackle bushing; late type dome head bushing; all models
HS-104N	rear spring shackle; all models
K-64	king bolt set; 5 passenger Detroit models up to 31006517; Los Angeles up to 45022935
K-342	king bolt set; 5 passenger Detroit models from 31006517 to 31057047 and after 31084245; Los Angeles models from 45022935 to 45029117

K-361	king bolt set; original type; 7 passenger models
K-362	king bolt set; optional bronze type; 7 passenger models

Tung-Sol—Auto Lamps and Flashers

Tung-Sol developed and sold the all glass, sealed beam "Vision-Aid" headlamp that made for safer, more comfortable night driving in all kinds of weather. Headlamps provided more light on the low and high beam, and greater projection distance of night light than ordinary headlamps. Low beam light was directed more to the right to reduce the amount of light toward approaching vehicles. Tung-Sol Electric Inc., was located in Newark, New Jersey.

51	turn signal indicator lamp
55	instrument lamp (one of two lamps that are used)
63	parking; tail light; license plate lamp
81	instrument lamp (one of two lamps that are used)
87	dome lamp
1129	stoplight lamp; courtesy or step light lamp
1158	directional lamp; front and/or rear
5040	headlight lamp
C-229-D8	flasher unit
P-229-D	universal flasher that may substitute for C-229-D8

Tungsten—Ignition and Electrical Replacement Parts

Tungsten started as a small laboratory in 1930 that produced tungsten discs for contact points and by 1939 was located in a 25,000 sq. ft. building that housed the manufacture of quality ignition, starter and generator replacement parts. Tungsten Contact Mfg. Co., was located in North Bergen, New Jersey.

4264	starter bearing; drive end
4270	distributor bushing
4278	generator bearing; commutator end
AGL-1	terminal connection
AGL-9	ground lead terminal
AL-18	ignition contact arm (for contact points)
AL-18H	ignition contact arm (heavy duty)
AL-21	ignition contact bar (for contact points)
AL-21H	ignition contact bar (heavy duty)
AL-97	distributor rotor
AL-97H	rotor (heavy duty)
AL-104	distributor cap
AL-104H	distributor cap (heavy duty)
AL-1821	distributor ignition contact set
AL-1821H	ignition contact set (heavy duty)
AL-2021MV	distributor point set; ventilated; heavy duty
ALC-114	distributor condenser

ALC-114H	distributor condenser (heavy duty)
DS-2	headlight dimmer switch
E-16X	starter motor brush set (2) E-16 brushes and (2) E-18 brushes
E-16-18	starter motor brushes (2) E-16 brushes and (2) E -18 brushes
E-37X	starter brush set
E-45	generator brushes (2) E-45 brushes
E-45X	generator brush set (2) E-45 brushes
E-57X	generator brush set; excludes GGJ model generator
HR-3	horn relay
SLS-22	stop light switch
SS-300	starter switch
UC-1	ignition coil; 6 volt
UC-1H	ignition coil (heavy duty); 6 volt
UC-11	regular duty coil; 6 volt
UC-11E	epoxy coil; 6 volt
UC-110H	distributor condenser
VR-30	voltage regulator
VR-34	voltage regulator; 6 volt; excludes GGJ model generator
VRF-20	voltage regulator fuse

Union—Ignition, Electrical Replacement Parts

Union specialized in aftermarket ignition repair parts for passenger cars and trucks. Parts were made with the highest quality materials and production was carefully controlled in the manufacture of standard and heavy duty replacement parts. All parts were tested before being shipped to jobbers, garages and repair shops nationwide. Union Electrical Parts Company, Inc., was located in Weehawken, New Jersey.

4258	starter bushing; drive end
4259	starter bushing; commutator end
4270	distributor bushing
4278	generator bushing; commutator end
AGL-1	distributor ground wire; 2$\frac{7}{16}$" long; all models
AL-97	distributor rotor; all models
AL-104	distributor cap; all models
AL-1821	distributor contact set; arm and bar; all models
AL-1821M	matched and assembled contact set; all models
AL-1821MV	matched, assembled and ventilated contact set; all models
ALC-114	distributor condenser; all models
DS-2	dimmer switch; all models
E-17X	starter brush set; all models
E-45X	generator brush set; GDZ generator
E-46X	generator brush set; GEG and/or GGJ generator
HR-1	horn relay; models with 3-terminal relay
HR-3	horn relay
SLS-22	stoplight switch; all models

SS-300	starter solenoid switch; all models
UC-1	ignition coil; all models
VR-34	voltage regulator; GDZ generator
VR-37	voltage regulator; GEG and/or GGJ generator
VX-105	distributor vacuum control; all models

Unit Parts (UP)—Fuel Pumps

Unit Parts Co. supplied a line of factory remanufactured fuel pumps for most U.S. automobiles, trucks and tractors. Pumps were remanufactured in accordance with original specifications, using quality component parts and available from dealers and jobbers throughout the country. Unit Parts Co. was located in Oklahoma City, Oklahoma.

| FP-588 | remanufactured fuel pump; all models |

United—Brake Parts

United Brake System supplied new and rebuilt brake parts for passenger cars and trucks nationwide through the NAPA stores. United Parts Division was located in McHenry, Illinois.

112	front and rear wheel brake cylinder repair kit; all models
201	front wheel brake cylinder repair kit; all models
202	rear wheel brake cylinder repair kit; all models
3241	brake master cylinder; all models
5550	stoplight switch; all models
10304	rear wheel hydraulic brake hose; all models
10580	front wheel brake cylinder; upper left; all models
10581	front wheel brake cylinder; upper right; all models
10582	front wheel brake cylinder; lower left; all models
10583	front wheel brake cylinder; lower right; all models
10588	rear wheel brake cylinder; right and/or left; all models
10595	front wheel hydraulic brake hose; right and/or left; all models
46421	speedometer cable; all models with fluid drive
46428	speedometer cable; all models without fluid drive
48300	speedometer cable and casing; all models
91702	emergency brake cable; all models with fluid drive
91703	emergency brake cable; all models without fluid drive

Victor—Gaskets

Victor was the largest supplier of gaskets and oil seals for use as original equipment in passenger cars, trucks and heavy equipment. Gaskets were available as single replacement envelopes or in complete sets and sold nationwide through NAPA stores. Victor Manufacturing and Gasket Co. was located in Chicago, Illinois.

| 924 | cylinder head gasket; all models |
| 1029 | cylinder head gasket; all models |

1059C	cylinder head gasket; copper; all models
1059S	cylinder head gasket; steel; all models
2066C	spark plug gasket
2125	oil pan drain plug gasket
5176BK	manifold intake and ends gasket; all models
5435-CS	exhaust pipe flange gasket
15017	one piece manifold gasket; all models
17186	intake to exhaust manifold gasket
17371	manifold to carburetor gasket
17917	oil pressure relief valve gasket
18005	manifold center gasket; all models
22348	water outlet gasket
24210	oil pump body gasket
24315	water pump by-pass elbow gasket
24384	fuel pump mounting gasket
24456	valve spring cover stud nut gasket
24503	universal joint housing gasket
24579	crankshaft rear main bearing oil seal gasket
24822	steering gear cover shim gasket
24972	oil pump cover gasket
25229	transmission drive pinion retention gasket; models with fluid drive
25238	chain cover oil seal gasket
25845	water pump body to cylinder block gasket
26239	air cleaner to carburetor gasket
26251	transmission case cover gasket
27055	water pump body cover plate gasket
27343	transmission extension case gasket
27453	transmission case to clutch housing gasket
27590	timing case gasket; up to engine 79100
27662	differential carrier gasket; 5 passenger
27748	timing case gasket; after engine 79100
35743	oil pan front and rear gasket
36054	valve spring cover gasket
45205	thermostat gasket
45208	rear main bearing cap oil seal gasket; right
45209	rear main bearing cap oil seal gasket; left
45237	oil pan front end plate gasket
45251	control lever shaft seal gasket
49318	transmission shaft bearing assembly gasket
49359	steering cross shaft oil seal gasket
49521	timing chain cover oil seal
FS-1046	motor gasket set; full, complete; iron head; excludes aluminum head
JS-1046	valve grinding or head gasket set; iron head
JV-134-6	engine rear main seal; after engine number 57933

JV-134-8   engine rear main seal; up to engine number 57933
JV-756   1946 to early 1947; timing case cover set
JV-757   late 1947 thru 1948; timing case cover set
MR-924   motor rebuilding gasket set; complete overhaul set; all models
MS-18005   manifold gasket set; all models
MS-18006   manifold gasket set; all models
OS-30893   oil pan gasket set
S-27662   rear axle gasket; excludes 7 passenger models
S-27843   rear axle gasket; all 7 passenger models
TS-27347   transmission gasket set; without fluid drive
TS-27453   transmission gasket set; with fluid drive
VS-36054   valve cover gasket set
WP-27055   water pump gasket set in envelope

Vitalic—Fan/Generator Belt

Vitalic fan and generator belts were high quality, low stretch, long lasting and advertised as "The Trouble Proof V-Belt." The logo on the packaging was an elephant head with the words "Tougher Than Elephant Hide." Vitalic belts were made by the Continental Rubber Works (CRW) of Erie, Pennsylvania. CRW also produced the highly collectible black rubber insulators used on telephone poles.

590   fan/generator V belt; all models

Vulcan Motor Products—Ignition, Electrical Replacement Parts

Vulcan Motor Products started in 1920 as a distributor of automotive replacement parts manufactured by Paragon Products Corp. Their goal was fast service of high quality ignition and electrical service parts to the automotive parts jobber and rebuilder at competitive prices. Vulcan Motor Parts, Inc., was located in Newark, New Jersey.

135   arm for contact points
136   bar for contact points
2415   Canadian "power-flyte" dual ignition plate assembly
2418   Canadian "power-flyte" standard ignition plate assembly
2440   "power-flyte" dual ignition plate assembly
2442   "power-flyte" standard ignition plate assembly
3203   generator drive end bearing
4258   starter bushing; drive end
4259   starter bushing; commutator end
4270   distributor bushing
4278   generator bushing; commutator end
4459   piston pin bushing
AC-2   standard ignition coil
AC-2X   heavy duty ignition coil

ALC-1	distributor condenser
ALC-1HD	heavy duty distributor condenser
CB-13	ignition coil bracket
CC-11	universal speedometer cable and casing; for 67½" casing
CC-20	universal speedometer cable and casing; for 68 5/8" casing
D-510	distributor lead; 2" length
D-511	distributor lead; 1$^{15}\!/_{16}$" length
D-300 C	distributor cap
D-330 R	distributor rotor
DS-36	dimmer switch
EX-37-38	starter brush set
EX-45	generator brush set
G-10	starter brush spring
G-12	generator brush spring
G-579	generator end plate; fits GDZ-4801 generator; uses EX-45 brush set, 4278 bushing and G-625 end plate
G-623	generator pulley; fits GDF and GDZ generator
G-625	generator drive end plate; uses 3203 bearing
G-627	starter end plate; commutator end; MAW starters
G-2608	generator pulley; fits GGU-6001 A, B and E generators
GK-201	generator repair kit; standard; complete with ball bearing
GKX-201	generator repair kit; standard; without ball bearing
HR-12	horn relay
HS-16	headlight switch
P-40	standard contact points
PM-40	matched contact points
PM-40H	matched heavy-duty contact points
PM-400	matched ventilated contact points
PS-40	heavy-duty contact points
PS-400	ventilated contact points
SK-207	starter repair kit; MAW starter
SK-208	starter repair kit; MZ starter
SL-101	stop light switch
SS-24	starter solenoid
SS-30	starter button
TK-73	tune-up kit with heavy duty points
TK-73 M	tune-up kit with matched heavy duty points
TK-730	tune-up kit with matched ventilated points
V-105	distributor vacuum chamber
VR-10	voltage regulator

Wagner-Lockheed—Brake Lining, Wheel Cylinders and Cylinder Repair Kits

Wagner-Lockheed brakes had friction characteristics that provided quick, safe smooth stops and extra-long operating life as bonded brake replacement for most cars and trucks. Brakes did not injure drums, absorb moisture, compress, or deteriorate with age. All lining withstood high operating temperatures and gave fade resistant stopping action with quick recovery characteristics. Wagner-Lockheed Brakes was a member of Wagner Electric Corporation, St. Louis, Missouri.

192-A	front wheel brake shoe set; 11 × 2 × ³⁄₁₆" brake size; excludes 7 passenger models
993-A	clutch facing; 9¼" O.D.
1008-A	clutch facing; 10" O.D.
1105-A	front or rear wheel brake shoe set; 12 × 2 × ³⁄₁₆" brake size; 7 passenger and limo models
1161-A	rear wheel brake shoe set; 11 × 2 × ³⁄₁₆" brake size; excludes 7 passenger models
FC-5395	master cylinder repair kit; discontinued number
FC-5550	stoplight switch; all models
FC-8451	wheel cylinder repair kit for wheel cylinder with one-piece piston
FC-10268 F	front hydraulic brake hose
FC-10304 R	rear hydraulic brake hose
FC-10580	upper front wheel cylinder assembly—left side
FC-10581	upper front wheel cylinder assembly—right side
FC-10582	lower front wheel cylinder assembly—left side
FC-10583	lower front wheel cylinder assembly—right side
FC-10588	rear wheel cylinder assembly—left or right
FC-11110 F	front hydraulic brake hose
FC-12222	wheel cylinder repair kit for wheel cylinder with two-piece piston
FC-13504	master cylinder repair kit; new number
FE-3241	master cylinder assembly
WC192A-1161ADC	combination brake lining set for front and rear wheels; brakes for 11" drum

Walker—Oil Filters, Exhaust Pipes and Mufflers

Walker was chosen by many of the U.S. automakers as the original exhaust system for their passenger cars and light trucks. Walker mufflers were "Precision Tuned" for each engine to preserve full power, and smooth quiet performance. Complete exhaust systems were available for school buses, heavy duty trucks, tractors and dual muffler systems. Walker Manufacturing Company was located in Racine, Wisconsin.

274	muffler; 5 passenger models; excludes convertible and 7 passenger models; replaces MoPar 676 955
2023	tail pipe; 5 passenger models; excludes convertible and 7 passenger models; replaces MoPar 1122 759
4002	exhaust pipe; 5 passenger models; excludes conv. coupe and 7 passenger models; replaces MoPar 958 122

RC-62   oil filter cartridge; all models; replaces 1121 694

WD-62   oil filter cartridge; all models; replaces 1121 694

Weatherhead—Brake Hoses and Fittings

The Weatherhead Company specialized in hydraulic brake, fuel and oil hoses and fittings. Display cabinets on garage walls, shelves and counter tops provided a complete assortment of hard-to-find parts that were identical in every way to the original equipment Weatherhead supplied to car manufacturers. The Weatherhead Company was located in Cleveland, Ohio.

7783   rear axle hydraulic brake fitting

7785   frame tee hydraulic brake fitting

7786   master cylinder hydraulic brake fitting

11001   flexible oil line assembly

11057   flexible fuel line assembly; all 1946–1947 models

11083   flexible fuel line assembly; all 1948 models

BH-10268   front; flexible hydraulic brake hose

BH-10304   rear; flexible hydraulic brake hose

BH-10362   front; flexible hydraulic brake hose

SL-5550   "clip type" stop light switch

Wells—Ignition and Electrical Replacement Parts

Wells Manufacturing Corporation started the manufacture of electrical parts for automobiles in 1903 with the production of magneto ignition parts. They expanded over the decades to advertise "Complete Coverage" of dependable quality electrical parts for "Starting, Lighting and Ignition." Parts were fully guaranteed to fit perfectly and function to the complete satisfaction of the purchaser. Wells was located in Fond Du Lac, Wisconsin.

4264   starter bushing; drive end

4278   generator bushing; commutator end

AL1-1   Vu-Pak tune-up kit

AL2-18   contact point set

AL2-18MV   point set; matched; ventilated

AL3-6   distributor condenser

AL3-13   universal strap condenser

AL4-4   distributor rotor

AL5-9   distributor cap

AL6-1   ignition coil

AL7-8   voltage regulator

AL10-1   dimmer switch

AL-923   distributor rotor

AL-930   distributor cap

CU6-6   universal ignition coil

DU10-1   universal dimmer switch

EX-17   starter brush set

EX-45	generator brush set
LU9-5	stoplight switch
RU20-12	horn relay
SS9R	starter Bendix spring

Wesco—Universal Joints and Universal Joint Repair Kits

Wesco produced a complete line of universal joints for car, truck, industry, agriculture and foreign car replacement. Their products were engineered to the exact standards of bearing cup and retainer type joints found as original equipment. They advertised their "Golden 500 Joints" as the finest available heavy duty universal joint assemblies in the replacement industry. Wesco was located in Chicago, Illinois.

D-4200HD	front or rear universal joint kit with body; lace boot; 5 passenger models; late 1946–1948
D-4202HD	front or rear universal joint kit with body; neoprene boot; 5 passenger models; late 1946–1948
D-4210	front or rear universal joint kit without body; lace boot; 5 passenger models; late 1946- 1948
D-4212	front or rear universal joint kit without body; neoprene boot; 5 passenger models; late 1946–1948
D-4500	front universal joint kit; 5 passenger models; early 1946
D-4579	rear universal joint kit; 5 passenger models; early 1946
D-4579C	rear universal joint kit; 5 passenger models; early 1946
D-7225	front or rear universal joint kit; 7 passenger models
G-7225	front or rear universal joint kit; 7 passenger models

Western Auto (Wizard)—General Line of Replacement Parts

Western Auto started its first retail store in 1921 to supply replacement automobile parts and accessories. The company brand name, "Wizard," advertised their offered products to be "Original Equipment Replacement" and to meet "Original Equipment Performance." Over 6000 company owned and associate owned stores sold "Wizard" parts nationwide. Headquarters was located in Kansas City, Missouri.

2L-6176	turn signal wiring kit; self-canceling switch kit
2L-6179	turn signal wiring kit
3R-5010	lowering block kit; 2" drop; all models
3R-6950	fiberglass-muffler
3RX-4910	lowering block kit; 3" drop; all models
4R-1011	starter drive
4R-1160	replacement generator for all models with GDZ generator
4R-5061	pressure plate assembly; models with fluid drive
4R-5375	4 piece brake shoe set; front; excludes 7 passenger sedan and limousine
4R-5376	4 piece brake shoe set; rear; excludes 7 passenger sedan and limousine

4R-5377	4 piece brake shoe set; front or rear; 7 passenger and limousine models
4RF-3230	rebuilt Stromberg carburetor; all models with fluid drive
4RF-3231	rebuilt Stromberg carburetor; all models with standard transmission and without fluid drive
4RF-5060	pressure plate assembly; models without fluid drive
4RF-5656	transmission ball joint suspension; all hand shift models
L-1086	Wizard twin-fire spark plug
L-1245	Wizard standard spark plug
L-2735	stoplight switch
L-3345	starter switch
L-3670	voltage regulator; all models
L-3762	starter brushes
L-3765	generator brushes for GDZ generator
L-4234	distributor cap
L-4273	rotor
L-4414	ignition points
L-4680	matched ventilated tune-up kit
L-4766	ignition coil
L-4830	tune-up kit
L-4877	distributor condenser
L-4916	battery cable; battery to starter switch; 16½"
L-4926	battery cable; battery to ground; 31 inches
L-4954	cable; starter to starter switch; 20 inches
L-5020	metal battery hold down band
L-5035	plastic battery hold down band
R-2330	super chrome piston rings; standard to .019"
R-2381	super chrome piston rings; .020" to .039"
R-2623	super power piston rings; standard to .019"
R-2624	super power piston rings; .020" to .039"
R-5476	engine intake valve
R-5477	engine exhaust valve
R-5659	engine valve spring; intake or exhaust
R-6056	cylinder head gasket
R-6175	valve grind gasket set
R-6281	manifold gasket set
R-6367	oil pan gasket set
R-6410	exhaust pipe flange gasket
R-6499	valve cover gasket
R-6842	water outlet gasket and thermostat housing gasket
R-7160	carburetor repair kit for Stromberg 3-39, 3-76, and 3-77; 1946–1947
R-7161	carburetor repair kit for Stromberg 3-82, 3-83, and 3-93; 1947–1948
R-7240	single action fuel pump
R-7320	double action pump
R-7821	single action fuel pump diaphragm kit

R-7850	overhaul kit for single action fuel pump
R-7866	double action diaphragm kit for vacuum pump
R-7869	double action diaphragm kit for fuel pump
RF-2381	super chrome piston rings; .020" to .039"
S-1037	front or rear universal joint; excludes 7 passenger sedan, limousine and early 1946 models
S-1147	clutch plate; 6 cylinder models with standard clutch without fluid drive
S-1149	clutch plate; 6 cylinder models with fluid drive
S-1360	front wheel grease retainer; 1946–1948; excludes 7 passenger sedan and limousine
S-1366	rear wheel inner grease retainer; late 1948; excludes 7 passenger sedan and limousine
S-1367	rear wheel inner grease retainer; 1946-early 1948; excludes 7 passenger sedan and limousine
S-1369	rear wheel outer grease retainer; 1946–1948; excludes 7 passenger sedan and limousine
S-2259	spindle bolt set
S-2811	tie rod end; left side or right side-inner end
S-2812	tie rod end; right side—outer end
S-2813	tie rod end; left side—outer end
S-2900	Wizard Magic Ride shock absorber; front
S-2905	Wizard Magic Ride shock absorber; rear
S-3002	Monroe EZ Ride shock absorber; front
S-3011	Monroe EZ Ride shock absorber; rear
S-3102	front motor mount
S-3116	rear upper motor mount
S-3118	rear lower motor mount
S-4803	rear spring shackle set; all models
S-5347	4 piece brake lining set; rear; excludes 7 passenger sedan and limousine
S-5348	4 piece brake lining set; front; excludes 7 passenger sedan and limousine
S-5770	master cylinder repair kit with piston
S-5831	master cylinder repair kit without piston
S-5921	front wheel cylinder repair kit
S-5922	rear wheel cylinder repair kit
S-6723	master cylinder; complete assembly
S-6779 U	left front upper wheel cylinder assembly
S-6780 L	left front lower wheel cylinder assembly
S-6781 U	right front upper wheel cylinder assembly
S-6782 L	right front lower wheel cylinder assembly
S-6783	left or right rear wheel cylinder assembly
S-6839	rear wheel brake hose
S-6840	front wheel brake hose

S-7101	speedometer housing with cable; all models
S-7161	speedometer cable only; all models
S-9310	front wheel—outer bearing; complete assembly
S-9807	Trico blade; early 1946 models with vacuum wipers
S-9817	Trico blade; all electric wipers and late 1946 to 1948 vacuum wiper models; electric models must use S9888 arm
S-9886	Trico wiper arm; all models with vacuum wipers
S-9888	Trico wiper arm; all models with electric wipers
T-1037	Dynatone muffler
T-1357	Westline standard muffler
T-1358	Wizard Supreme muffler
T-1740	muffler inlet clamp
T-1741	muffler outlet clamp
T-2170	exhaust pipe; excludes conv. coupe, 7 passenger sedan and limousine
T-3322	tail pipe; excludes conv. coupe, 7 passenger sedan and limousine
T-8025	high temperature thermostat
T-8087	standard temperature thermostat
T-8550	water pump
T-9088	fan and generator belt
T-9168	fan and generator belt

Westling Manufacturing Co.—General Line of Replacement Parts

Westling was one of the oldest rebuilders of replacement parts for the automotive industry and supplied exchange units that were precision built and thoroughly tested. Westling Manufacturing Company was located in Minneapolis, Minnesota.

AP-5	rear shock absorber; left or right
AP-6	front shock absorber; left or right
AT-588	fuel pump; all models
B-12	starter drive; all models; barrel type
B-12 A	starter drive; all models; barrel type
BB-192 A	front bonded brake shoe set; 5 passenger models; 11" × 2" brake drum
BB-608	drive shaft emergency brake band
BB-1105	front or rear bonded brake shoe set; 7 passenger models; 12" × 2" brake drum
BB-1161 A	rear bonded brake shoe set; 5 passenger models; 11" × 2" brake drum
CADO-104	exchange carburetor; replaces Stromberg 3-65, 3-76, 3-83; standard transmission
CADO-106	exchange carburetor; replaces Stromberg 3-66, 3-77, 3-82; fluid drive models
CL-952	clutch assembly; fluid drive transmission; 9¼"—1¼"
CL-360957	clutch assembly; standard transmission; 10"—1"

HCD-728	clutch disc; standard transmission; 10"—1"
HCD-756	clutch disc; fluid drive transmission; 9¼"—1¼"
HS-30	matched clutch set; standard transmission; HCD 728 disc and CL 360957 clutch assembly; 10"—1"
HS-31	matched clutch set; fluid drive transmission; HCD 756 disc and CL 952 clutch assembly; 9¼"—1¼"
M-3241	master brake cylinder; all models
PL-102	water pump; casting number CA 637437; all models
W-10580	upper left front wheel cylinder
W-10581	upper right front wheel cylinder
W 10582	lower left front wheel cylinder
W-10583	lower right front wheel cylinder
W-10588	rear wheel brake cylinder; left or right

WGB—Oil Filters

WGB (WGB Oil Clarofier, Inc.) started producing oil "Clarofiers" and oil cartridges in 1927. Filters were produced for passenger cars, trucks and military vehicles. WGB was located in Kingston, New York.

S-16-C   replacement oil filter; all models; replaces 1121 694

Winslow—Oil Filters

Winslow produced a line of sock type and cartridge type oil filters for passenger cars and trucks. Their replacement filters neutralized acid and absorbed foreign particles that caused excessive motor wear and bearing corrosion. Winslow Engineering Company was located in Oakland, California.

WP-70   replacement oil filter; all models; replaces 1121 694

Wix—Oil Filters

Wix advertised that their oil filters were engineered to "Out-Perform" competitive products. Wix also supplied filter kits, oil lines and tools to repair or replace factory equipment. The Wix corporation was located in Gastonia, North Carolina.

PC-80-N   oil cartridge filter; premium depth type multi-cell filtrant; replaces 1121 694; all models

PC-80-NP oil cartridge filter; "Porosite" pleated paper; replaces 1121 694; all models

Wohlert—General Line of Replacement Parts

Wohlert was a leader in the field of oil pump and water pump repair kits for passenger cars and trucks. In addition they supplied replacement parts for exhaust, engine, suspension, clutch and steering. Wohlert was located in Lansing, Michigan.

3 B   water pump repair kit; bushing type
3 CB 3   clutch throwout bearing assembly; models without fluid drive

3 CB 4	clutch throwout bearing and sleeve with springs; models without fluid drive
3 CF 3	clutch fork set; models without fluid drive
3 CP 1	clutch pilot bearing
3 DX 1	clutch fork ball
3 DX 4	clutch fork screw
3 DX 8	clutch release sleeve spring
3 DX 9-B	king bolt set; 1946–1947; excludes 7 passenger sedan and limousine
3 DX 13	clutch torque shaft bearing
3 KB 10-B	king bolt set; 1948; excludes 7 passenger sedan and limousine
3 P 3	water pump; bushing type
11 KB 12	king bolt set; 7 passenger sedan and limousine
146 CF	flywheel gear
2504	tail pipe hanger assembly; rear
2508	tail pipe hanger; rear
2509	tail pipe hanger grommet; rear
3001	oil deflector cap
3002	piston pin bushing; solid bushing
3006	battery hold down; for 15 plate $7\frac{1}{4}$" × $9\frac{1}{4}$" battery
3007	battery hold down; for 17 plate $7\frac{1}{4}$" × $10\frac{5}{8}$" battery
3008 A	steering gear arm insulator
3009	oil pump; gear type
3009 A	gear type oil pump repair kit
3010 A	valve springs
3011	valve spring retainers
3011 A	valve spring retainer lock
3021	starter housing bushing
3022	upper fan pulley
3023 A	crankshaft pulley hub
3026	valve guides
3027	front motor mount; 1 required
3031	rear upper motor mount; 2 required
3032	rear lower motor mount; 2 required
3035	motor mount set
3037	valve tappet adjusting screw
3038	valve tappet; standard
3038 A	valve tappet; .001" oversize
3038 B	valve tappet; .003" oversize
3038 C	valve tappet; .005" oversize
3040 A	water pump by-pass elbow
3041 B	water distribution tube; zinc plated
3077 B	transmission repair kit
3508	shock absorber rubber bushing; front and/or lower rear; all regular shocks
3508 A	shock absorber rubber bushing; front; all oversize shocks

3508 EH	front tail pipe bracket set
3509	wheel bolt; right hand thread
3509 B	wheel bolt; left hand thread
3514 A	spring hanger set; rear of rear spring; left or right
3515	spring and shackle rubber bushing; rear; early style
3515 A	spring and shackle rubber bushing; rear; late style
3516 A	eye bushing; front or rear spring
3536 A	steering sector bushing
3548	steering sector set
5511 B	universal joint repair kit
12510	steering tube and worm assembly
T-60	tie rod ends; for right hand assembly
T-131	tie rod ends; for left hand assembly

Appendix I

Additional Features
of the Floating-Power-Flow Engine

_____ camshaft driven by "silent chain" from crankshaft

_____ four camshaft bearings

_____ distributer driven by camshaft

_____ pressure oil spray to pistons, piston pins, valve stems, camshaft and tappets

_____ timing chain drive lubricated by oil stream from camshaft

_____ fuel pump driven from camshaft; fuel pump with screen filter and sediment bowl

_____ shunt-type generator with voltage and current voltage regulator

_____ generator ventilated and cooled by centrifugal fan at pulley

_____ generator with ample capacity to carry all approved accessories at all driving speeds

_____ exhaust chamber of manifold is extended to the carburetor flange which warms and vaporizes fuel faster

_____ crankshaft and connecting rod bearings are the precision-steel backed removable type for longer life

_____ equipped with vibration damper on the front of the engine.

_____ oil-bath air intake and air intake silencer

_____ automatic choke

_____ larger carburetor to provide increased fuel mixture required by the larger engine

_____ less rpm's (reduced rear axle ratio) means less wear on all moving parts of the engine and on the cylinder walls

_____ valve spring cover assembled to engine by cap screws (not studs) for easier access and repairs

Appendix II

Additional Features
of the Full Floating Ride

_____ independent action front wheel springs

_____ synchronized spring action—front with rear

_____ airplane-type hydraulic shock absorbers

_____ "hush-point" body mountings

_____ rubber insulated spring shackles

_____ rubber cored rear spring bushings

_____ shockless steering mechanism with worm and roller tooth selector and roller thrust bearings

_____ floating power engine mountings

_____ helical transmission gears and 7 ball and roller bearings give smoother ride in all gears

_____ tubular propeller shaft balanced at rest and rotation for smoother ride

_____ matched front coil springs of Amola steel

_____ working steering joints sealed against dirt and water for smoother operation and longer life

_____ ball thrust bearings at king pins give smoother turns without sway

_____ semi-elliptic rear springs with leaves designed to prevent squeaks

_____ rear springs with metal covers resist dirt and dust accumulation for a smoother ride

_____ transverse rear sway bar

_____ rear axle—hypoid bevel gears and axle shafts of Amola steel

_____ pressure grease system of chassis lubrication

_____ body supported on rubber-insulated "hush-point" mountings with no metal to metal contact of body to frame

_____ insulation reduces transmission of road noises from frame to body

_____ welded steel floor, sides and roof are reinforced with steel pillars, braces and gussets for a smoother ride

_____ Hotchkiss-type tubular propeller shaft balanced at rest and in rotation

_____ ball and trunnion type universal joints with roller bearings

_____ matched front coil springs of Amola steel

_____ wheel fight eliminated—steering gear unaffected by up and down motion

_____ Hotchkiss drive force is transmitted through the axle and cushioned by the rear springs for a smoother ride

_____ large air wheel tires at 28 pounds pressure cushion road shocks
_____ lengthened rear spring softens the action of the rear spring
_____ front coil spring and rear leaf spring are "synchronized" in matched up and
down motion

Appendix III

Easily Seen Features
of the D24 "New Dodge"
in the 1946 Showroom

This section is arranged as a checklist. Walk around your car and check each line on the list that you find on your car.

Easily Seen Features Outside the Car

_____ safer night driving with headlamps set wide apart on the outermost part of the fender

_____ headlamps separate from the grille

_____ larger rectangular shaped parking lights set wide apart on the fenders to improve visibility and enhance safety

_____ massive grille of stainless steel (egg crate grille) resists pitting and corrosion

_____ massive chrome plated bumpers

_____ heavier bumper braces to give greater stability and lifting support when changing tires

_____ blended front fenders that swing back smoothly to become part of the door panel

_____ "freeze-proof" outer door locks are covered with a moveable metal shield that resists water

_____ rear fenders are redesigned with smaller wheel openings

_____ tire chain strap slots in the wheels are increased in size for easier application of tire chains

_____ five 16" "Aerodisc Wheels" (1946 models; 15" wheels 1947–1948)

_____ deep and wide rain gutters

_____ concealed running boards

_____ lowerable rear windows in convertibles

_____ Dodge branded hubcaps

_____ "Dependenamel" paint finish

_____ dual windshield electric two speed wipers (Custom) dual windshield vacuum wipers (Deluxe)

_____ front and rear gravel shields behind bumpers

_____ swing type ventilator glass in front door windows and rear quarters (sedan)

_____ rear center license plate bracket with light

_____ front and rear bumper guards

_____ chrome bead around windshield and rear window

_____ one-piece-roof safety steel body

_____ safety glass in all windows

_____ double-acting airplane type shock absorbers at each wheel

_____ rubber weather strip around the doors

_____ independently sprung front wheels

_____ dual tail lights

_____ forward opening cowl ventilator

_____ wrap around bumpers give extra protection

_____ screen guarded cowl ventilator—forward opening

_____ safety steel construction

_____ straight up and down rear doors are wider and permit easier and safer entrance and exit

_____ corners of the deck lid are rounded for safety

Easily Seen Features Under the Hood

_____ horns relocated behind the radiator grille for sharper signal and easier access

_____ voltage regulator case is dust and waterproof

_____ carburetor accelerator linkage is redesigned for smoother accelerator pedal

_____ radiator drain cock on front of the radiator is easily accessible in the space between radiator and the grille

_____ nothing hung on the cylinder head studs but the cylinder head—makes for easier servicing

_____ horn relay unit is sealed from dirt and moisture

_____ dual airtone horns

_____ crankcase ventilator at rear of the engine to draw fumes out, down, under and behind the car

_____ coil moved away from firewall and bolted to the side of the engine block to reduce static and increase reception

_____ vibration damper on front of engine

_____ cellular core type radiator

_____ all cables heat resistant and waterproof

_____ battery is located under the hood and protected by new hood locks that can only be released from inside the car

_____ battery under the hood is easily accessible for testing and filling

_____ rubber isolated and protected steering gear

Easily Seen Trunk Features

_____ ratchet type bumper jack—no stoop, no kneel to lift car

_____ hinges alone hold the trunk lid open without aid from obstructing props

_____ luggage compartment lid is raised or lowered by the touch of a finger

_____ luggage compartment is lighted inside by the deck lid light when the car lights are turned on

_____ lid is prevented from falling by a "spring balanced" hinge—lid is spring counter-balanced

_____ a slight upward movement raises the deck lid of the roomy luggage compartment

_____ luggage compartment has increased capacity yet is protected and concealed under the deck lid

_____ luggage compartment floor insulation

_____ trunk floor level with opening, luggage easily slides in

Easily Seen Features Inside the Car

_____ small red light in speedometer that activates when the headlight high-beam is on

_____ instrument panel offers new beauty and utility

_____ more intense "edge lighting" of the instrument panel for greater legibility of the indicators

_____ steering wheel with only three spokes (right, left, down, not up) allows unobstructed view of instruments

_____ improved action of window regulators

_____ Dodge radios are designed to fit the car and not look like afterthought add-ons

_____ Dodge radios provide both automatic push-button preselected tuning and manual tuning control

_____ driver and passenger sun visor

_____ gearshift lever on the steering column

_____ easily viewed instrument panel includes electric fuel gauge, oil-pressure gauge, temperature gauge and ammeter

_____ "ribbed" rubber pad brake and clutch pedals

_____ leather scuff pads on the bottoms of the doors

_____ leather scuff pad on the rear seat cushion

_____ foot rest (sedans only)

_____ extra-spacious glove compartment easily opens with a pushbutton—lock is keyed differently from ignition

_____ front and rear ash receivers

_____ front door padded arm rest

_____ new complementary color interior plastics

_____ assist straps (sedans) can be adjusted to stay just where desired and will not sway when the car is in motion

_____ rear window is both deeper and wider with 47% more visibility rearward for the driver

_____ robe cord on back seat

_____ horn ring that works at the touch of a thumb from either hand—no need to remove hand from wheel to work horn

_____ ash receptacle within easy reach

_____ instrument panel map light

_____ space for outstretched comfort

_____ button starter on instrument panel—works only when ignition key is turned on

_____ luxurious comfort with extra leg and head room

_____ easy lubrication of the speedometer is possible with the installation of an accessible oil cap

_____ driver's seat provides a forward and back adjustment

_____ chair height seats with generous legroom front and rear

_____ clear view from the front seat with "airplane-vision" V-shaped front divided windshield

_____ scientifically calculated "pitch" of the windshield eliminates reflection hazards

_____ adjustable rear view mirror

_____ pistol grip parking brake lever

_____ light dimmer switch foot controlled

_____ headlight beam indicator

_____ pedal type accelerator

_____ all-weather air-control heating and cooling system

_____ three spoke steering wheel gives clear view of the instrument panel

_____ gauges with white numbers on a dark background

_____ all instruments indirectly lighted

_____ safety light speedometer

_____ beautiful finish of the window and door moldings

_____ harmonizing interior hardware

_____ deep rich upholstery is beautifully "tailored"

_____ clear vision in every direction by driver and passengers

_____ full width front and rear seats are roomier in every way and more comfortable than ever

_____ careful detail to interior trim and fittings

_____ inside handles are the vertical-lift type that prevent accidental opening— handles must be lifted up to release catch

_____ passengers sit at normal sitting position

_____ two speed electric wipers (Custom models)

_____ rotary door latches that continuously keep the door "tight"

_____ woodgrain interior finish

APPENDIX IV

Unseen Features of the D24 "New Dodge" Outlined in Brochures, Showroom Literature and Magazine Articles to Perspective Buyers and Customers in 1946

_____ new rust protection for inside the door

_____ new rust protection for exposed under parts of the body

_____ "Oilite gas filter" (developed during the war) installed in the tank protects clogging and plugging of the fuel line

_____ new hydraulic brake system requires one-third less foot pedal pressure for safer, softer stops

_____ sway eliminator

_____ rear axle stabilizer

_____ 3.9:1 hypoid type rear axle (excludes 7 passenger 4.3:1)

_____ new brakes increase stopping power with a reduction of 30% less pedal pressure

_____ fuel tank designed with sediment collecting sump with drain plug

_____ Hotchkiss type tubular propeller shaft

_____ two cylinder front brake

_____ separate, external-contracting hand brake for parking, mounted at rear of transmission

_____ new intake manifold design improves atomization of gas/air mixture

_____ cross-type universal joint and roller needle bearings are fully enclosed

_____ transmission is quiet because of helical mesh gears and seven ball and roller bearings

_____ new brakes—hydraulic, internal expanding, self-equalized and weatherproof

APPENDIX V

1946–1948 Dodge D24 Paint Colors

What do you answer when asked the question "What color is your Dodge?" Most of us would simply answer it's red or blue or green. It does not take long in the paint department of a home improvement center to discover that there are dozens of red, blue and green colors. Each color has a name, and the name does not always describe the color. The same holds true for automotive paints. A quick search of the internet will generally show a list of a dozen or more paint chip charts for the D24 Dodge and a color printout of the chart will quickly identify the name of the color of your car and if the color is original for 1946–1948.

Dodge did not come up with a brand new paint color list for the new postwar cars. Nine paint colors for the D24 were holdover colors from the 1942 Dodge.

Holdover Colors from 1942

Black	LaPlata Blue	Fortress Gray
Orinoco Green	Windward Green	Squad Red
Patrol Blue	Forest Green	Panama Sand

New Colors for 1946–1948 D24

Air Cruiser Red (also on paint charts as Air-cruiser Red)	Stone Beige No. 1	Lullaby Blue
	Opal Gray	
	Gypsy Green	

Appendix VI

D24 MoPar Factory Engineered
and Inspected Accessories

In addition to the new features built into the D24 Dodge, Chrysler Corporation offered factory engineered and inspected MoPar accessories that could be installed at the factory, at the dealership, or ordered from the dealership and installed by the owner of the car. Accessories can often be found in the original MoPar packaging at flea markets and on the internet that includes the words "MoPar Accessories Parts Division Products" or "MoPar Parts And Accessories Factory Engineered And Inspected." The MoPar trademark on the box was Chrysler Corporation's way of saying "These accessories are made right! They fit right! They work right!" These parts are not considered as aftermarket accessories but as original NOS and are suitable, with the proper documentation, for passing judges' inspection at regional and national AACA meets. Good "used" MoPar accessory items are also available at flea markets and on the internet. It was a common practice, especially on the Custom models, to add a few accessories to a car at the factory before reaching the dealership. The MoPar accessory numbers, with a brief description of each, are listed below in numerical order. Any of the following can be found on any Custom or Deluxe D24.

Check the list of Factory Engineered and Inspected Accessories below to determine which, if any, are on your D24 Dodge.

656 592	MoPar License Plate Trim Frame—telescopic type construction; telescopic sections of highly polished metal that hide the rusty and unfinished edges of the rectangular license plates; lends a finished look to license plates and adds a touch of beauty to the car.
664 543	MoPar Vanity Mirror—handy mirror for checking appearance on entering or leaving the car; folds out of sight when the visor is turned up; convenient for recording service or mileage data on etched spaces with pencil or pen.
830 197	MoPar Spare Tire Valve Extension—a high pressure hose with fittings that extends the valve of the spare tire to the outside of the car where it can be easily checked and serviced without opening the trunk lid.
830 253	MoPar Exhaust Extension—a rust resistant heavy gauge steel exhaust pipe extension designed to deflect exhaust gases downward and prevent sooty deposits and heat from discoloring the body and bumper.
864 927	MoPar Heater Windshield Defroster Package—
904 042	MoPar Skyway Header Type Antenna—a center mounted two section

antenna mounted above the windshield divider strip and operated by an inside knob.

947 597 MoPar View Master Rear-View Mirror (Inside Type)—new type glass eliminates glare from sealed beam headlights and makes night driving safer; increased size provides greater view of all road conditions.

986 332 MoPar Fog Light Package

1064 749 MoPar License Plate Trim Frame—round type construction; overlapping sections of highly polished metal that hide the rusty and unfinished edges of the rectangular license plates; lends a finished look to license plates and adds a touch of beauty to the car.

1064 770 MoPar Evr-Dry Shielding Ignition System—designed for easy starting in wet weather; water-tight shielding protects the ignition when driving in rain, snow or fog; keeps moisture, dirt and grease from distributor, coil and spark plug connections.

1064 853 MoPar Replacement Lighter Element—replacement element for the 1163 907 lighter.

1064 863 MoPar Auto Compass—instrument mounts on dash within easy view of driver or passenger; provides accurate, dependable compass driving direction.

1117 771 MoPar Fuel Tank Locking Cap—gas cap is hinged and attaches to the gasoline filler neck; cap locks automatically when closed and springs open when unlocked with a key; cap spins freely when locked and cannot be opened without a key.

1134 446 MoPar Deluxe Grille Guard—heavy gauge chrome plated steel "U" shaped bar that provides sturdy protection for the grill; rigidly mounted behind the front bumper guards.

1154 229 MoPar Glove Door Clock

1161 428 MoPar Radio Package Model 802

1161 430 MoPar Radio Package Model 602

1163 608 MoPar Skyway Concealed Type Antenna—a telescopic three section antenna that extends to 50" above the cowl.

1163 672 MoPar Deluxe Heater Package Model 36—passenger side

1163 841 MoPar Supplementary Heater Package Model 54—driver side

1163 853 MoPar Skyway Concealed Long Type Antenna—a telescopic three section antenna that extends to 83" above the cowl.

1163 907 MoPar Automatic Cigar Lighter. D24 models provide a special pre-drilled location on the instrument panel for the lighter. There is no hole to drill. Replacement elements are available (see 1064 853).

1232 607 MoPar Underhood Light. Designed for the D24 models with hood opening at the side. The light turns on automatically by a mercury switch that is operated when the hood is raised or lowered.

1232 608 MoPar Glove Compartment and Map Light. Light comes on automatically when the glove compartment door is opened. An adjustable reflector around the bulb throws the light into the glove box or back towards the seat for maps.

1232 639   MoPar Back-Up Light—back-up light with a specially designed lens that throws diffused light behind the car when backing up; chrome plated light mounts on the lower rear driver's side above the bumper; controlled by a back-up switch knob on the dash that illuminates when the back-up light is turned on.

1232 712   MoPar Directional Signal Package—flashing lights in the parking and taillights enable the driver to indicate either a right or left turn; easily operated by the driver with a lever on the steering column; a flashing green dot light indicates when the signal is operating; signal turns off automatically after the turn is completed.

1237 316   MoPar Jiffy Jet Windshield Washer Solvent (for use in 1241 006 Jiffy Jet Washer)

1239 367   MoPar Comfort Master Heater Package Model 53—passenger side

1239 369   MoPar All Weather Air Control System Package—system includes heater models 53 and 54, and fresh air adapter.

1241 006   MoPar "Jiffy Jet" Windshield Washer Package. Designed for the D24 V-Type split windshield controlled by the driver with just a light pressure of the foot on a floorboard "button" located just to the left of the clutch pedal. A positive pressure of the foot reduces the possibility of a nozzle becoming clogged and supplies a strong two-stream spray at all times to the driver and passenger windshield. All parts in contact with the washing fluid are noncorrosive for long life and smooth quiet operation. A two quart storage jar for the washing fluid is readily accessible under the hood and can be easily refilled. Uses 1237 316 Mopar "Jiffy Jet" windshield Washer Solvent.

1243 618   MoPar Pneumatic Cushion—air comfort cushion that is easy to inflate and fits the contour of the body; can be used as a backrest or a seat cushion.

1244 493   MoPar Outside Rear-View Mirror—universal outside rear-view mirror that can be adjusted for right or left hand door mounting; easily attaches with a screwdriver; no drilling necessary; convertibles excluded.

1244 497   MoPar Outside Rear-View Mirrors (Cowl Mounting Type—Pair). The Package contains one 1244 498 and one 1244 499 mirror. The mounting base of the mirror replaces the cowl molding of the D24 and is shaped to conform to the adjacent molding on the car. Extra-large mirror (4⁷/₁₆") gives a wide range of vision.

1244 498   MoPar Outside Rear-View Mirror (Cowl Mounting Type—see 1244 497)

1244 499   MoPar Outside Rear-View Mirror (Cowl Mounting Type—see 1244 497)

1244 922   MoPar Trunk Compartment Light. The light is mounted inside of the trunk compartment lid and provides light at night to the far corners of the luggage compartment.

1253 102   MoPar Spotlight Package—

1254 677   MoPar Outside Sun Visor Package—A one piece sun visor especially designed to blend into the roof contours of the D24 Dodge (many cars were equipped at a later date with an aftermarket 3 piece "Fulton" sun visor that is not MoPar approved).

APPENDIX VII

MoPar Seat Covers

MoPar seat covers are designed to protect your car seat and provide lasting beauty. All colors, fabrics, and patterns are carefully selected to harmonize with the new Dodge interiors. Each is custom tailored to fit your model exactly right and stay snugly in place. "Seat-drag" is eliminated by the smooth glossy surface so that you and your passengers can effortlessly slide in and out of the car. Seats are "water-repellent" and "fade-resistant." Elastic cord and hook fasteners provide quick installation and easy removal for cleaning. Each seat cover package includes a booklet of cleaning instructions and well as complete installation instructions. Three different styles based on color blend, pattern and price range to be found: (1) Deluxe, (2) Aristocrat, and (3) Imperial.

Mopar Deluxe Seat Covers

1243 698	MoPar 4-Door Town Sedan Seat Covers
1243 700	MoPar 4-Door Sedan Seat Cover (Without Robe Cord Trim Panel or Center Rest)
1243 703	MoPar 2-Door Sedan Seat Cover (Without Rear Center Rest)
1243 705	MoPar Club Coupe Seat Cover
1243 707	MoPar 3-Passenger Coupe Seat Cover

Mopar Aristocrat Seat Covers

1243 709	MoPar 4-Door Town Sedan Seat Cover
1243 711	MoPar 4-Door Sedan Seat Cover (Without Robe Cord Trim Panel or Center Rest)
1243 714	MoPar 2-Door Sedan Seat Cover
1243 716	MoPar Club Coupe Seat Cover
1243 718	MoPar 3-Passenger Coupe Seat Cover

Mopar Imperial Seat Covers

1243 759	MoPar 4-Door Sedan Seat Cover (Green)
1243 770	(Maroon)
1243 781	(Blue)
1243 761	MoPar 4-Door Town Sedan Seat Cover (Green)

1243 772	(Maroon)
1243 783	(Blue)
1243 762	MoPar 2-Door Sedan Seat Cover (Green)
1243 773	(Maroon)
1243 784	(Blue)
1243 765	MoPar Club Coupe Seat Cover (Green)
1243776	(Maroon)
1243 787	(Blue)
1243767	MoPar 3-Passenger Coupe Seat Cover (Green)
1243 778	(Maroon)
1243 789	(Blue)

APPENDIX VIII

MoPar Protective and Maintenance Materials for the D24 Dodge

Many D24 owners like to collect approved Protective and Maintenance Material products that were distributed and sold only through approved Chrysler Corporation dealers when their car was new. Collections can be displayed with the 1946–1948 Dodge at car shows or in a garage or "man cave" at home. Items are usually found as a single tin, bottle or tube on a flea market table or for sale on the internet. Rare but not impossible to find is a dealer carton containing a dozen or more items. All have the MoPar logo and are generally found in a red, yellow and blue color scheme. The MoPar numbers for Protective and Maintenance Materials are listed below in numerical order.

638 669	MoPar Spring Lubricant (quart)
680 177	MoPar Shock Absorber Fluid (quart)
680 183	MoPar Fabric Cleaner (pint)
680 184	MoPar Fabric Cleaner (gallon)
680 185	MoPar Automobile Polish (pint)
680 186	MoPar Automobile Polish (gallon)
680 191	MoPar Auto Wax Paste (8 ounces)
680 194	MoPar Radiator Rust Resistor (pint)
680 195	MoPar Radiator Rust Resistor (gallon)
830 096	MoPar Fluid Drive Fluid (gallon)
830 660	MoPar Pre-Wax Cleaner (pint)
830 661	MoPar Pre-Wax Cleaner (gallon)
830 663	MoPar Black Rubber Finish (gallon)
830 667	MoPar Radiator Stop Leak (10 ounces)
830 668	MoPar Dripless Penetrating Oil (4 ounces)
830 670	MoPar Liquid Auto Wax (pint)
830 672	MoPar Shock Absorber Fluid (gallon)
830 673	MoPar Spot Remover (5 ounces)
996 399	MoPar Glass Cleaner (12 ounces)
1057 794	MoPar Perfect Seal Sealing Compound (16 ounces)
1063 642	MoPar Fluid Drive Fluid (5 gallons)
1063 700	MoPar Chromium Polish (8 ounces)
1064 580	MoPar Cooling System Cleaner (pint + 2 ounces powder)

1064 704   MoPar Super Brake Fluid (pint)
1064 705   MoPar Super Brake Fluid (quart)
1064 706   MoPar Super Brake Fluid (gallon)
1064 707   MoPar Super Brake Fluid (5 gallons)
1064 768   MoPar Lubriplate All Purpose Lubricant (2 ounces)
1064 769   MoPar Door Ease Surface Lubricant (paper wrapped stick)
1064 861   MoPar Super Rubber Cement (pint)
1237 316   MoPar "Jiffy Jet" Windshield Washer Solvent (6 ounces)
1241 691   MoPar Glass Cleaner (10 ounces)
1243 667   MoPar Tar and Road Oil Remover (16 ounces)
1316 224   MoPar Polishing Cloth (1 cloth per tin)

Appendix IX

Abbreviations

The following abbreviations are used in the Field Guide, aftermarket catalogs, counter catalogs, and factory parts manuals.

Not all of the abbreviations are used in any one publication.

bbl.—barrel (carb.)

carb.—carburetor

cl.—clutch

conv.—convertible

cyl.—cylinder(s)

dc.—direct current

d.c.—double contact (lamp, bulb)

diaph.—diaphragm

dist.—distributor

dr.—door

eng.—engine

ex.—exhaust

exc.—excludes

F.—Fahrenheit

f/d.—fluid drive

fl.dr.—fluid drive

ga.—gauge

h.p.—horsepower

hyd.—hydraulic

ign.—ignition

in.—inch(s)

int.—intake

L.—length

limo.—limousine

mech.—mechanical

no.—number

opt.—optional

pass.—passenger

s.c.—single contact (lamp, bulb)

sdn.—sedan

spl.—splines

std.—standard

T.—thickness

trans.—transmission

v.—volt(s)

W.—width

w/—with

w/o.—without

2d.—2 door

4d.—4 door

Appendix X

Aftermarket Catalog List

The following is a brief alphabetical guide to aftermarket suppliers and the parts they manufactured.

ABC—ball and tapered roller bearings

AC—fuel pumps, oil filters, and spark plugs

Accurate—clutch assemblies, bearings and clutch plates

ACE—voltage regulators and water pumps

Aetna—clutch release bearings

Airtex—fuel pumps and water pumps

Alco—universal joints and universal joint repair kits

Allied (A.P.C.)—water pumps and engine rebuild parts

Alloy—universal joints and universal joint repair kits

Allstate (Sears)—full line of popular auto replacement parts

American Brakeblok—fan/generator belts, brakes, clutches and hoses

American Hammered—piston rings

Amoco—fan/generator belts

Ampco—ignition, fuel pump and electrical replacement parts

Andrews Bearing Corp.—clutch assemblies and clutch release bearings

Andrews Line—ignition, voltage regulators and electrical replacement parts

AP—exhaust clamps, pipes and mufflers

Apeco—remanufactured water pumps

Arco Products Co.—ignition, filters, fuel pumps and thermostats

Armor-Flex—bushings, motor mounts and replacement rubber parts

Arrow—armatures, clutch assemblies, generators, starters, fuel pumps and water pumps

ATB—clutch release bearings

Atlas—fan/generator belts, brake cylinders and chassis replacement parts

Auburn—spark plugs

Autoline—master cylinder and wheel brake cylinders

Auto-Lite—ignition, generators, starters and electrical replacement parts

Automotive—armatures, generators, starters and electrical replacement parts

Autostat—thermostats

Babcock—thermostats

Badger—pistons

Baldwin—oil filters

Balkamp—general line of popular replacement parts
BCA—bearings
Bendix—brake shoes
Benson Industries—armatures, generators, starters and voltage regulators
Besco—clutch bearings
B.G. Engineering—master cylinder and wheel cylinders
B.H.T.—brake shoes, fuel pumps and clutch assemblies
Bishop & Babcock—thermostats
Bishop Thermostats—thermostats
Blackstone—fuel pumps
Blue Crown—spark plugs
Blue Streak—ignition and electrical replacement parts
Bohnalite—water pumps
Borg-Warner—clutch assemblies, bearings, plates and chassis replacement parts
Bower—bearings
Bowes—fan/generator belts
Bridgeport—thermostats
Briggs—shock absorbers
Buffalo—oil filters
Bull Dog—motor mounts
Burd—piston rings
Caltherm—thermostats
Camco—armatures, generators and starters
CaPaC—fuel pumps
Capsul-Pac—carburetor tune-up kits
Cardo—carburetors and fuel pumps
Carter—fuel pumps and thermostats
Casco—distributors, vacuum controls
Celoron—timing gears
Cepco—brake shoes
Champ-Items—cables, fasteners and springs
Champion—spark plugs
Champion ReNu—water pumps
Chefford-Master—clutch bearings, fuel pumps and universal joints
Cities Service—fan/generator belts
Clawson and Bals—engine bearings
Clevite—engine bearings
Cloyes—timing gears and chains
Columbus—shock absorbers
Crown—armatures, generators and starters
Crown—fan/generator belts
Cyclone—oil filters
Dayton—fan/generator belts and radiator hoses
Delco—shock absorbers
Detroit—universal joints

Dittmer—transmission gears

Dole—thermostats and radiator caps

Dorman—clutch bearings, fasteners and hardware

Double Diamond—flywheel ring gears

Duckworth—timing chains

Dueco—clutch assemblies

Durkee-Atwood—fan/generator belts and hoses

Echlin—ignition and electrical replacement parts

Eclipse—brake shoes

EIS—hydraulic brake parts

Ennis Manufacturing—water pumps

Ertel Products—engine rebuild parts, bushings, chassis and suspension replacement
     parts

Eveready—electric lamps and electric bulbs

EZ-Ride—shock absorbers

Federal—clutch release bearings

Federal-Mogul—engine replacement parts, pistons, bearings, rods and bushings

Federated—thermostats, fuel, radiator and oil caps

Fel-Pro—gaskets

Filko—ignition and electrical replacement parts

Firestone—fan/generator belts

Fitzgerald—gaskets

Gabriel—shock absorbers and thermostats

Gates—fan/generator belts, hoses, thermostats and fuel, radiator oil caps

General Armature Manufacture (GAMCO)—armatures, generators and starters

General Automotive Products—ignition and electrical replacement parts

G-H (Geary-Hershey)—chassis and suspension replacement parts

Gibson—brake shoe hold down parts

Gilmer—fan/generator belts

Globe—fan/generator belts, hoses and rubber replacement parts

Goerlich—exhaust mufflers and pipes

Gold Seal—oil filters

Gould—armatures, generators and starters

Grand—mufflers

Green—clutch bearings

Grey-Rock—brake shoes and clutch plates

Grizzly—brake shoes

Guaranteed Parts (GP)—ignition and electrical replacement parts

HaDees—thermostats

Hampden—brake shoes and water pumps

Harrison—thermostats

Hastings—piston rings, fuel pumps and oil filters

Hastings Company (The)—brakes, clutch assemblies and water pumps

HE—ignition

Hoosick Engineering (HE)—ignition

Hoover—bearings and tie rod ends
Houdaille—shock absorbers
Hygrade—fuel pumps
Imparco—exhaust mufflers and pipes
Imperial—rebuilt armatures, generators and starters
Inlite—brake linings
International Parts—general line of replacement parts
Jiffy-Kit—carburetors
Johns-Manville—clutch facings and brake shoes
Johnson—piston rings
K.O. Lee—valve inserts
Kem—ignition and fuel pumps
King Products—engine and suspension replacement parts
KM (Ken Mar)—water pumps
Lasco—brake shoes
Lempco—clutch bearings, timing chains and axle shafts
Limpco—clutch assemblies and clutch plates
Link-Belt—timing chains and gears
Lion—fuel pumps and suspension replacement parts
Maremont—exhaust mufflers and pipes
Martin—oil filters
Master—clutch bearings, fuel pumps and universal joints
McCord—gaskets
McQuay-Norris—general line of popular engine and suspension replacement parts
Merit—exhaust clamps, pipes and mufflers
Metro Auto Electric—generators
Michigan—engine and camshaft bearings
Micro-Test—axles and gears
Mo-Car—starter drives
Modac—fan/generator belts and hoses
Molec—armatures, generators and starters
Monmouth—engine, clutch and suspension/chassis replacement parts
Monroe—shock absorbers
Moog—chassis and suspension replacement parts
Morse—timing chains
Monteith—armatures, generators and starters
Motor Master—universal joints
MRC—clutch bearings
Muskegon—piston rings
National—grease and oil seals
Nice—clutch assemblies and bearings
Norwalk—fan/generator belts
Nylen—pistons
Ohio Pistons—pistons
P&D—ignition

Pacco—carburetors

Packard—wires and cables

Partex—fuel pumps

Parts Specialties—water pumps

Pedrick—piston rings

Perfect Circle—piston rings and chassis/suspension replacement parts

Perfect Parts—clutch bearings, wheel bearings and engine rebuild parts

Perfection, clutch assemblies, bearings and plates

Permite—engine bearings and pistons

Pick—brake shoes

Pierce—fuel pumps

Pilot—master cylinders, wheel cylinders, universal joints and universal joint repair kits

Powell—exhaust muffler and pipes

Pratt—exhaust mufflers and pipes

Purolator—oil filters

Quality Service Parts—ignition and electrical replacement parts

Ramco—piston rings

Raybestos—brake shoes, brake cylinders and cylinder repair kits

Rayloc—brakes shoes, clutch assemblies, fuel, oil and water pumps

ReNu—fuel pumps

Republic Automotive—timing chains, universal joints and universal joint repair kits

Robertshaw—thermostats

Rusco—brakes and fan/generator belts

Sachs—clutch assemblies and water pumps

Safeguard—fuel pumps

Scandinavian—brake shoes and clutch lining

Sealed Power—piston rings

Shurhit—ignition and electrical replacement parts

Silv-O-Lite—pistons

Sorensen—ignition and electrical replacement parts

Soundmaster—exhaust clamps, pipes and mufflers

Springfield Electrical Specialties—ignition

Standard—thermostats

Standard/Blue Streak—ignition and electrical replacement parts

Stant—thermostats, gas, oil and radiator caps

Sterling—thermostats

Sterling Products—pistons

Stromberg—carburetors and carburetor repair kits

Superior—armatures, generators and starters

Superior—piston rings

Thermoid—brake lining, clutch facing, belts and hoses

Thompson Products—engine rebuild and suspension replacement parts

Timken—bearings

Toledo Steel—engine rebuild and suspension replacement parts

Triangle—springs
Triplex—pistons
Tru-Power—carburetor repair kits
Tru-Torque—brake part kits
TRW—engine rebuild and suspension replacement parts
Tung-Sol—auto lamps and flashers
Tungsten—ignition and electrical replacement parts
Union—ignition and electrical replacement parts
Unit Parts (UP)—fuel pumps
United—hydraulic brake cylinders and cylinder repair kits
Victor—gaskets and seals
Vitalic—fan/generator belts
Vulcan—ignition and electrical replacement parts
Wagner-Lockheed—brake lining, wheel cylinders and cylinder repair kits
Walker—oil filters, exhaust pipes and mufflers
Weatherhead—brake hose and fittings
Wells—ignition and electrical replacement parts
Wesco—universal joints and universal joint repair kits
Western Auto—general line of replacement parts
Westling—general line of replacement parts
WGB—oil filters
Winslow—oil filters
Wix—oil filters
Wohlert—general line of replacement parts